THE SECRETS OF
STATION X

THE SECRETS OF STATION X

HOW THE BLETCHLEY PARK CODEBREAKERS HELPED WIN THE WAR

MICHAEL SMITH

First published in Great Britain in 2011 by
Biteback Publishing Ltd
Westminster Tower
3 Albert Embankment
London
SE1 7SP

ISBN 978-1-84954-095-7

10 9 8 7 6 5 4 3 2 1

A CIP catalogue record for this book is available from the British Library.

Set in Garamond and Steelfish by Namkwan Cho
Cover design by Namkwan Cho

Printed and bound by CPI Group (UK) Ltd, Croydon, CR0 4YY

CONTENTS

ACKNOWLEDGEMENTS

I must thank a number of people for their assistance in the writing of this book, most notably Simon Greenish, Kelsey Griffin and the staff and volunteers of the Bletchley Park Trust, who work so hard to keep the memory of the codebreakers alive. I am particularly grateful to the late Keith Batey, and to Mavis Batey, Bill Bonsall, Frank Carter and Brian Oakley for their assistance on technical matters, although I would like to stress that any errors that appear in this book are mine alone. I would also like to thank all the former codebreakers I have interviewed over the past fourteen years and whose memories appear in this book. The work of Bletchley Park codebreakers undoubtedly did much to assist the Allies in winning the war. This book is an unashamed tribute to them and the astonishing organisation that Bletchley Park was.

I thank the Bletchley Park Trust for providing most of the photographs used in this book, Iain Dale and James Stephens at Biteback for their support and their work on this project, Hollie Teague for a superlative piece of editing and Namkwan Cho for a brilliant cover. Thanks are also due to my agent Robert Kirby and to my wife Hayley who, as ever, suffered far more than the author while this book was being written.

Michael Smith, July 2011

CHAPTER 1

CAPTAIN RIDLEY'S SHOOTING PARTY

The sudden increase in activity up at the old Leon estate led to a great deal of excitement in the sleepy Buckinghamshire town of Bletchley in the last few months of 1938. Amid the deteriorating situation in Europe, where war with Hitler and Nazi Germany seemed unavoidable, there was no shortage of suggestions as to why workmen might be so busy laying concrete, installing a new water main, digging in power cables and laying telephone lines to connect the old mansion house at Bletchley Park to Whitehall's corridors of power.

Then there was that rather odd-looking group of people, mainly middle-aged 'professor types' accompanied by surprisingly young women, who arrived at the Park in August 1938. They stayed in local hotels and called themselves 'Captain Ridley's Shooting Party', as if they were there for a weekend in the country. No one in Bletchley was fooled by such a fancy name. Something very odd and very 'hush-hush' was going on up at the Park.

The small town of Bletchley had been a tiny hamlet until the arrival of the locomotive turned it into a major railway junction in the mid-nineteenth century. The estate itself had been owned by the Leon family since 1883, when the wealthy city financier Herbert Leon bought it as a country estate. He built a mansion house and used his money and influence to turn himself into a pillar of the local community, first as Liberal Member of Parliament for Buckingham and later as a minor member of the aristocracy. But when he and his wife Fanny died the estate was sold off to a builder who wanted to demolish the mansion and build on the land. The removal of the mansion would certainly have been no loss to Britain's architectural heritage. It was an ugly mix of mock-Tudor and Gothic styles, built in red brick and dominated on one side by a large copper dome turned green by exposure to the elements. The grounds around the mansion were more pleasant. It looked out over a small lake, rose gardens, a ha-ha and even a maze, all put in place by the Leon family.

As war loomed and Members of Parliament worried over the country's lack of air defences in the face of increasingly warlike noises from Germany, the mansion was rescued from the demolition ball. A mysterious government official paid the then enormous sum of £6,000 to buy the entire estate and an army of workmen moved in. The story was put about that the mysterious new owner had bought Bletchley Park on behalf of the government to turn it into an air defence training school. The *Bletchley District Gazette* told its readers that this story had been dismissed out of hand by its sources in Whitehall, but whenever the subject was broached with any of the new arrivals they insisted they were working on Britain's air defences. Who knew what the truth was? Whatever it might be, it was clearly related to the threat of war, and very, very 'hush-hush'.

It was in fact far more secret than anyone then living in Bletchley was ever likely to imagine. In June 1938, Bletchley Park had been bought by Admiral Sir Hugh Sinclair, the head of the Secret Intelligence Service – now known as MI6 – to be used as a 'war station' for various parts of his organisation, which were scheduled to be evacuated from London in the event of war to remove them from the threat of German bombing. 'Sinclair bought Bletchley Park out of his own pocket,' said a former MI6 officer who later worked as the service's archivist. 'He could not get any joy out of the War Office or anyone else to provide him with a site so he went and bought it. We know he paid for it, we're not even sure if he was ever repaid. He died soon afterwards, so he probably wasn't.' Sinclair left the estate to his sister Evelyn, which suggests that he had not been paid back, since he could scarcely have left her something he did not own. But he was a wealthy man and he and his sister were extremely close. She shared in the family fortune and had no more need of the money than he did. She had in fact joined the Government Code and Cypher School (GC&CS) before the war began and was one of those sent to Bletchley Park. There is no doubt that she would have been aware of what Sinclair wanted to happen to the estate and she swiftly signed it over to the chief administrative and financial officers of MI6, Captain William Ridley RN and Paymaster-Commander Percy Sykes.

Sinclair certainly planned for Bletchley Park to be the wartime home of the vast bulk of MI6, to keep them safe from German bombs and spies. One group destined to move to the Park at the start of the war mirrored the work of James Bond's 'Q', designing special explosive gadgets for British secret service officers tasked with sabotaging the German war effort. Another included the communications experts who had equipped Britain's spies abroad with wireless sets to cut the time it took to obtain their intelligence reports and ran the wireless network, together with the 'decoders' who unravelled the messages the British secret agents sent back to London. By far the most secretive of the people Sinclair intended to send to Bletchley were the government's top secret codebreakers, whose existence was virtually unknown to all bar the most senior officials in Whitehall.

The British had been renowned as expert codebreakers since the fourteenth century when King Edward II ordered the seizure of 'all letters coming from or going to parts beyond the seas'. A royal writ dated 18 December 1324 reminded ports officials that it was part of their duties to 'make diligent scrutiny of all persons passing from parts beyond the seas to England to stop all letters concerning which sinister suspicions might arise'. By the sixteenth century, the British were infamous for their interception of diplomatic correspondence, with the

Venetian Ambassador to Britain complaining that 'the letters received by me had been taken out of the hands of the courier at Canterbury by the royal officials and opened and read'. Sir Francis Walsingham, Queen Elizabeth I's spymaster, set up a decyphering department in his London home under the guidance of John Dee, the Queen's astrologer, to detect Spanish intrigues. Walsingham's codebreakers foiled the Babington plot, which aimed to replace Elizabeth with Mary Queen of Scots and was the main cause of the latter's execution.

John Thurloe, who was Oliver Cromwell's spymaster, placed a 'Secret Man' in the Post Office to intercept suspicious mail, a process authorised by Parliament 'to discover and prevent many dangerous and wicked designs'. During the eighteenth century, the Foreign Office had a 'Secret Department' which monitored the correspondence of foreign diplomats based in London and had its own 'Secret Decyphering Branch', run by the Reverend Edward Willes, an Oxford don who later became the Bishop of Bath and Wells and who was succeeded by other members of his family. The vast majority of the secret messages they read were Russian, Swedish or French, reflecting Britain's main enemies at the time, but the branch was closed down in 1847 to save cash with one official complaining that the then incumbent, the bishop's grandson Francis Willes, had cracked 'scarcely any' codes and was merely 'a fraudulent trickster who leads a life of pleasure and relaxation at his home in Hanger Hill out of sight of the office.'

The First World War and the military use of the new invention of the wireless led to an inevitable resumption of British interception of other countries' messages. The War Office used the excuse of 'censorship' to obtain the diplomatic communications transmitted by relay stations of international telegraph companies based in British territory, setting up a codebreaking operation to decypher the secret messages. The British Army intercepted German military wireless communications with a great deal of success. E. W. B. Gill, one of the Army officers involved in decoding the messages, recalled that 'the orderly Teutonic mind was especially suited for devising schemes which any child could unravel'. One of the most notable successes for the British cryptanalysts came in December 1916 when the commander of the German Middle East signals operation sent a drunken message to all his operators wishing them a Merry Christmas. With little other activity taking place over the Christmas period, the same isolated and clearly identical message was sent out in six different codes, only one of which, up until that point, the British had managed to break.

The Army codebreaking operation became known as MI1b and was commanded by Major Malcolm Hay, a noted historian and eminent academic. It enjoyed a somewhat fractious relationship with its junior counterpart in the Admiralty, formally the Naval Intelligence Department 25 (NID25) but much better known as Room 40, after the office in the Old Admiralty Buildings in Whitehall that it occupied. Room 40 was set up shortly after the start of the war on the orders of Winston Churchill, then First Lord of the Admiralty. Churchill directed that Sir Alfred Ewing, the Navy's Director of Education, who had dabbled in codes and cyphers as a hobby before the war, should lead the codebreakers:

> An officer should be selected to study all the decoded intercepts, not only current but past, and to compare them continually with what actually took place in order to penetrate the German mind and movements and make reports. The officer selected is for the present to do no other work. I shall be obliged if Sir Alfred Ewing will associate himself continuously with this work.

Ewing set up a series of listening stations around the country, all manned by the Post Office. He also recruited a small number of language experts, firstly from the Naval colleges at Dartmouth and Osborne and then from the universities. One of the first of these naval instructors turned codebreakers was Alastair Denniston, a diminutive Scot known to his colleagues as A.G.D. and by close friends as Liza, who would become the first head of Bletchley Park. But by far the most productive source of codebreakers was the universities. Ewing went back to his old college, King's, Cambridge, to bring in two Old Etonians: Dillwyn 'Dilly' Knox, one of the most brilliant and most eccentric of the codebreakers, and Frank Birch, a talented comic and famous actor, who would later appear in pantomime at the London Palladium as Widow Twanky in *Aladdin*. Other eminent recruits, almost entirely Old Etonians, included William 'Nobby' Clarke, a lawyer whose father had been Solicitor-General and had represented Oscar Wilde during his 1885 trial for gross indecency, and Nigel de Grey, a publisher whose diminutive stature and unassuming nature led the more extrovert Birch to dub him 'the Dormouse'. It was de Grey who is credited with giving Room 40 its greatest First World War triumph: the decyphering of the so-called Zimmermann Telegram (although it was in fact Knox who initially broke into the cypher). The telegram showed that Germany had asked Mexico to join an alliance against the United States, offering Mexico's 'lost territory' in Texas, New Mexico and Arizona in return, and brought the United States into the war.

There was little or no cooperation between the Army and navy codebreaking departments, with Denniston, who ran Room 40 at the end of the First World War, lamenting the turf war between the two organisations: 'Looking back over the work of those years, the loss of efficiency to both departments caused originally by mere official jealousy is the most regrettable fact in the development of intelligence based on cryptography.' The Army and Navy codebreakers did eventually begin to exchange results in 1917, but there remained little love lost.

At the end of the First World War, there were a number of people within Whitehall who were keen to axe the codebreakers as part of a peace dividend. But they were far outnumbered by those anxious not to lose the intelligence that the codebreakers had been producing. The Army and Navy codebreaking operations were amalgamated into a single organisation in 1919. Denniston was given charge of the Government Code and Cypher School (GC&CS), as it was to be known, with a staff of just over fifty employees, around half of whom were actual codebreakers.

'The public function was "to advise as to the security of codes and cyphers used by all government departments and to assist in their provision",' Denniston later recalled. 'The secret directive was "to study the methods of cypher communications used by foreign powers".'

The main source of those communications was the international cable companies, who were told to continue to pass over diplomatic telegrams to GC&CS which copied them and returned them within twenty-four hours. 'Secrecy is essential,' noted Lord Curzon, the then Foreign Secretary. 'It must be remembered that the companies who still supply the original messages to us regard the intervention of the government with much suspicion and some ill-will. It is important to leave this part of our activity to the deepest possible obscurity.' Amid concern that the process could fall apart if any of the telegraph companies chose to object, a clause was inserted into the 1920 Official Secrets Act allowing the Home Secretary to order the companies to hand over the cables to the codebreakers. Two Royal Navy intercept sites at Pembroke in South Wales and Scarborough, Yorkshire, also provided GC&CS with coded wireless messages.

GC&CS came under the control of the Director of Naval Intelligence Admiral Hugh Sinclair, a noted bon-viveur who installed it in London's fashionable Strand, close to the Savoy Grill, his favourite restaurant. It worked almost entirely on the diplomatic telegrams handed over by the commercial cable companies. The main target countries for the codebreakers were America, France, Japan and Russia, with the last providing what Denniston said was 'the only real operational intelligence'. When Sinclair was transferred to another post, in 1921, the Admiralty handed GC&CS over to the Foreign Office. The codebreakers moved to Queen's Gate, Knightsbridge, and were told to forget about military and naval communications and concentrate on decyphering the diplomatic cables, not just of Britain's enemies, but also of some of its friends. 'It was a very small organisation for the Treasury had, throughout the nego-tiations, been insistent on cutting down the expense,' recalled Nobby Clarke.

> The inevitable had happened. There seemed no longer any need to study the communications of a naval and military nature. The Navy and Army of Germany had disappeared, never were they supposed to rise again. To show the extent of the change, in the early days of 1920, the strongest section of the GC&CS was the United States section, to which Knox and Strachey and a number of lesser lights were attached.

Perhaps understandably, the Admiralty saw little reason to fund the collection of diplomatic intelligence, and Britain's codebreakers were soon placed once more in the hands of the Foreign Office. When Admiral Sinclair was made head of MI6 in 1923, he also took over control of GC&CS, Denniston said. 'It became in fact an adopted child of the Foreign Office with no family rights and the poor relation of MI6 where peacetime activities left little cash to spare.'

The codebreakers were recruited, as with their MI6 colleagues, from a limited circle of people within the estab-lishment. Joshua 'Josh' Cooper, who would become a leading member of Bletchley Park and subsequently its Cold War successor GCHQ, recalled being recruited as a 'Junior Assistant' in October 1925 when he was twenty-four.

> Like many other recruits, I had heard of the job through a

personal introduction – advertisement of posts was at that time unthinkable. In my case introduction came through the family of the novelist Charles Morgan, whose father Sir Charles Morgan of the Southern Railway was an old friend and chief of my father. I was one year down from University of London King's College with a first in Russian and had found nothing better to do than teach at a preparatory school at Margate. My father was bewailing this at tea with the Morgans one day, and one of Charles's sisters remarked that she had a friend called Sybil Pugh who worked at a place in Queens Gate where Russian linguists were actually wanted. So in due course I took an entrance exam which included a number of puzzles, such as filling in missing words in a mutilated newspaper article and simple mathematical problems calling for nothing more than arithmetic and a little ingenuity. I wasted a lot of time on these, thinking there must be some catch and rechecking my work and so did not finish the paper. Nevertheless I got top marks. There was also an interview board where I found Denniston, whom I had already met, and for the first time met 'C' (Admiral Sinclair) the Director of GC&CS. I do not think this exam was ever repeated but selection continued on a fairly haphazard basis right up to the [Second World] War.

Cooper was set to work on Russian cyphers alongside Ernst Fetterlein, who had been codebreaker to the Tsar, where one of his main jobs was solving British codes, a role that was now reversed. 'Fetterlein was a devotee of his art,' one of his former colleagues in the Russian *Cabinet Noir* recalled.

I was told that once, when he was sent to London with dispatches, he sat morosely through breakfast until suddenly a complete change took place. He beamed, began to laugh and jest, and when one of the embassy officials asked him what the matter was, confessed that he had been worried by an indecypherable word which occurred in one of the English telegrams he had decyphered. Someone had in conversation mentioned the name of a small English castle to which the King had gone to shoot and this was the word in the telegrams which had bothered him.

Fetterlein, who was by then fifty-two, had a large ruby ring given to him by Tsar Nicholas in gratitude for his achievements, which included breaking a German Navy message which enabled the Russian Navy to sink a number of German ships in the Baltic in 1914. This was helpful to Fetterlein's future employers. The Russians recovered a naval codebook from the light cruiser the *Magdeburg*, which they passed on to the British.

Fetterlein fled Russia during the Bolshevik takeover in November 1917, later telling William Filby, one of his new British colleagues, that he and his wife narrowly evaded a search of the ship by trigger-happy Bolsheviks. 'As the top cryptographer in Russia he held the rank of admiral,' said Filby. 'His stories of the day the revolution occurred, when workmen stripped him of many decorations and bullets narrowly missed him, were exciting. It is said that the French and the British organisation were anxious to get him and Fetterlein simply sat there and said: "Well gentlemen, who will pay me the most?"'

The British evidently offered the most money. Fetterlein was recruited by Room 40 in June 1918, working on Bolshevik, Georgian and Austrian codes, Filby said.

Fetty, as we addressed him, would arrive precisely at 9.30 and read his *Times* until ten when he would adjust a pair of thick-lensed glasses and look to us expecting work to be given to him. He was a brilliant cryptographer. On book cypher and anything where insight was vital he was quite the best. He was a fine linguist and he would usually get an answer no matter the language.

Josh Cooper already knew Fetterlein, having been introduced to him by one of the teaching staff at King's College.

His experience and reputation were both great, and I was fortunate to find myself assigned to work with him on Soviet diplomatic, which at that time consisted of book cyphers, mostly one part, re-cyphered with a 1,000-group additive key. He took very little notice of me and left it to an Army officer who had been attached to GC&CS, to explain the problem. Traffic was scanty and it was hard to get adequate depth. It took me some time to realise that almost every group had two meanings. After about six weeks' work, during which I rubbed holes in the paper with endless corrections, at last I read my first message which was from Moscow to the Soviet representative in Washington and was concerned with repudiation of debts by American states. Later we got much better material from Tehran, where traffic was a great deal heavier and was obtained from the Persian post office by MI6. Hitherto it had been exploited locally by an Army officer resident in Tehran, but now the work was transferred to GC&CS. Later still we got even more voluminous material obtained in the same way from the post office in Peking, and were able to solve for the first time whole additive tables.

Despite Cooper's problems with the cypher he was put to work on, the amount of Soviet messages continued to increase with the opening of a new Royal Navy intercept site at Flowerdown, near Winchester, an Army site at Chatham and an RAF site at Waddington, in Lincolnshire.

The Russian messages disclosed a concerted attempt to provoke a Bolshevik revolution in Britain in 1920 and repeated attempts to subvert British society throughout the 1920s and 1930s, but this success was a double-edged sword. First in 1920 and then again in 1923 and 1927, the British government used Russian messages broken by the codebreakers as evidence of the communist threat to Britain, leading to changes in Soviet cypher systems that by the late 1920s had all but ended the codebreakers' success against Russia's diplomatic cyphers. After the government's 1927 admission that GC&CS was reading Moscow's secret messages, the Russians began using the one-time-pad system which, when used properly, was unbreakable.

The codebreakers had little in the way of formal training, Cooper recalled.

> The structure of the office was pretty hopeless. It had begun as six Senior Assistants and eighteen Junior Assistants but by the time I joined it was, I think, one Senior Assistant with a responsibility allowance (Denniston), twelve Senior Assistants and twelve Junior Assistants. Supporting staff consisted of a few misemployed typists, some women on MI6 books and, I believe, a few women employed as 'JAA' (Junior Assistant's Assistant). For it was the Treasury's understanding that Senior Assistants broke new cyphers and Junior Assistants decyphered and translated the texts. Recruitment by personal introduction had produced some very well-connected officers, especially among the seniors. At best they were fine scholar linguists, at worst some of them were, frankly, 'passengers'.

Very little interest was shown in naval or military messages in the immediate wake of the First World War and responsibility for assessing the value of these was left largely to naval and military intelligence. But in 1924, GC&CS set up a small Naval Section under William 'Nobby' Clarke, a veteran of Room 40 and then forty-one years old. It obtained its intercepts from the Scarborough station; from the new Royal Navy site at Flowerdown, which had replaced Pembroke; and from operators on board Royal Navy ships who intercepted foreign naval messages in their spare time. The Army still had its intercept site at Fort Bridgewoods, Chatham and in 1930 a military code-breaking section was formed at GC&CS under the command of Captain John Tiltman. The RAF had set up its own intercept station at Waddington, Lincolnshire, in 1927, but it was not until 1936 that an Air codebreaking section was created in GC&CS

with Cooper in charge. Two years later, the RAF intercept site moved from Waddington to Woodhead Hall at Cheadle, in Staffordshire. There were also a number of intercept stations at various sites overseas at the end of the First World War, including Malta, Sarafand in Palestine, Baghdad, and Abbottabad on the North-West Frontier. A Royal Navy intercept station was set up in Hong Kong in 1934 as the threat from Japan became more evident. The messages provided by this network and the international cable companies were augmented by diplomatic and clandestine messages intercepted by a small Metropolitan Police wireless unit based initially in the attic at Scotland Yard and from the mid-1930s in the grounds of the Metropolitan Police Nursing Home at Denmark Hill, south London. The unit, which was controlled by Harold Kenworthy, a Marconi wireless expert, was co-opted by Sinclair to provide GC&CS with both intercepts and technical advice.

By now, Sinclair had moved both the codebreakers and his MI6 staff to a new joint headquarters at 54 Broadway, close to Whitehall and the centre of power. The resurgence of Germany under Adolf Hitler and the Nazis had led to a realisation that war was inevitable and determined efforts were being made to try to break the German cyphers. Cooper recalled that the British codebreakers had almost totally ignored them since the end of the First World War assuming they must be unbreakable:

Another grave fault in the old GC&CS was the tradition, which I found firmly established when I joined, that German cyphers were invincible. Considering what Room 40 had achieved in 1914–18 it seems extraordinary that anyone should believe this, but it was generally assumed that no civilised nation that had once been through the traumatic experience of having its cyphers read would ever allow it to happen again, and that after the wide publicity given to Room 40's results, together with unfortunate leakages to the Germans during the Peace Conference it would be waste of time to work on German high-grade systems. The result was that for twenty years one man was employed to read the German diplomatic low-grade code traffic which was of no intelligence value whatever.

Germany had indeed learned its lesson from the publication of the Zimmermann Telegram and, during the 1919 Paris Peace Conference, its delegation used the one-time-pad system, blocking British attempts to read its communications with Berlin. It also began looking at the possibility of using cyphers generated by a machine. The publicity given to the success of the British codebreakers during the First World War led a number of nations to adopt machine cyphers, which were seen as more difficult to break. The most famous of these was the Enigma machine. The first British contact with the machine came in 1921, when it was still in development. It was shown to the British military attaché in Berlin, in the hope of persuading the British armed forces to use it.

The German Navy introduced the Enigma machine cypher in 1926 and for a brief period it remained a possibility that both the British and the German armed forces might use it. In 1927, Commander Edward Travis, a member of GC&CS who oversaw the construction and security of British codes and cyphers, asked Hugh Foss, a specialist in machine cyphers, to test the commercially available machine.

The Enigma machine resembled a small typewriter encased in a wooden box. It had a typewriter-style keyboard, set out in the continental QWERTZU manner, which differed slightly from the standard British/American QWERTY keyboard. Above the keyboard, on top of the box, was a lampboard with a series of lights, one for each letter of the alphabet. The operator typed each letter of the plain-text message into the machine. The action of depressing the key sent an electrical current through the machine, which lit up the encyphered letter on the lampboard.

The encypherment mechanism consisted of three or four teethed wheels or rotors which were inserted into the machine. The wheels had twenty-six different electrical contacts on each side, one electrical contact for every letter of the alphabet. Each electrical contact was connected to one of the contacts on the other side of the wheel by internal wiring. The order of these contacts and their wiring was different for each of the three wheels, which could be set at twenty-six different starting positions with any one of the twenty-six contacts at the top. They could also be placed in different orders within the machine to add further difficulties for anyone trying to break the cypher.

The action of depressing each key turned the first wheel one position. When that wheel had moved a set number of times, the second wheel moved round one position, and when the second wheel had turned a set number of times, the third wheel moved round one position. The point at which the next wheel moved was known as 'the turnover'.

The Enigma machine had two crucial features which Foss realised would help anyone trying to break it. A letter could not be encyphered as itself (so if the operator pressed 'T', for example, the only letter that would not light up on the lampboard was 'T' itself), and the machine was reciprocal, i.e. if 'P' was encyphered as 'T', with the machine set at the same position, 'T' would be encyphered as 'P'.

The number of different settings for the commercial machine was put at several million. But Foss determined that while it had a 'high degree of security', it could be broken if accurate 'cribs' were available. 'Cribs' were predictions of possible original plain text, usually standard parts of routine messages, such as situation reports sent out every day. One of the most common was *Keine besondere Ereignisse*, 'nothing to report', which because of its brevity and common usage in situation reports was easy to spot.

Foss later recalled: 'I wrote a paper entitled "The Reciprocal Enigma" in which I showed how, if the wiring was known, a crib of fifteen letters would give away the identity and setting of the right-hand wheel and how, if the wiring was unknown, a crib of 180 letters would give away the wiring of the right-hand and middle wheels.'

The British decided not to buy the machine, although the RAF used it as the inspiration for a much more secure rotor-based cypher machine known as Type-X which British armed forces used with great success during the Second World War. A year after Foss's investigation, the German Army began using the Enigma machine and within two years had introduced an enhancement that greatly improved its security.

The *Stecker*-board was an old-fashioned telephone-style plugboard, which allowed the operator to introduce an additional encypherment, using cables and jacks to connect pairs of letters: 'B' to 'Z', 'V' to 'L', etc. This made the machine very much more secure, increasing the variations of encypherment to 159 million million million possible settings and blocking British attempts to read the *Wehrmacht* systems for around eight years.

The Spanish Civil War brought a flood of operational Enigma messages and on 24 April 1937 Dilly Knox managed to break the basic non-steckered machine supplied by Germany to its Italian and Spanish allies. Shortly afterwards, he began working on the steckered systems used by the *Wehrmacht* for high-grade communications between Spain and Germany. Knox made some progress, but while he knew that the *Stecker*-board was what made the *Wehrmacht* machines more secure, he was unable to decypher any German Enigma messages.

CHAPTER 2

CONFIDENTIAL WORK FOR THE FOREIGN OFFICE

The German annexation of Austria in March 1938 and the subsequent threats to Czechoslovakia made clear that war with Nazi Germany was inevitable. Hitler warned on 30 May 1938 that it was his 'unalterable will to smash Czechoslovakia by military action in the near future'. British Prime Minister Neville Chamberlain flew to Germany to try to persuade Hitler to modify his demands, but at the same time Britain was preparing for war and on 18 September 1938, the bulk of the Government Code and Cypher School (GC&CS) and a number of sections of MI6 were moved to Bletchley Park as 'a rehearsal'.

The move was in keeping with the rather genteel atmosphere enjoyed by the codebreakers at Broadway Buildings, the result of Sinclair's belief that they were fragile characters who needed careful treatment. 'There had been a tragic case of suicide shortly before I joined,' recalled Cooper. 'A man called Fryer threw himself under a train at Sloane Square and "C" had formed the opinion that the work was dangerous and people must not be overstrained.' No doubt reinforced in these opinions by the eccentricity of many of the codebreakers, Cooper included, Sinclair ordered that they should only work between 10am and 5.30 in the afternoon, with a one-and-a-half hour break for lunch.

Barbara Abernethy joined GC&CS in August 1937 at the age of sixteen. She was fluent in French, German and Flemish and was working at the Foreign Office. When Denniston asked for a new typist, she found herself sent across to Broadway. 'I was posted over there for a week not knowing what I was doing and told that it was strict secrecy,' she said. 'I was there for a week and they apparently approved of me because I was kept on and I stayed there. Life was very civilised in those days, you know, we stopped for tea and it was brought in by messengers. I was very impressed by this, first job I'd ever had and it seemed paradise to me. I thought: "Well, this is the life, isn't it. Thank God I'm not back in the Foreign Office".'

The 1938 Bletchley 'rehearsal' began on 18 September 1938 and was managed by Captain William Ridley RN, the chief MI6 administrative officer, hence the nickname of 'Captain Ridley's Shooting Party'. It involved the Military, Air and Naval Sections of GC&CS, the Enigma research party under Dilly Knox, and a number of sections of MI6. They were to stay at Bletchley for three weeks. Cooper recalled:

> We were told that this was just a 'rehearsal', as in fact it turned out to be. But we all realised that the international situation was such that the 'rehearsal' might well end in a real war with Germany, and probably also with Italy. All personnel of every grade were accommodated in hotels in Bletchley and surrounding towns and villages. The Admiral sent out an excellent chef from London and we all sat down to lunch together at one long table in the house. All this was simply paid for out of MI6 funds. MI6 also provided some cars for transport, but many people used their own cars and gave lifts to others. It fell to my lot to be driven in from Stony Stratford by Knox, who had a remarkable theory that the best way to avoid accidents was to take every cross-road at maximum speed.

The mix of young female secretaries and rather elderly and eccentric male codebreakers, many of whom had worked in Room 40 or its War Office equivalent during the First World War, scandalised the staff of the hotels where they were staying. The head of the Naval Section 'Nobby' Clarke, by now fifty-five years old, recalled booking into the Bridge Hotel in

Bedford with two male and three very young female colleagues. 'The men were all in their late fifties and the females somewhat younger,' Clarke said. 'Each day to the astonishment to the hotel staff they all went off in a car and did not return until late in the evening. It seems to have been thought that these must be a party of elderly gentlemen with their young women. A chambermaid at the hotel who was complaining of over-work, on being told that times were serious and that she should not complain, said: "It's alright for you, but some of us have to work." Little did she realise what these odd people were doing.'

The chef sent in by Sinclair was in fact his favourite chef from the Savoy Grill and the meals were very much *haute cuisine*. But after a few days of trying to deal with the demands of the some of the more difficult codebreakers, the chef also attempted suicide. Clarke was forced to telephone the Buckinghamshire Chief Constable in an attempt to keep the story out of the papers and ensure that the codebreakers' presence at Bletchley Park remained secret. 'Then we learned that Chamberlain had flown to Munich and made an agreement with Hitler,' Cooper recalled. 'We all trooped back to London with mixed feelings of shame and relief.'

Despite Chamberlain's claims of 'peace in our time', all he had actually done was buy time, at the expense of the Czechs, for Britain to prepare for war. The race to break the Enigma cyphers now had added urgency, but despite his undoubted brilliance Dilly Knox was having no success. In search of an answer, Denniston invited his opposite number in the French *Deuxième Bureau*, Colonel Gustave Bertrand, to London. The meeting was so secret that it was held away from Broadway Buildings with Bertrand referred to, even in correspondence between Denniston and Sinclair, as 'Mr X'.

The British had exchanged information on Russian cyphers with the *Deuxième Bureau*'s codebreaking operation since 1933. But it was not until late 1938 that the two sides began to discuss the Enigma machine in any detail. Given that the exchange on Russian material had been somewhat one-sided, with the British providing far more than they received in return, the French had a surprisingly large amount of material on the Enigma machine. Denniston wrote to Sinclair suggesting that the dialogue was worth continuing. The French had clearly not got far themselves but had produced some 100 documents, some of which were of more value than others. They included 'photographs of documents relating to the use of the Enigma machine which did increase our knowledge of the machine and have greatly aided our researches', Denniston said. Bertrand made clear that some of the French material had been obtained by secret agents. In fact, it was largely from one *Deuxième Bureau* agent codenamed *Asche*.

Hans Thilo Schmidt worked in the German War Ministry's cypher centre and, in exchange for money and sex, had provided the French with comprehensive details of the *Wehrmacht* Enigma systems. Schmidt was a 'walk-in', calling at the French embassy in Berlin in 1931 and offering to sell them documents on the use of Enigma in return for 10,000 marks. The critical handover came at a meeting between *Asche* and Bertrand at a hotel at Vervier, on the French-German border, in late 1932, when *Asche* produced two operators' manuals, one of which had a message which had been encyphered using a real Enigma machine, and a schedule of daily Army keys for September and October 1932. They were photographed by the French allowing *Asche* to return the documents to the safe in the German War Ministry from which he had taken them before their absence could be spotted. Over the next six years, *Asche* produced numerous documents which were offered to the British and – until the November 1938 meeting with 'Mr X' – turned down, but which were passed on to the Poles.

Following the meeting with 'Mr X', Denniston asked Sinclair's permission to continue the liaison with the French, explaining that

> our main reason for seeking this liaison in the first place was
> the desire to leave no stone unturned which might lead to a

solution of the Enigma Machine as used by various German services. This is of vital importance for us and the French have furnished us with documents which have assisted us but we are still doubtful if success can be obtained without further documents. During the coming meetings, we hope to show Mr X the lines on which we are working and make clear to him what other evidence we need in the hope that his agents may produce it.

The liaison with the French brought GC&CS a number of interesting documents, Cooper recalled. Since they arrived via the MI6 station in Paris in the same red jackets the British secret service used for all its reports, the French contributions were nicknamed 'Scarlet Pimpernels'. They included documents on how to use the machine as well as photographs showing the *Stecker* system and how it worked, Cooper recalled. They also suggested that the French were not working alone.

> They had not disclosed that they had other signals intelligence partners. But a Scarlet Pimpernel on the German Air Force Safety Service traffic had obviously been produced from material intercepted not in France but on the far side of the Reich. It gave data on stations in eastern Germany that were inaudible from Cheadle, but was weak on stations in the north-west that we knew well. Eventually, the French disclosed that they had a liaison with the Poles, and three-sided Anglo-Franco-Polish discussions began on the Enigma problem.

Denniston, Knox and Foss attended a meeting in Paris in early January 1939 with the French and representatives of the *Bureau Szyfrow*, Polish codebreaking organisation. The British codebreakers had high hopes that the meeting with the Polish codebreakers would help them to find a way to break Enigma. But it was to be a major disappointment. All three sides appear to have been too cautious to give anything of value

away with Denniston describing the conference as having been
held in 'an atmosphere of secrecy and mystery'. The French
codebreakers explained their own method of breaking Enigma,
which was even less refined than the basic system used by Foss
in 1927. Knox described his improved version of Foss's system,
which used a process known as 'rodding'. The Poles were under
orders to disclose nothing substantive and explained only
how lazy operators set the machines in ways that produced
pronounceable settings, such as swear words or the names of their
girlfriends. This was something the British had already worked
out and it was a great disappointment that they had nothing
more to add, Foss recalled. 'Knox kept muttering to Denniston,
"But this is what Tiltman did," while Denniston hushed him
and told him to listen politely. Knox went and looked out of
the window.'

Knox was dismissive of the claims made by both the French
and the Poles, in the latter case wrongly but largely because
the officer explaining them was clearly not a codebreaker
himself and did not speak with any authority on the subject.
Knox's assessment of the Polish work was damning: 'Practical
knowledge of QWERTZU Enigma nil. Had succeeded in identifying indicators on precisely the methods always used here,
but not till recently with success. He [the Polish officer] was
enormously pleased with his success and declaimed a pamphlet,
which contained nothing new to us.'

The main problem for Knox was what he called 'the
QWERTZU', by which he meant the way in which the letters
on the keyboard of the *Wehrmacht* Enigma machines were wired
to the letters on the wheels inside the machine, and he left the
meeting in Paris none the wiser. One good thing did however
come out of the January 1939 meeting. It became clear that the
Poles were using mathematicians to try to break Enigma and,
when they returned to the UK, Denniston recruited two mathematicians to assist Knox. One was Alan Turing, a 27-year-old
fellow of King's College, Cambridge, who began working part-

time, coming in on occasional days with the intention of joining full time when the war began. The other was Peter Twinn, a 23-year-old mathematician from Brasenose College, Oxford, who started work immediately.

'When I joined GC&CS in early February 1939 and went to join Dilly Knox to work on the German services' Enigma traffic, the outlook was not encouraging,' Twinn recalled. Knox and the other leading GC&CS codebreakers were largely classicists or linguists, he said.

> They regarded mathematicians as very strange beasts indeed and required a little persuasion before they believed they could do anything practical or helpful at all. The people working on Enigma were the celebrated Dilly Knox and a chap called Tony Kendrick, quite a character, who was once head boy [Captain of the School] at Eton. There was a slightly bizarre interview from Dilly who was a bit of a character to put it mildly. He didn't believe in wasting too much time in training his assistant; he gave me a five-minute talk and left me to get on with it, which was actually rather good for me. Before I arrived Dilly was a lone hand, he always was, assisted by one secretary/assistant and enjoying a total lack of other facilities – though it is by no means clear that he would have used any. He was notorious for being very secretive about his ideas and I am not sure whether he had any hopes of ultimate success.

Dilly Knox was an exceptional man whose brilliance has only rarely been acknowledged. With the possible exception of John Tiltman, Knox was the only codebreaker of this era who proved as adept at breaking the old-fashioned codebooks of the First World War as the machine cyphers of Second World War. The son of a bishop, and the brother of the Roman Catholic theologian Ronnie Knox, he was fifty-five at the start of the war and so wildly eccentric as to put his fellow codebreakers in the shade. A fellow of King's College, Cambridge, he walked with a limp, the result of a motorcycle accident, and wore horn-rimmed glasses without which he could see nothing. Knox was so absent-minded that he forgot to invite two of his three brothers to his own wedding. He believed so strongly in the relaxing powers of a bath to give him inspiration that during the First World War he had a bath installed in a room in the Admiralty. A fellow codebreaker recalled how, early in the war, the fellow lodgers in Knox's billet became so concerned at the length of time he was spending in the bathroom that they felt compelled to break in. 'They found him standing by the bath, a faint smile on his face, his gaze fixed on abstractions, both taps full on and the plug out. What was passing in his mind could possibly have solved a problem that was to win the war.'

Knox was in fact very close to breaking Enigma and there was just one major thing that was holding him up, Twinn recalled.

> What we did not know was the order in which the letters of the keyboard were connected to the twenty-six input discs of the entry plate. Dilly, who had a taste for inventing fanciful jargon, called this the QWERTZU. We had no idea what the order was. We had tried QWERTZU, that didn't work. There are twenty-six letters in the alphabet. Our ordinary alphabet has them in a certain order, but the Germans weren't idiots. When they had the perfect opportunity to introduce a safe-guard to their machine by jumbling it up that would be the sensible thing to do. After all, there were millions of different ways of doing it.

The introduction of mathematicians to help Knox in his investigations of the Enigma problem was fortunately not the only good thing to come out of that first meeting with the Poles in Paris in January 1939. Knox might not have been initially impressed with the Poles, but they were certainly impressed with him and specifically asked that he be present at a second meeting between the Polish, British and French codebreakers, to be held at the *Bureau Szyfrow*, the Polish cypher bureau, in the Pyry Forest just outside Warsaw, in July 1939. It was only then that the Poles revealed the full extent of the progress they had made in reconstructing the *Wehrmacht*'s steckered Enigma machine.

The *Bureau Szyfrow* had broken a number of German codes during the early 1920s but the introduction of Enigma had left them unable to read the *Wehrmacht*'s messages. Their response was to recruit mathematics students and put them through a codebreaking course. Only three passed. Their names were Jerzy Różycki, Henryk Zygalski and Marian Rejewski. All three were recruited but worked initially on a part-time basis and it was only in September 1932 that Rejewski, the best of the three, was given the steckered Enigma machine and asked to solve it. By the end of that year, assisted by Enigma key lists obtained by the French from *Asche*, he had reconstructed the wiring mathematically, using permutation theory. By the beginning of 1938, assisted by the fact that the Germans were not changing the settings frequently, Rejewski and his colleagues were able to solve 75 per cent of the Poles' intercepts of German Army Enigma messages. 'We were deciphering every day and often at a record speed,' he recalled.

In the autumn of that year, they began using electro-mechanical machinery known as *Bomby* – literally 'bombs', a name that derived from the ticking noise they made. The *Bomby* were used to identify 'females', repetitive letters in the Enigma keys, to break the messages. But the introduction, in December, of two additional wheels, allowing further different permutations of wheel order, brought the Polish successes to a halt. Rejewski succeeded in reconstructing the wiring of the two new wheels but the Poles no longer had enough *Bomby* to run through the much greater number of possibilities the new wheels had created. They needed help and believed the British could provide it, said Colonel Stefan Mayer, the officer in charge of the *Bureau Szyfrow*. 'As the danger of war became tangibly near we decided to share our achievements regarding Enigma, even not yet complete, with the French and British sides, in the hope that working in three groups would facilitate and accelerate the final conquest of Enigma.'

The Poles explained how they used the *Bomby* and the *Netzverfahren* or 'grid system' invented by Zygalski. These were lettered sheets of paper with holes punched in them to help to break the keys and wheel orders by identifying the 'females'. But the introduction of the fourth and fifth wheels had meant they had to use far more *Bomby* and sheets than they could possibly produce. Knox was furious to discover that the Poles had got there first, sitting in 'stony silence' as they described their progress and produced a clone of the Enigma machine, reconstructed using the knowledge they had built up over the previous six years. But his good humour soon returned after they told him that the keys were wired up to the encypherment mechanism in alphabetical order, A to A, B to B, etc. Although one female codebreaker had suggested this as a possibility, it had never been seriously considered, Twinn recalled. 'It was such an obvious thing to do, really a silly thing to do, that nobody, not Dilly Knox or Tony Kendrick or Alan Turing, ever thought it worthwhile trying,' he recalled. 'I know in retrospect it looks daft. I can only say that's how it struck all of us and none of the others were idiots.'

A few weeks later the Poles gave both the French and British codebreakers clones of the steckered Enigma. Bertrand, who had been given both machines and asked to pass one on to the British, later described taking the British copy to London on the Golden Arrow express train on 16 August 1939. He stepped down from the train at Victoria station to find the deputy head of MI6 Colonel Stewart Menzies standing on the platform, swathed in smoke and wearing a dinner jacket on which was pinned the rosette of the *Legion d'Honneur*. Bertrand handed the machine over to Menzies with the words, '*Accueil Triomphal*' – 'a triumphant welcome'.

As well as setting up the meetings with the French and the Poles, which would ultimately give the British the additional information they needed to break Enigma, Denniston began building up the organisation for war, touring the universities to search out academics, particularly mathematicians, linguists and classicists, with potential to become the new codebreakers his organisation would desperately need to first break the German cyphers and then keep on top of them. Sinclair got authorisation from the Treasury for the recruitment of 'fifty-six senior men or women, with the right background and knowledge' as well as thirty young female language graduates. Josh Cooper recalled:

> It was often said, in the old GC&CS, that if we had another war we should have to mobilise the dons again. Denniston now went on a round of visits to the universities in order to sound out his former colleagues from the 1914–18 war, to find whether they would be prepared to rejoin in an emergency, and whether they could introduce him to other university teachers who might be useful and would be prepared to come. He dined at several High Tables in Oxford and Cambridge and came home with promises from a number of dons.

Denniston, who was by now fifty-seven, recalled that

> it was naturally at that time impossible to give details of the work, nor was it always advisable to insist too much in these circles on the imminence of war. At certain universities, however, there were men now in senior positions who had worked in our ranks during 1914–18. These men knew the type required. Thus it fell out that our most successful recruiting occurred from these universities. During 1937 and 1938 we were able to arrange a series of courses to which we invited our recruits to give them a dim idea of what would be required of them.

The 'territorial training course' lasted about a fortnight; the first day was taken up with security indoctrination, after which the trainees visited a number of sections spending two or three days in each, with programmes arranged to suit the interests and qualifications of individuals. At the end of the course they were asked to say whether they would undertake to come to Bletchley on receipt of a telegram, and to say which section they would prefer to work with. Their pay was fixed at £600 a year with their colleges making up the balance of their normal salaries. The young female language graduates were not so fortunate, receiving just £3 a week.

Denniston is in many ways a tragic figure, never given the credit he deserved for his astute decision to work with the French, which led to the cooperation with the Poles, and to bring in mathematicians, a proposition that was never going to be welcomed by many of his more experienced staff. He would later be unceremoniously pushed aside and when he died in 1961 there were no obituaries pointing out the good work he had done for his country. But the work he put into recruiting academics, and particularly mathematicians, and preparing them to be called up on the outbreak of war showed a large degree of prescience and, as Cooper recalled, laid the foundations for the breaking of the Enigma cyphers that was to make such a major contribution to the Allied war effort.

> It would I think be hard to exaggerate the importance for the future development of GC&CS. Not only had Denniston brought in scholars of the 'humanities', of the type of many of his own permanent staff, but he had also invited mathematicians of a somewhat different type who were specially attracted by the Enigma problem. I have heard some cynics on the permanent staff scoffing at this course; they did not realise that Denniston, for all his diminutive stature, was a bigger man than they.

Those recruited included Gordon Welchman, a 33-year-old

mathematics lecturer and fellow of Sidney Sussex College, Cambridge, who would bring in a number of his students. Other more distinguished academics recruited to work at Bletchley included Professor Leonard Forster, a distinguished scholar of German and Renaissance Studies from Selwyn College, Cambridge; Norman Brooke Jopson, Professor of Comparative Philology at Cambridge, who was said to be 'able to converse in most of the living languages of Europe'; Hugh Last, Professor of Ancient History at Brasenose College, Oxford; Tom Boase, Director of the Courtauld Institute and Professor of History of Art at the University of London; W. H. Bruford, Professor of German at Edinburgh, who had also served in Room 40; Gilbert Waterhouse, Professor of German, Queen's University, Belfast; A. H. 'Archie' Campbell, Barber Professor of Jurisprudence at Birmingham; and J. R. R. Tolkien, Professor of Anglo-Saxon at Oxford University, who – sadly perhaps for codebreaking but not for the world of literature – eventually elected to remain at Oxford and write *Lord of the Rings* rather than join his fellow academics at Bletchley.

Patrick Wilkinson was one of those swept up by Denniston in his tour of the universities.

One day in the summer of 1938, after the Nazis had taken over Austria, I was sitting in my rooms at King's when there was a knock on the door. In came F. E. Adcock, accompanied by a small, birdlike man with bright blue eyes whom he introduced as Commander Denniston. He asked whether, in the event of war, I would be willing to do confidential work for the Foreign Office. It sounded interesting, and I said I would. I was thereupon asked to sign the Official Secrets Act form. By now I had guessed what it was all about. It was well known to us that Adcock had been a member of Admiral 'Blinker' Hall's Room 40 at the Admiralty in the First World War, famous since its existence was revealed in 1928, which had done pioneering work on the decoding of enemy messages. A totally secret organisation, the GC&CS, had carried on in peacetime, under the Foreign Office since 1922, and was now run by Denniston, always known as 'A.G.D.', a retired naval schoolmaster, whom I sensed to be a kind and civilised man.

Adcock, who would himself join Cooper's Air Section on the outbreak of war, had been involved in more surreptitious recruitment of some of his Cambridge colleagues for some time. E. R. P. 'Vinca' Vincent, professor of Italian Studies at Cambridge, recalled how Adcock summoned him to a discreet dinner in the spring of 1937.

> We dined very well, for he was something of an epicure, and the meal was very suitably concluded with a bottle of 1920 port. It was then that he did something which seemed to me most extraordinary; he went quickly to the door, looked outside and came back to his seat. As a reader of spy fiction I recognised the procedure, but I never expected to witness it. He then told me that he was authorised to offer me a post in an organisation working under the Foreign Office, but which was so secret he couldn't tell me anything about it. I thought if that was the case he need not have been so cautious about eavesdropping, but I didn't say so. He told me war with Germany was inevitable and that it would be an advantage for one of my qualifications to prepare to have something useful to do.

Many of the young women were recruited in a way typical of the recruitment of clerks and secretaries into the intelligence services during the inter-war years. They were daughters of 'somebody who knew somebody'. Diana Russell Clarke, a 25-year-old, whose father had worked in Room 40, was typical of the pre-war codebreakers recruited through family connections. 'My mother simply rang up Commander Denniston, whom we'd known all our lives. She said: "Liza, have you got a job for Diana?" He replied: "Yes, send her along," so that's where I started. We were on the third floor. There were MI6 people upstairs. They were always known as "the other side". We didn't have any truck with them.'

The signing of the Molotov–Ribbentrop Pact between the Soviet Union and Germany on 23 August 1939 left little doubt that war was now inevitable. Preparations were made to move to the MI6 'War Station' at Bletchley Park, which was given the covername Station X, not as a symbol of mystery but simply because it was the tenth of a number of MI6 sites all designated using Roman numerals. Telegrams were sent out calling the dons to Bletchley and the existing members of GC&CS moved there on 15 August 1939.

Despite what now seems with hindsight to be the obvious imminence of war, the move to Bletchley in August 1939 was regarded very much as 'a test', similar to the visit of Captain Ridley's Shooting Party the previous year. The memo ordering staff to prepare to move to the War Station said that 'in order to carry out communications tests' it would be manned from the morning of 15 August 1939 'by those detailed in GC&CS first wave'. From the outset the codebreakers and their support workers were told that there must be 'absolute secrecy' about what was going on at Bletchley Park, even among themselves. 'The staff are warned against any conversations regarding the work with other members of the staff whilst in their billets. If occasion should arise as to what you are doing the answer should be that you are part of the aerial defence of London,' the memo warned. It ended with the words: 'This test is to be treated with absolute secrecy by all members of this department. Gas masks are to be taken.'

If this sounded distinctly ominous – indeed a reflection of the very real, dangerous and lonely position in which Britain would soon find itself – the reality of the move was entirely different. The first wave comprised only around 110 members of the pre-war establishment and in the last peaceful weeks of the summer of 1939 war could not have seemed further away, said Nigel de Grey, a 53-year-old veteran of the First World War codebreaking organisation Room 40, who was recalled for the move to Bletchley.

There is no moment in time more beautiful than the early days of a fine English autumn such as were the last days of August 1939 and the last days of peace. In such richly romantic atmospheric conditions even the architectural vagaries of Bletchley Park were wrapt in a false mellowness and almost, but never quite, achieved the appearance of a stately home. The house, its 'carriage sweep' and backyards had been enclosed in posts and rails to mark the narrow confines of the ground that had been bought for the War Station of GC&CS and its richer relation the MI6. So much that happened afterwards seems, in retrospect, to have sprung from the decision to house GC&CS in Bletchley Park that we may be forgiven perhaps this brief recollection of its exterior features. They form the background against which so many difficulties of signals intelligence were fought out and so much was achieved; the conditions of work there reflected upon so many problems of staff and efficiency that Bletchley Park and its gradual complete transformation became an historical factor that it is impossible to ignore. On mobilisation, the house was already too small to accommodate the number of people for whom office space was required. A neighbouring boys' school was acquired at short notice and the Commercial Section, some of the Enigma party and some of the so-called Diplomatic Sections of GC&CS were pushed into it before the proprietor had had time to remove his furniture.

The second floor of the mansion was reserved for the staff of MI6 who had moved to Bletchley, while the Naval, Military and Air Sections of GC&CS were on the ground floor along with the telephone exchange, the teleprinter room, the kitchen and the dining room for the entire staff, de Grey recalled.

Recruits previously earmarked began to drop in with the slightly unexpected effect of carrier pigeons and were dispatched to the billets provided by the neighbourhood. A curious air of unreality pervaded this collection of strangers and friends. None of the new arrivals had any idea of the general organisation or, indeed, of what other sections existed beside the one to which they had been appointed and it was no one's business to explain. This was not like reservists rejoining the colours. It was more like the prim first day at a public school. The sight of a professor of some erudition struggling with an unfamiliar task on the blankets of a boy's bedstead in the dormitory is one not easily forgotten.

Not the least striking feature of the list of people who moved to Bletchley in that first wave is how few of them were actually working on German material. Aside from Denniston and his deputy Commander Edward Travis, there were twenty-nine people in the diplomatic and commercial sections, none of whom were working on German cyphers (the largest number of people focusing on any specific language were the nine working on Italian diplomatic cyphers, with the next largest number the six working on the cyphers of Britain's ally France). The Military Section comprised eighteen people of whom only four were working on German material, half the number who were working on the Italian Army systems. The Air Section had a staff of just eleven, of whom only three were trying to break German systems. The Naval Section had more people, a total of twenty-five, but only two of them were German experts, as opposed to eleven working on Italian systems.

'There was virtually no yield whatever from German codes and cyphers – diplomatic, naval, military or air – other than partial decrypts of low-grade, air-to-ground *Luftwaffe* traffic,' said Frank Birch, a famous actor and Room 40 veteran recalled in 1939 to take over as head of the Naval Section. 'On the civil side, the two high-grade German diplomatic systems had not been seriously tackled since their introduction in 1919, and, owing to the wartime diversion of experienced research cryptanalysts to service tasks, were not to be subjected to concerted attack until 1941.'

The only section focusing exclusively on Germany was Dilly Knox's research section, which was solely interested in Enigma. It comprised just four codebreakers – Knox himself, Turing, Twinn and John Jeffreys, another Cambridge mathematician – and was working on its own in a cottage adjoining the mansion. So out of the 110 members of GC&CS who moved to Bletchley, only thirteen were actually working on the codes or cyphers of the country which was now the main threat to the UK.

The inside of the mansion was impossibly crowded and it was difficult to manage, recalled Edmund Green, one of the senior members of the Naval Section, who became the office manager and acquired the nickname 'Scrounger'. He recalled that this was a result of the determined manner in which he ensured that the naval codebreakers had any equipment they needed.

Chaos is a mild term to describe our condition at the outset. We had very few plans, nowhere to lay our heads – no furniture, books of reference, maps, atlases, dictionaries or any tools with which we might be expected to finish the job. Our difficulties were increased by the fact that our work was so 'hush hush' that we were not able to specify the reason for our importunities – for so they were regarded. Then we were a government office tied and bound by the red tape of rules and regulations which none of us, even the heads of the organisation, really understood. It was like playing a game with an umpire who did not know the rules. Was it then surprising if some of us resorted to methods frowned upon by the Civil Service? Lastly we were expanding at a speed only equalled by rabbits breeding in a warren. I not only had to scrounge tools but if we acquired a typewriter, our next headache was to find a typist to work it. I had always understood that the most difficult and temperamental personalities were prima donnas.

I soon discovered that many of those with whom I had to do could give stones and a beating to any Patti or Tetracinni. As far as our own staff were concerned, once one had discovered the human end of them, they were worth their weight in gold. If we did strike a dud, it was my business to sell him or her. I am told that I once swopped a small and incompetent typist for a large and priceless card index.

Secrecy was paramount, Josh Cooper recalled. Service personnel initially wore civilian clothes in an attempt to suggest that the site had nothing to do with the military.

We were all instructed not to tell friends and relations where we were, but to give as our address a Post Office Box Number in Victoria Street. Letters addressed to this box were delivered to Broadway and forwarded to Bletchley by MI6 courier. The system broke down when large parcels were addressed to the Box Number. In one case a grand piano was consigned in this way.

Most staff were put up in hotels until Parliament authorised the billeting of personnel vital to the war effort on ordinary households. Private cars were used for transporting staff into work and taking them back to their rooms. 'A great friend lent me his Bentley for the duration of the war because he decided it was better for it to be driven than being put up on blocks,' recalled Diana Russell Clarke. 'So I had this beautiful grey Bentley and of course they were useful because we used to collect people to come into work and then drop them home afterwards.'

The two things that stuck in the mind of Phoebe Senyard, a 48-year-old spinster, who was a senior clerk in the Naval Section, were the great secrecy surrounding the whole affair and the wonderful food the staff were provided with.

A great deal of secrecy had to be observed of course and we were given instructions to inform inquisitive persons that we were attached to the Air Ministry for the aerial defence of London. What I remember very well were the wonderful lunches with which we were served. Bowls of fruit, sherry trifles, jellies and cream were on the tables and we had chicken, hams and wonderful beef steak puddings. We certainly could not grumble about our food.

The threat of war seemed to leave the staff at Bletchley completely unruffled. As Barbara Abernethy recalled, at lunchtime, most of the codebreakers would troop out onto the lawn in front of the house to play rounders.

We had a tennis ball and somebody managed to commandeer an old broom handle, drilled a hole in it and put a leather strap in it. It was all we had, things were getting a bit tough to get. If it was a fine day, we'd all say rounders at one o'clock, we'd all go out and play, just to sort of let off steam. Everybody argued about the rules and the dons just laid them down, in Latin sometimes. We used trees as bases. 'He got past the deciduous,' one would say. 'No he didn't,' another would argue. 'He was still between the conifer and the deciduous.' That was the way they were.

Malcolm Muggeridge, who served in MI6 during the war, recalled visiting Bletchley and watching the codebreakers debate the finer points of the rules of rounders.

They adopted the quasi-serious manner dons affect when engaged in activities likely to be regarded as frivolous or insignificant in comparison with their weightier studies. They would dispute some point about the game with the same fervour as they might the question of free will or determinism, or whether the world began with a big bang or a process of continuing creation. Shaking their heads ponderously, sucking air noisily into their noses between words.

For most of the university dons recruited as codebreakers since the First World War this was the life to which they had become accustomed, a mixture of Oxbridge high table and Foreign Office gentility. But to many of the more junior staff it was a world they had never seen before. 'It was beautiful,' said Barbara Abernethy. 'Lovely rose gardens, mazes, lovely old building, wonderful food.' For a brief moment, Bletchley Park really did have the relaxed air of a weekend party at an English country mansion.

'None of us quite knew what would happen next,' said Abernethy. 'War had not been declared and most people thought and hoped that nothing would happen and we would go back to London.' Given their experience the previous year, when Chamberlain's agreement with Hitler at Münich had averted war, most of the staff were highly sceptical about the likelihood of Britain becoming involved in war. 'As one cynic put it: "The Poles are going to be sold down the same river the Czechs were sold down last year",' said Henry Dryden, a member of the Military Section. The codebreakers began mounting a 'sleeping watch' with duty officers staying overnight in the few bedrooms that had not been taken over as offices, or simply putting up a cot in their own offices. 'The news in the papers was grave enough but there was still nothing in our material to indicate that Germany was on the brink of war,' recalled Cooper. 'Early in the morning of 1 September 1939, I met the admiral's deputy, Colonel Menzies, over breakfast in the old dining room in the house. I must have made some fatuous remark about another quiet night, to which he replied tersely: "Heavy fighting all along the Polish frontier".'

In the early hours of the morning, the German Army had swept into Poland. The Polish infantry divisions were unable to hold back the *Blitzkrieg* launched by the highly mechanised *Wehrmacht*. When the British told Hitler to withdraw, he responded by accusing the Poles of being the aggressors. Neville Chamberlain, the British Prime Minister, then gave him an ultimatum. If he did not withdraw his troops from Poland, Britain would declare war on Germany. At 11am on 3 September 1939, the deadline set in the ultimatum expired without any response. Britain was at war with Germany, standing virtually alone against the might of Hitler's forces. Bletchley Park was now faced with a race against time to break the German Enigma cypher.

With more and more people arriving, the cramped conditions in the mansion were soon getting on everyone's nerves. Sinclair died of cancer shortly after the start of the war, so Denniston wrote to Menzies, who had taken over as head of both MI6 and Bletchley, suggesting that the MI6 sections be moved elsewhere.

> Many of our recruits are men of considerable distinction and it is definitely felt that in the allocation of accommodation such facts should be taken into account. It appears to me improper to invite such as these to try to do work requiring a high degree of concentration in overcrowded rooms. There is a real spirit of discontent growing among my colleagues. I have congratulated them on the good work that is being done under trying conditions and the natural reply is 'improve our conditions and you will get more results'. The Naval Section is now grossly overcrowded and we have to remember that we have added to our staff volunteers of very considerable standing and the research work they will undertake is of extreme national importance and one which calls for some degree of comfort in their surroundings in order to get the best out of them. It seems that there is not room to house MI6 and GC&CS in Bletchley Park efficiently. The only alternative therefore is to separate. It therefore remains to examine whether alternative accommodation can be found for some or all sections of MI6.

MI6 sections began to move out; the GC&CS Commercial and Diplomatic Sections had already moved into the neighbouring

Elmer's School and a programme of construction of temporary wooden huts began. Soon the various sections began to move out of the mansion into the newly constructed buildings, adopting the name of the hut they were in as their section title, in part for security reasons. The first to move was the Naval Section, which moved into Hut 4, next to the mansion, in November 1939.

The accommodation remained primitive and as late summer turned first into autumn and then into winter, the codebreakers found the heating to be woefully inadequate. 'It was dreadful," said Barbara Abernethy. 'We had an electric stove which didn't work and a very poor heating system. We all froze. We had to wear coats and mittens.' It was even colder in the huts, which were bleak after the comfort of the house. Bare concrete floors disguised with a coating of red tile paint, windows with blackout curtains, wooden trestle tables, light bulbs with no shades and inefficient electric heaters, or worse, cast iron coke stoves with metal chimneys going up through the asbestos roof or inefficient paraffin heaters. 'They were awful,' said Phoebe Senyard.

> When the wind was high, long flames would be blown out into the room frightening anyone nearby. Alternatively, the fire would go out and smoke would come billowing forth filling the room with a thick fog. It was a familiar sight to find Mr Green on his hands and knees wearing thick motor gloves endeavouring to light a recalcitrant fire, whilst the shivering occupant would be dressed in a thick overcoat, scarf and gloves endeavouring to cope with his work, with all the windows open to let out the smoke.

But it was wartime and across Britain there was very much a spirit of make-do and live for the day. Funding for all that was required to take place at Bletchley was low and there had been no real breakthrough into the German Enigma cypher but morale remained remarkably high. 'Christmas was now drawing near and the question of leave arose,' said Phoebe Senyard.

> It was impossible for all to be away together so we arranged among ourselves who should stay. Jocelyn and I drew lots and I lost and resigned myself to a miserable Christmas, the first one for some years that I had spent away from home. When the day arrived I found there were more people at BP than I had thought there would be. For the travel ban which had been imposed had prevented quite a number from going home. Mr Birch invited me to a small celebration and I arrived afterwards in the dining room for lunch feeling quite happy and being rather late to find the hall decorated magnificently with everyone sitting down wearing the peculiar paper hats one gets from Christmas crackers and blowing whistles which shot out a terrific length of paper. Every seat was occupied with the exception of one seat round the corner but there I sat quite happily with a wonderful lunch in front of me. All the Christmases which I spent in Bletchley were extremely good, everyone going all out to make everyone else enjoy themselves.

CHAPTER 3

EARLY BEGINNINGS
VERY SMALL BEER – FULL OF FOREIGN BODIES

When German forces crossed the border into Poland, Rejewski and his fellow codebreakers were forced to flee to Bucharest. Hoping to join Knox and resume their work breaking Enigma, they went first to the British embassy where the ambassador told them he could do nothing to help them until he had spoken to London. Sadly for the British, the staff at the French embassy were far better briefed on the importance of the Polish codebreakers and arranged for them to leave for Paris immediately. Attempts by Knox, Denniston and Menzies to bring them to Bletchley Park failed and they were incorporated into the French intercept site – the *Poste de Commandement Bruno*, based in the beautiful Château de Vignolles, in Gretz-Armainvilliers, on the north bank of the Marne, twenty-five miles south-east of Paris. British codebreakers were posted to the château, with one of them, Henry Dryden, recalling his time at what the British called the 'Mission Richard' for reasons quite separate from the codebreaking he carried out. 'My enduring memories of the two months I spent there have no military connotations,' Dryden said. 'Never before or since have I seen such a remarkable display of roses, nor heard so many nightingales singing against each other, nor eaten so much Brie in so short a time.'

Turing had spent his time since arriving in the Cottage working on Naval Enigma, which Knox had put to one side since it was a more difficult problem than German Army and *Luftwaffe* Enigma. He had also been busy devising a machine, called the Bombe, after the *Bomby*, although it was a more complex piece of equipment than its Polish namesake. This would test the encyphered messages against commonly used streams of text – known to the codebreakers as cribs – to narrow down the possibilities for the keys, settings and wheel orders of the Enigma machines. Turing enjoyed a good degree of progress on both. Menzies agreed funding of £100,000 for the construction of the first Bombes and the British Tabulating Machinery company (BTM) was commissioned to build it, with the work supervised by the BTM research director Harold 'Doc' Keen. Then in December 1939, Turing managed to work out the indicator systems for five days of pre-war Naval Enigma traffic. But neither the Poles in France nor the British could manage to break a wartime Enigma message. Dennis Babbage, one of the young mathematicians who had joined the small party in the cottage, recalled that attacks were made on numerous days' traffic. 'One after the other they went down and a general gloom descended.'

This period was not entirely wasted because the codebreakers discovered one feature of the way in which the ordinary signals operators set up the machine. The operators were using pronounceable sequences of letters for the three-letter message settings on the machine, these were usually the first three letters of a word, or their girlfriends' names, sometimes even the first three letters of obscenities. They became known as Cillies because one of the first that was spotted was CIL, an abbreviated form of the German girl's name Cilli. 'Just occasionally you would get a chap who was rather fond of the same letters,' said Susan Wenham, who was twenty-eight and one of the young female codebreakers recruited from Newnham College, Cambridge. 'It might be for some personal reason. Perhaps one chap might use his girlfriend's initials for the setting of the wheels or his own initials. Something like that, you know, silly little things. They weren't supposed to do it but they did.' Searching for Cillies became something of an art, said Mavis Lever, another of the young female codebreakers, who also worked on four-wheeled

Enigmas. 'One was thinking all the time about the psychology of what it was like in the middle of the fighting when you were supposed to be encoding a message for your general and you had to put three or four letters in these little windows and in the heat of the battle you would put up your girlfriend's name or dirty four-letter German words. I am the world's expert on dirty German four-letter words!'

But no actual cyphers were being broken and the pressure got to Knox, who had just been appointed Chief Assistant, effectively the chief cryptographer. He threatened to resign, an approach he was prone to take when he felt the battle to break the cyphers was not being pursued with sufficient vigour by those in charge. At the Pyry conference, he and Denniston had promised to send the Poles more of the Zygalski sheets, which they had been unable to procure. These had been produced, but never sent. In a letter to Denniston, Knox insisted that the Zygalski sheets must be taken to the Poles in France immediately. 'My personal feelings on the matter are so strong that unless they leave by Wednesday night I shall tender my resignation,' he said. 'I do not want to go to Paris but if you cannot secure another messenger I'm actually at the moment completely idle.'

In fact, Turing was sent to Mission Richard with the Zygalski sheets and a brief to find out why the codebreakers were unable to get into the wartime cyphers. The Zygalski sheets allowed Rejewski to make the first break into the German wartime Enigma: a German Army message in what the codebreakers dubbed the *Green* cypher for the 28 October 1939. Turing's visit also uncovered the reasons for the British codebreakers' failure to break any wartime Enigma. The information the Poles had given them was inadvertently wrong, providing the incorrect turnover points for two of the wheels. Shortly after Turing's arrival back in the UK, Knox used the corrected information to break the *Green* Army Enigma settings for 28 October and, within days, an Enigma key known as the *Red* was broken for 6 and 17 January 1940. (The first Enigma cyphers to be worked on by GC&CS were given the names of colours because progress was listed on boards using coloured crayons, the green and red crayons simply being the first that came to hand.)

Despite Knox's undoubted brilliance as a codebreaker, there were those who felt that something more intensive along the lines of a codebreaking production line would be required once the Phoney War came to an end and British troops became involved in the fighting.

'One decision had been taken just prior to the first success,' noted Nigel de Grey, who took charge of intelligence production.

> Among the younger men engaged on the Enigma problem, Commander Travis had found not only the knowledge required to grapple with the Bombe theory but men with an active sense of urgency. He felt that the atmosphere of research work tended to cloud the practical attack, the 'chuck and chance it' spirit that might hook the fish while the more experienced fisherman still considered the colour of his fly. Both were necessary but one should be tried not independently of, but separately from, the other. The decision to make this change was taken at a meeting held on 5 December 1939 and it was further determined to move the exploitation party into a new wooden hut erected in the garden of Bletchley Park, named Hut 6. This they occupied in January and as Hut 6 they were ever after known.

Commander Edward Travis, Denniston's deputy, had been the government's main adviser on what type of codes and cyphers to use before the war, a secondary role of GC&CS. Short, stout and bald, with small round spectacles, 'Jumbo' Travis was fifty-one years old and an able and forceful administrator who did not feel himself bound by the traditions of the veteran codebreakers. He put one of the impressive new younger men identified by de Grey in charge of Hut 6. Gordon Welchman, a studious, pipe-smoking man in his early thirties with dark hair and a moustache, who was far more dynamic than his academic appearance suggested, had already begun recruiting his own people to man the section. Stuart Milner-Barry, the 33-year-old Chess Correspondent of *The Times* and a fellow student of Welchman's at Trinity College, Cambridge, was one of the first to join Hut 6, as Welchman's deputy. When the war broke out he had been in Argentina playing chess for Britain, along with his friends 30-year-old Hugh Alexander and 28-year-old Harry Golombek. They too soon joined, as did the 31-year-old Scottish chess champion J. M. 'Max' Aitken; 30-year-old Dennis Babbage, from Magdalene College, Cambridge and Howard Smith, also thirty and like Welchman a Fellow of Sidney Sussex. (Smith would later serve as British Ambassador to the Soviet Union and then as head of MI5.) Continuity with Knox's efforts was provided by John Jeffreys. Knox continued to carry out research into various problems in the Cottage while Hut 6 prepared to carry out what was hoped to be the day-to-day breaking of Enigma. It is important to realise that at this stage no one was sure whether the success would continue. Indeed, there were concerns that it might not last at all, that the Germans were bound eventually to realise that Enigma was not secure, de Grey recalled.

> There were, in January 1940, no means within GC&CS of assessing the value of Hut 6's achievement in terms of intelligence. The material available from the Poles was fragmentary or rather, perhaps, spasmodic. It was long out of date. But, since the Germans had not made a change on 1 January, and the methods of attack were proving themselves, it seemed that at least GC&CS might look to have a run for its money, especially when the Bombe could be brought into action. The achievement, it was true, hung by a hair, for it was really mostly lack of good cypher discipline that so far had made the Enigma vulnerable and the Germans were regarded as

masters of disciplinary regulations and slaves of the iron rule. It was clear that steps must be taken to put the deciphered material into English and in some measure order it for expert examination. If the pearl were indeed of great price, crypt-analytically a triumph achieved after years of investigation, a potential source of first-rate intelligence both on the German Army and on their Air Force and a good omen for the attack upon the German Naval machine, then it must be guarded as none other.

The break into the Enigma cypher led to strict security being imposed on the work going on at Bletchley Park. Menzies issued orders giving GC&CS the covername 'Government Communications Headquarters' – the name by which it is still known to this day – adding that 'this should be sufficient expla-nation for the curious to account for the presence of personnel from so many different government departments.' Hut 6 and Dilly Knox's Enigma Research Section became 'barred zones' for anyone who was not working there.

The potential intelligence haul from Bletchley Park's 'Most Secret Source' was immense. But de Grey was right. It hung by a very slim thread. The British had managed to penetrate the Enigma cyphers only because the Germans had been careless and did not adhere strictly to their signals instructions. If they found out and strengthened or even changed their cypher systems, all the codebreakers' efforts would be wasted. There were already strict regulations in place preventing staff from talking about their work, but these were now reinforced to the point that most of the people at Bletchley who were not working on Enigma, or a related issue – the vast bulk of the people working there – were not even aware that it had been broken. 'We knew nothing about Enigma at all until long after the war,' said Julie Lydekker, one of the clerks in Cooper's Air Section. 'It was a very strange set-up. We were very much in water-tight compartments because of the security so one really only knew one's own sections.'

The lack of understanding in the services and in Whitehall of the extent of what was going on at Bletchley led them to send people who while fluent in German were never going to match up to the very tight vetting procedures, Josh Cooper recalled.

> The German-speaking ladies that Air Ministry sent down to Bletchley pretty obviously failed to meet these requirements. There was for example the elderly and very imposing typist-secretary whom the Section immediately nicknamed 'Queen Mary', and a younger and rather promising recruit who made her position impossible scandalising her Bletchley billetors by saying to all and sundry that the only friends she had ever had were Germans. This seems to have been true; she had had a troubled and unhappy life at home in England, but had found kindness and sympathy when she went to Germany. It was a pity that she had to go, for she had evident aptitude for the work.

When Gwen Davies was sent to Bletchley Park, as an 18-year-old member of the Women's Auxiliary Air Force (WAAF), she was told she was being posted to nearby RAF Chicksands. 'When I arrived at Chicksands I was taken into the administration office where there was a driver waiting and he said with perfect seriousness: "Do we blindfold her or do we use the covered van?" and ultimately they used the covered van, I was shut into the back of a blacked out van and taken to Bletchley.'

She was dumped with her luggage outside the gates of the park and told by a young guard that she couldn't come in because she didn't have a pass. 'I was by this time hungry, thirsty and very, very annoyed. "Look," I said, "I don't know where I am, and I don't know what I'm supposed to do." "Come to the right place then," said the guard, "most of 'em here look as if they didn't know where they was and God knows what them doing". An elderly guard told him to leave me alone, and said that I was to go to the hut at the left of the gates. "Somebody will come and see to you," he said, "and if you want to know where you are, you're at Bletchley Park." "And if you want to know what that is," added the younger guard, sniggering, "it's the biggest lunatic asylum in Britain.'"

Davies was given a security lecture and told never to reveal, even to her close family, what she did at Bletchley.

> I had to sign the Official Secrets Act and I was told that I must never ever say to anyone where I was working, except to say Box 101, Bletchley, and that I must never ever tell anyone about any of the work I was doing. You never talked even to your own watch about your traffic, about what you were doing. So you talked about personalities. That was the great thing. Gossip at Bletchley was absolutely wonderful, apocryphal stories about everybody flew everywhere; personalities were safe to talk about.

Similarly, those in Hut 6 knew nothing of what went on elsewhere in the Park. 'It was a very curious organisation,' said Susan Wenham, one of the Hut 6 codebreakers.

> We were very, very departmentalised. You never discussed your work with anyone except your little group that you worked with. I hadn't a clue what was going on in the rest of the Park and nobody else had a clue what we were doing, except the real high-ups. It was a curious world of its own.

At the outset of war, Bletchley Park was at the centre of a web of intercept sites around the country where wireless operators carefully logged all German radio messages before sending them to the codebreakers by teleprinter, or initially at least from some of the smaller stations by motorcycle courier. These 'Y Service' stations were operated by the Army, Navy and Air Force; the Foreign Office; the Post Office; and the Metropolitan Police.

The main Navy and Army intercept sites were as they had been for much of the inter-war period with the Navy sites at Scarborough and Flowerdown and the Army site at Fort Bridgewoods, near Chatham. The RAF Y Service site had moved from Waddington to Cheadle in 1938. In the months leading up to the war, the Post Office had been building a number of other intercept sites for diplomatic traffic to allow the armed forces to concentrate on military and naval traffic and one of these, at Sandridge, near St Albans, was already in place working directly to Bletchley Park. Two more would shortly be opened in Scotland at Cupar and Brora.

'GC&CS had always tended to take too little interest in the radio by which they lived,' Cooper recalled. Similarly the three services had little understanding of the work of the codebreakers and believed that their intercept sites produced sufficient intelligence simply by analysing the activities of the radio networks they were monitoring, a process known as 'log-reading', or later 'Traffic Analysis'. But without the service, Post Office and Metropolitan Police intercept operators, Bletchley would have had no Enigma traffic to work on in the first place.

Joan Nicholls talked her way into the female equivalent of the Army, the Auxiliary Territorial Service (ATS), at the age of fifteen by pretending she was two years older. She was posted to one of the intercept sites where she was taught to operate a radio set and how to transcribe German messages sent out in Morse code. 'When there was a lot of excitement the wires would be absolutely humming with Morse,' she said.

> They would be transmitting all over the place and we would really have cramp in our fingers sometimes trying to write it down non-stop, because you only had one chance to get it.
>
> We had to get the preamble and the first three blocks absolutely accurate because that was the key to decoding the message. If we missed a letter we had to know exactly what position it was in and if the signal faded and we lost information, we had to know how many blocks we missed. Every one of our sets had access to three aerials. We had what looked like

a little switchboard in the set room and, if the reception wasn't good from one aerial, we could switch over to another. It could be quite exciting but sometimes we had a very quiet shift and not an awful lot happened. Nights were very boring, hour after hour of listening for the station to open. It was a little bit like a cat sitting outside a mousehole waiting patiently for the mouse to appear and that's how we were. We'd be sitting there listening, waiting for them to come to life. Then suddenly we'd hear the signal of them coming back, transmitting again and then all your adrenaline was running and it didn't matter how tired you were, how sleepy or bored you felt, the minute that station came alive again, you would be alive too, tearing pieces of paper off the pad and scribbling away like mad.

The intercept operators had several additional weapons in their armoury that would assist in the identification of stations and therefore in building up the intelligence picture. The first was direction-finding (DF), a technique in use since the First World War in which a directional aerial or an array of aerials was set up in such a way as to produce a bearing to the enemy transmitter and by using two or more 'DF stations' against the same target, a number of different bearings could be plotted on a map using triangulation to determine the enemy location. The second was identification of the specific wireless transmitter in use, on the basis that every transmitter contained vagaries that could be identified from analysis of its pattern of transmission in a process known as radio finger-printing (RFP). The last was the operator's 'hand', the way in which the German operator sent his Morse code messages, known as TINA.

'It is like a voice,' said Joan Nicholls.

When a member of your family comes through the door and says something to you, you don't have to look to see who it is because you know the voice. You recognise the voice of your friends and family on the telephone because the minute they speak you know it's them and it's the same with the operators. They each had their own particular sound, that lilt or staccato way of sending Morse dots and dashes. So if they changed frequency and we lost them, we would go looking for them and we would listen first of all for the sound of the transmitter and then we would tune in to that transmitter and listen for the operator and the minute we found him, that was him, there was no question of 'We think we have him'. As soon as we heard the sound of our man, the way he sent the letters, he was our man.

The Army site at Chatham had been intercepting most of the Enigma traffic, including both the *Red* and the *Green* cyphers. It was not clear when the first breaks occurred in early 1940 that the *Red*, rather than the *Green*, would become the most important of the keys. But what was clear was that the *Red* was not, as had always been assumed until it was actually broken, an Army cypher. When it first appeared, shortly after the formation of the *Wehrmacht* in March 1935, it was clearly passing traffic between a number of ground stations. The British military intelligence section that controlled the Army Y station at Chatham, MI8, ruled that since the messages were between land-based stations they must be military rather than air force and therefore the responsibility of Army intercept operators rather than RAF operators. But once the codebreakers managed to crack it they soon discovered it was being used to encypher communications between various *Luftwaffe* headquarters.

Since the end of 1938, the *Red* Enigma traffic had been the Army's main priority. It came as something of a shock to MI8 to discover that for more than a year it had been funding an expensive operation which should have been carried out by the RAF. But trying to persuade Air Ministry that it should be intercepted by the RAF site at Cheadle rather than by Army operators at Chatham was a difficult task and Group Captain Lyster Blandy, who was in charge of the RAF intercept operation, but unaware of the potential importance of the Enigma traffic, refused to allow his men to take encyphered messages, Cooper recalled. 'Even after Enigma had begun to be read, early in 1940, when I suggested to Blandy that Air Ministry ought to take a hand in intercepting it, he replied: "My Y Service exists to produce intelligence, not to provide stuff for people at Bletchley to fool about with".' The Army was equally adamant that its men should not be tied up with intercepting *Luftwaffe* traffic and the row continued for several months at the beginning of 1940.

The RAF eventually decided to allocate twenty sets to the *Red* traffic but this was not enough to provide sufficient messages and the operators at Cheadle did not have the same appreciation of the level of accuracy that was required in taking down the five-letter Enigma traffic. As a result, Chatham had to continue taking it as well.

A section which could liaise with Chatham, Cheadle and the other intercept sites taking German Army or *Luftwaffe* messages was set up in Hut 6 with Travis ringing round the top London banks and begging them to loan him their brightest young men to coordinate between the academics who broke the cyphers and the service Y stations. This liaison section, known as Bletchley Park Control, was to be manned twenty-four hours a day and to stay in constant touch with the intercept sites to ensure that their coverage of radio frequencies and networks was coordinated and that as little as possible was missed. Where an important station was difficult to hear, it was to be 'double-banked', taken by two different stations so that the chances of picking up a false letter that might throw a spanner into the works were cut down and that the material that came to Hut 6 could be worked on with some degree of confidence by the Hut 6 codebreakers.

'We were told what we would cover and that came from Station X, the intercept control there would tell us what to cover that day with what priority,' Joan Nicholls recalled.

They would tell us if they wanted them double-banked, two

people to take them, or if one good quality operator would be sufficient. We didn't know that Station X was Bletchley Park. We never knew where it was. You were only told what you needed to know and we just needed to know that Station X was controlling what we actually monitored.

Many of the messages themselves arrived from the outstations by motorcycle courier. But Traffic Registers giving the preambles and first six groups of the messages intercepted by the outstations were sent by teleprinter to the Hut 6 Registration Room. Here a number of female graduates recruited by Milner-Barry from Newnham College, where his sister had been vice-principal, tried to establish the specific Enigma cypher in use from the preambles, carefully examining them to see if there was any intelligence that could be garnered before the code-breakers got to work. A description of each message, containing the frequency and callsigns; the number; whether or not it was urgent; and the first two groups, was carefully logged on so-called B-Lists. These became known colloquially as Blists and the female graduates were dubbed the 'Blisters'.

At this stage, the Bombes had not yet been built and Enigma was being broken purely by hand, a difficult, if not virtually impossible, task with a machine cypher. The first step in breaking any cypher is to try to find features which correspond to the original plain text. Whereas codes substitute groups of letters or figures for words, phrases or even complete concepts, cyphers replace every individual letter of every word with another letter. They therefore tend to reflect the characteristics of the language of the original text. This makes them vulnerable to studies of letter frequency; for example the most common letters in English are E, T, A, O and N. If a reasonable amount, or 'depth', of English text encyphered in the same simple cypher were studied for 'letter frequency', the letter that came up most often would represent E. The second most common letter would be T and so on. By working this out and filling in the letters, some will form obvious words with letters missing, allowing the codebreaker to fill in the gaps and recover those letters as well.

Another basic weapon used by the codebreaker, 'contact analysis', takes this principle a step further. Some letters will appear frequently alongside each other. The most obvious example in the English language is TH as in 'the' or 'this'. So by combining these two weapons, the codebreaker could make a reasonable guess that where a single letter appeared repeatedly after the T which had already been recovered from letter frequency, the unknown letter was probably H, particularly if the next letter had already been recovered as E. In that case, he might conclude that the letter after the E was probably the start of a new word and so the process of building up the message would go on.

Machine cyphers like Enigma were developed to try to protect against these tell-tale frequencies and letter pairings, which is why the wheels of the Enigma machine were designed to move around one step after a number of key strokes. By doing this, the Germans hoped to ensure that no original letter was ever represented by the same encyphered letter often enough to allow the codebreakers to build up sufficient depth to break the keys. But it still left open a few chinks of light that would permit the British codebreakers to attack it. They made the assumption, correct far more often than not, that in the part of the message being studied the right-hand wheel would not have had the opportunity to move the middle wheel on a notch. This reduced the odds to a more manageable proportion. They were shortened still further by the Enigma machine's great drawback. No letter could ever be represented by itself. This was of great assistance in using cribs, pieces of plain text that were thought likely to appear in an Enigma message. This might be because it was in a common proforma, or because there was an obvious word or phrase it was expected to contain. Sometimes it was even possible to predict that a message passed at a lower level, on a system that had already been broken, would be repeated on a radio link using the Enigma cypher. If the two identical messages could be matched up, in what was known as a 'kiss', it would provide an easy method of breaking the keys.

The Germans, with their liking for order, were particularly prone to providing the British with potential cribs. The same words were frequently used at the start of the message to give the address of the recipient, a popular opening being *An die Gruppe* (To the group). Later in the war, there were a number of lazy operators in underemployed backwaters whose situation reports regularly read simply: *Keine besondere Ereignisse*, or 'nothing to report', said Peter Twinn, one of the leading Bletchley codebreakers.

'You can guess sometimes how messages are started even though you haven't seen the German text,' Twinn said.

> For example you might expect that a message might start '*An die Gruppe*' something or other, just an address. So you make a supposition that it started like this and you might be able to get a very little confirmation that if you wrote *An die Gruppe* something or other under the message, the one thing that the encoded message couldn't for instance have is the A of *An* as A, it could be any one of the twenty-five letters other than A and the second letter couldn't possibly be N and the sixth letter couldn't possibly be G of the word *Gruppe* so if you had quite a long thing you might have far from certain evidence but quite a feeling it might very well be right.

Cribs could appear at any point in the message. Even *Keine besondere Ereignisse* was likely to be preceded or followed by some piece of routine information. But the fact that none of the letters in the crib could ever be matched up with the same letter in the encyphered message made it much easier to find out where they fitted.

'Think of it as a sort of crossword technique of filling in what it might be,' said Mavis Lever, a member of Knox's team.

> I don't want to give the impression that it was all easy. You did

have inspired guesses. But then you would also have to spend a lot of time, sometimes you would have to spend the whole night, assuming every position that there could be on the three different wheels. You would have to work at it very, very hard and after you had done it for a few hours you wondered, you know, whether you would see anything when it was before your eyes because you were so snarled up in it. But then of course, the magic moment comes when it really works and there it all is, the Italian, or the German, or whatever it is. It just feels marvellous, absolutely marvellous. I don't think that there is anything one could compare to it. There is nothing like seeing a code broken. That is really the absolute tops.

But in Hut 6, the codebreakers would not sit and decypher whole messages. They broke the keys and once they had done that left it to other less qualified staff to decypher the actual message. 'When the codebreakers had broken the code they wouldn't sit down themselves and painstakingly decode 500 messages,' said Peter Twinn. 'I've never myself personally decoded a message from start to finish. By the time you've done the first twenty letters and it was obviously speaking perfectly sensible German for people like me that was the end of our interest.'

Diana Russell Clarke was one of a group of young women in the Hut 6 Machine Room, decyphering the messages. 'The cryptographers would work out the actual settings for the machines for the day,' she said.

We had these Type-X machines, like typewriters but much bigger. They had three wheels, I think on the left-hand side, all of which had different positions on them. When they got the setting, we were to set them up on our machines. We would have a piece of paper in front of us with what had come over the wireless. We would type it into the machine and hopefully what we typed would come out in German.

The decyphered message then had to be distributed in some way that made it clear the information was important and was authoritative while at the same time preserving the security of the source. It could not be revealed that the British were breaking Enigma. A new section was formed in Hut 3, next door to Hut 6, in what had previously been the Army section, in order to report the material down the line. The section was made up of just three men. It was headed by Commander Malcolm Saunders RN, even though Hut 6 only dealt with German Army and *Luftwaffe* messages. He was assisted by Squadron-Leader Courtley Nasmith Shaw, an MI6 officer with experience of running operations inside Germany, and by F. L. 'Peter' Lucas, a fellow of King's College, Cambridge, and a famous writer and poet who is best remembered now for his scathing attacks on the modernist poetry of T. S. Eliot.

The material was to be disguised as an MI6 CX report, the standard format for reporting information collected by MI6 agents abroad, de Grey recalled. MI6 was supposedly in contact with a German left-wing organisation which was feeding it the new material. 'Now the essence of the security of an agent is that he should never be recognised as such,' de Grey said.

He must always masquerade in sheep's clothing with a solid 'cover-story' in case suspicion is aroused. Some sort of cover-story had already been produced for Bletchley Park – the air defences of London or the like – cover-stories were in vogue. Since the orders were that the material was all to be cast in the form of a report from an agent, conventions had been adopted, such as 'source saw an order to ...', or in the case of corrupt messages 'from part of a torn document source was able to report ...' Only the pith of the messages was extracted. Ingenuity would be exercised but none the less the reports had none of the cut and dried smack of a service telegram such as would carry conviction to a service mind.

Therein, initially at least, lay the problem. The three services were already suspicious of anything that MI6 reported so while the format adopted by Hut 3 was secure, it took a while before the material began to be taken with the respect it deserved. At this stage, only thirty officers outside of Bletchley Park were aware that Enigma was broken – the six Royal Navy officers 'in the know' included Ian Fleming, the creator of James Bond, then the main naval intelligence officer liaising with MI6 and Bletchley Park. Hut 3 was only to pass the material out via MI6 itself so the reports had to be sent by teleprinter to the MI6 Air Section, Section II, if they were about the *Luftwaffe*, and to the MI6 Military Section, Section IV, if they were about the German Army, and at night they must be passed only to the MI6 duty officer. Although, initially, the standard of the intelligence Hut 6 was reporting did not appear to justify the stringent security measures surrounding it.

'On a snowy January morning in 1940, in a small bleak wooden room with nothing but a table and three chairs, the first bundle of Enigma decodes appeared,' said Lucas.

> The four of us who then constituted Hut 3 had no idea what they were about to disclose. Something fairly straightforward like German Police, or something more like diplomatic – neat and explicit documents straight from the office-tables of the *Führer* and the *Wehrmacht* that would simply need translating and forwarding to ministries?

They were neither. In after-years, even the *Führer's* orders were duly to appear. But meanwhile here lay a pile of dull, disjointed, and enigmatic scraps, all about the weather, or the petty affairs of a *Luftwaffe* headquarters no one had heard of, or trifles of *Wehrkreis* business; the whole sprinkled with terms no dictionary knew, and abbreviations of which our only guide, a small War Office list, proved often completely innocent. Very small beer in fact, and full of foreign bodies.

CHAPTER 4

THE FALL OF FRANCE AND THE BATTLE OF BRITAIN

In the early hours of 9 April 1940, the Phoney War came to an abrupt end with the start of Operation *Weserübung*, the first German military operation in the West. The *Wehrmacht* invaded first Denmark and then Norway, occupying Copenhagen and landing in the Norwegian ports of Narvik, Trondheim, Bergen and Stavanger that night. Almost immediately a new Enigma key made an appearance. Six days later, the *Yellow* key as it had been dubbed in Hut 6 was broken, producing a mass of intelligence on the German operations in Norway. The intercepted messages told the British virtually every detail of what the advancing Germans were doing, said Peter Lucas, one of just three intelligence reporters then working in Hut 3.

Very shortly Hut 6 began breaking it, not occasionally, but daily, and often within a few hours of the introduction of each fresh day's setting. The volume of traffic was considerable, the information important and often urgent: frequently it was read in Hut 3 within a few hours or even less than an hour after it had been sent out by the German station. Hut 3, and through them the ministries, were thus able to follow closely the Norwegian campaign from the point of view mainly (but not exclusively) of the *Luftwaffe*. They learned, not merely what had been done, but what was intended. They received information both strategic and tactical, information which covered not only air operations, but also military and naval operations, and not operations alone, but matters of supply, organisation and politics.

Both Hut 6 and Hut 3 were unprepared for such a huge amount of material and began working around the clock to break the keys and get the intelligence they were producing to London. Up until now, shifts had worked from 10am to 6pm with all the reports being bagged up at the end of the day and sent down by van to MI6 headquarters in Broadway. They were then passed on to the War Office, Air Ministry and the Admiralty, but with British troops deploying to Norway, and Royal Navy ships also taking part in the operation, the Bletchley intelligence was needed urgently. Initial attempts to pass Hut 3's reports by telephone were abandoned as insecure and a teleprinter was installed in Hut 3 so that the intelligence reports, carefully couched in the language of an MI6 report from a spy, a so-called CX Report, could be sent direct to either Section II of MI6, the Air Section, if they related to the *Luftwaffe* or Section IV (military) ground forces operations. Nigel de Grey said they were then distributed by hand to the War Office, Air Ministry, Admiralty and Foreign Office.

> The Enigma traffic, from having been interesting and informative, became suddenly highly operational. The business of Hut 3 and Hut 6 was to ensure that the facts as reported by the enemy reached the three Service Ministries in the shortest possible time. This entailed working round the clock seven days in the week and the Hut 3 party were formed into three eight-hour watches.

The authorities were so concerned over the propriety of having young women working alongside young men overnight in Hut 6 that they insisted that where women were working night shifts there must be at least six women, recalled Stuart Milner-Barry, the deputy head of Hut 6.

> The innovation was thought to be not only a strange fad but dangerous to the morals of a mixed community. Indeed, a

total of three girls, which was all that we required, was thought
to be insufficient to ensure the observance of the proprieties
and – presumably on the principle that the men would be
overworked by such large numbers – a minimum of six was
insisted upon.

As a result, three girls from another department had to be put
on the night shift, not to work but simply to act as 'dummies',
Milner-Barry said. Fortunately, this was 'a precaution that was
dropped by tacit consent after a short interval'.

The number of Hut 3 intelligence officers, all of whom
were at this stage male, only doubled to produce two-man
watches which rewrote the information completely to remove
any suggestion that it had come from decyphered Enigma
messages and to give the impression that it was the product of
Source Boniface, a supposedly left-wing German recruited by
the British and running a network of spies inside the German
armed forces. At this stage it was known only as 'Source CX/FJ',
the FJ being a designation for the supposed MI6 spy.

R. V. Jones, who as MI6 scientific adviser was a frequent
recipient of reports from Bletchley Park, said they were

disguised by some introduction such as 'A reliable source
recovered a flimsy of a message in the wastepaper of the Chief
Signals Officer of *Fleigerkorps* IV which read...', or in the case
of an incomplete decrypt, 'Source found a partly charred
document in the fireplace of...' I can remember handing a
disguised decrypt to Air Commodore [Charles] Nutting, the
Director of Signals, who exclaimed: 'By Jove, you've got some
brave chaps working for you.' Inevitably, there was speculation
about the identity of the supposed secret agent or agents who
were sending back such valuable reports. Gilbert Frankau, the
novelist, who had a wartime post in intelligence, told me that
he had deduced that the agent who could so effectively get into
German headquarters must be Sir Paul Dukes, the legendary

agent who had penetrated the Red Army so successfully after the Russian Revolution.

It wasn't easy by any means to give the Enigma messages the appearance of credible agent reports. They were in a very formatted, specialised military German that was very different from the language as studied by the German scholars who were working on it and were more used to the writings of Schiller and Goethe. It was 'a difficult and fundamental problem', recalled Peter Lucas.

> It was not a matter of receiving straightforward messages and translating them: it was always a matter of receiving material which was nearly always more or less imperfect, often incomplete, rarely intelligible with ease and at its worst totally meaningless even to the best German scholar.'

Mistakes by the German officer who drafted the original signal, or by the German operator who sent it, or by the British operator who intercepted it, or simply gaps in reception caused by bad atmospheric conditions all provided potential to make the deciphered message difficult to understand and were compounded by the military jargon or technical terms in use, or simply by colloquial usage of words and phrases that meant something quite different in '*Hochdeutsch*', the German equivalent of 'Oxford English', that the codebreakers had studied at university.

'The first task of the Hut 3 watch, from the very beginning, was to produce out of these corruptions, gaps, abbreviations and technical terms, a reliable and intelligible text, and to put that text into English,' said Lucas.

> To do this needed all the technique of the academic editor, with the great disadvantage, as compared with an academic editor, that the work generally had to be done in a hurry. Corruptions

had to be emended and reasonable conjectures had to be made as to the contents of missing passages, if this could all be done safely. Something more than 'academic' knowledge of the German language was necessary for this sort of work. Undoubtedly it was generally true that the best linguists did the best work. Nevertheless, there were one or two striking instances of men whose academic training was incomplete, or whose knowledge of German had apparently been more or less casually picked up, achieving remarkable success with Enigma texts. They were, however, exceptional.

Our experiences in Hut 3 demonstrated clearly enough, as a general proposition, that what we really needed – but did not get, at any stage, in sufficient numbers – were men with a first-class training in German, plus a sort of flair for handling these particular linguistic problems, which some of the less likely workers displayed, but some of the more likely did not. This flair is difficult to define and was impossible to predict in any untried watchkeeper. A combination of academic knowledge and flair carried a watch worker further than anything else, but not many watch workers possessed both in sufficient degree. The technical terms, many of them quite unknown at the beginning to anyone save a few specialists in Germany, and the abbreviations, and the plain bad German usages sometimes yielded to straightforward academic or technical knowledge, sometimes to more or less inspired guesswork, sometimes not at all.

The Norwegian campaign was an exhilarating time for both the Hut 6 codebreakers and the intelligence officers in Hut 3. There was a feeling of triumphant excitement that the system put in place by Welchman and Travis was actually doing its job, that the relatively sedate organisation that GC&CS had been between the wars was being turned into a codebreaking production line that was reading the Nazis' most secret signals. The Hut 6 codebreakers were also relieved to discover how much easier it was to crack the Enigma keys when there was a mass of operational signals on which to work.

While Bletchley was now producing valuable operational intelligence, it was not yet appreciated for what it was among the customers, not least because the tight security surrounding the break into Enigma still meant that a total of only thirty Army, Navy and RAF officers knew the truth about where the *Boniface* intelligence was coming from. Everyone else believed that it was the product of an MI6 agent network. Unfortunately, there was little confidence among the service intelligence departments in MI6 agent networks and their reports and among the vast bulk of recipients who knew nothing of the Bletchley secret, Source Boniface was regarded with outright suspicion. Nor had anybody given any thought as to how this intelligence might be passed to the troops on the ground where it could be of some use.

The solution came as a result of the fact that the MI6 head of station in Oslo Frank Foley was retreating through Norway with the Norwegian commander-in-chief Major-General Otto Ruge. Foley was passing messages back to MI6 from Ruge asking for assistance. He was encoding them in the MI6 emergency code. This was a 'book code' which used an 1865 edition of John Ruskin's book *Sesame and Lilies*. Both Foley and the MI6 decoding section based at Bletchley had exactly the same edition and the messages were made up of words taken from the text and identified by page number, line number and position of the word within the line. This link was used to send Foley details of German progress garnered from the Bletchley Park decodes and disguised as information 'from our own forces'.

The German occupation of Norway was still continuing, providing large amounts of intelligence from the *Yellow* Enigma, when the Germans invaded Holland, Belgium and Luxembourg, sweeping into France. Unfortunately, at the same time, they changed the Enigma indicating system on the Army and *Luftwaffe* cyphers they were using, preventing attempts by Hut 6 to break the Enigma cyphers and leading to concern among the codebreakers that they might not get back into it at all. No matter how hard they tried, they simply could not get back into the Enigma cyphers.

The solution came as a result of a moment of inspiration by John Herivel. The 21-year-old from Belfast was brought in at the end of January 1940 by Gordon Welchman, who had been his mathematics tutor at Sidney Sussex College, Cambridge, and recognised that he had exceptional talent as a mathematician. He was one of the new boys trying to think of ways to break into the *Red*. After being taught 'the mysteries of the Enigma' by Alan Turing and Tony Kendrick, Herivel was sent to Hut 6.

'I had been recruited by Welchman and I was going to work in his show,' Herivel recalled.

> I do remember that when I came to Hut 6, we were doing very badly in breaking into the *Red* code. Every evening, when I went back to my digs and when I'd had my supper, I would sit down in front of the fire and put my feet up and think of some method of breaking into the *Red*. I had this very strong feeling: 'We've got to find a way into the *Red* again.' I kept thinking about this every evening and I was very young and very confident and I said I'm going to find some way to break into it. But after about two weeks, I hadn't made any progress at all.

As he thought about how the system worked, and might be unravelled, Herivel tried to get into the mind of the operators who were setting up the Enigma machines. How did they go about it; what were they thinking when they did it? The operators using Enigma began each day by putting the correct wheels and ring settings into their machines. They then selected an opening position for the wheels themselves – there was no laid-down starting position – and then they sent that starting position as a three-letter indicator at the beginning of their first messages.

'Up until the middle of February, I had simply been think-ing in terms of the encyphered messages which were received daily and which came to Hut 6,' Herivel recalled.

Then one evening, I remember vividly suddenly finding myself thinking about the other end of the story, the German opera-tors, what they were doing and inevitably then I thought of them starting off the day. I thought of this imaginary German fellow with his wheels and his book of keys. He would open the book and find what wheels and settings he was supposed to use that day. He would set the rings on the wheels, put them into the machine and the next thing he would have to do would be to choose a three-letter indicator for his first message of the day. So I began to think, 'How would he choose that indicator?' He might just take it out of a book, or he might pluck it out of the air like ABC or whatever. Then I had the thought, suppose he was a lazy fellow, or in a tearing hurry, or had the wind up, or something or other and he were to leave the wheels untouched in the machine and bang the top down and look at the windows, see what letters were showing and just use them.

Then another thought struck me. 'What about the rings? Would he set them for each of the three given wheels before he put them into the machine or would he set them afterwards?' Then I had a flash of illumination. If he set them afterwards and, at the same time, simply chose the letters in the windows as the indicator for his first message, then the indicator would tend to be close to the ring setting of the day. He would as it were be sending it almost in clear. If the intercept sites could send us the indicators of all the *Red* messages they judged to be the first messages of the day for the individual German operators there was a sporting chance that they would cluster around the ring settings for the day and we might be able to narrow down the 17,576 possible ring settings to a manageable number, say twenty or thirty, and simply test these one after the other in the hope of hitting on the right answer. The next day I went back to Hut 6 in a very excited state and told my colleagues of this idea. 'Oh, brilliant,' they all said. Welchman immediately arranged, very discreetly, for first message indicators on the *Red* to be sent early each day to Hut. It was a simple matter to look for clusters. The idea, as my colleagues said, was a good one, and it was faithfully tested every day. Unfortunately, it never worked.

But with the large amount of Enigma traffic pouring into Bletchley as the German *Blitzkrieg* engulfed first Holland and Belgium, and then France, the chances of Herivel's idea working grew exponentially and, on 22 May, David Rees, another of the Hut 6 codebreakers, noticed that a number of the indicators in various messages for two days earlier were very close together. He tried all the different possibilities and managed to break the *Red*. It was one of the most decisive moments in the breaking of the Enigma cyphers, certainly of the Army and *Luftwaffe* cyphers. The *Red* would be broken from now on until virtually the end of the war and although the codebreakers clearly could not have known that, they were jubilant after weeks of only being able to break the *Yellow*, which was only used in Norway.

'I can remember most vividly the roars of excitement, the standing on chairs and the waving of order papers which greeted the first breaking of *Red* by hand in the middle of the Battle of France,' Stuart Milner-Barry recalled. 'This first break into the *Red* was the greatest event of all because it was not only, in effect, a new key, which is always exciting, but because we did not then know whether our number was up altogether or not.'

It became immediately clear that the *Red* was the most valuable of the keys to work on. Far from being just a simple *Luftwaffe* key, it was the system used by the *Luftwaffe Fliegerverbindungsoffiziere (Flivo)*, the *Luftwaffe* officers liaising with ground forces to provide air support, and provided copious details not just of what the German ground and air forces were doing at any one moment but of what they planned to do in the future. Although the invasion of France had brought a number of new Enigma keys, Hut 6 decided to concentrate its limited resources on the *Red* since following Herivel's breakthrough they were now able to break it on a daily basis.

'The volume of traffic on the one key was enormous,' Milner-Barry said.

> Over one thousand messages one day, which was broken by five in the morning. I cannot now imagine how, with our primitive methods of collecting and registering traffic, and our tiny staff for decoding it, we manage to cope at all. It is not at all easy now to recapture the atmosphere of those days. The main sensation of the newcomer was that he was participating in a miracle which he was entirely incapable of comprehending. I may say that this sensation has never entirely left me and that no amount of success staled the thrill of the break.

The long-term significance of the break into the *Red* using 'the Herivel Tip', or Herivelismus as it was dubbed by the other codebreakers, was not entirely clear at the time. But the *Red* key would never be lost again. It became Bletchley Park's staple diet. It was used by countless *Luftwaffe* units and, because they needed to liaise closely with both the Army and the navy in order to provide them with air support, gave an exceptional insight into all the *Wehrmacht's* plans for land operations.

'From this point on it was broken daily, usually on the day in question and early in the day,' recalled Peter Calvocoressi, one of the members of Hut 3. 'Later in the war, I remember that we in Hut 3 used to get a bit tetchy if Hut 6 had not broken *Red* by breakfast time.'

There was very little that the Bletchley Park material could do at this stage to influence the Battle for France, but efforts were made to develop the process previously used in Norway of passing the Enigma decrypts, now known by the codeword *Ultra*, to British commanders in France. This was done by an MI6 communications link to the headquarters of the British Expeditionary Force. A copy of the Hut 3 'agent report' was passed to the MI6 Codes Section, which was based in Bletchley Park and which enciphered it using one-time pads, which when used properly are unbreakable. The enciphered report was then sent by motorcycle dispatch rider to the wartime headquarters of Section VIII of MI6, which was based at nearby Whaddon Hall, and from there it was sent on the MI6 radio link to the MI6 representative at GHQ in France. The codebreakers were jubilant when they deciphered a message giving eight hours' notice of a meeting between the chiefs of staff and the four *Luftwaffe* formations involved but their joy turned to disappointment when the British commanders ignored the intelligence and the opportunity to bomb the meeting and kill key German commanders.

'Valuable as this mass of Special Intelligence might become after analysis as the foundation of strategic knowledge of such matters as the enemy's order of battle, it was clearly of little if any immediate tactical use,' Birch recalled.

> Hut 3 had not as yet the experience, the collateral information or even the reference books and maps wherewith to disentangle the obscurities of the German texts; few in the ministries could currently assess their significance in their disguised form, recipients in the operational theatre could only take them at their face value as agents' reports; not many of them arrived in time for action to be taken; and even if all the material had been available and correctly appreciated, it is doubtful whether in the prevailing confusion, any practical use could have been made of it. Disguised and mutilated to resemble an agent's report, it lost its integrity, did not inspire confidence and could not be correctly assessed.

But in real terms the dismissive attitude of the military at this time to any intelligence produced by Bletchley Park was irrelevant during the Battle for France, which was already lost by the time *Red* was broken. The Allied troops were already in full retreat and even if they had accepted that the intelligence was accurate, they would have been in no position to make proper use of it. Nevertheless, vital lessons were learned allowing the system to be revised so that *Ultra* intelligence could have a direct effect on any future campaigns fought by British troops. It was clear to Menzies and the directors of intelligence in the Admiralty, War Office and Air Ministry that they had to find a way to get the Bletchley Park intelligence, now distinguishable by the classification Most Secret *Ultra* which appeared at the top and bottom of each sheet of the reports, to commanders in the field, with someone involved in the reporting process on the ground fully aware of where the information came from and its true value while at the same time protecting it and limiting knowledge of the fact that the British codebreakers were reading the Enigma messages.

The issue was discussed at cabinet level and in mid-June 1940, the War Office set up a mobile Special Signal Unit, the role of which was to provide liaison with major commands so that *Ultra* intelligence from Hut 3 could be passed on direct. The unit was in fact run by Richard Gambier-Parry, head of Section VIII of MI6, and its original title of Special Signal Unit did not last long because the abbreviation SSU was assumed to be Secret Service Unit. The units were later split into two with Secret Communications Units attached to all major command posts to provide the communications links via which the *Ultra* intelligence would be passed and Special Liaison Units set up and controlled by Frederick Winterbotham, the head of the MI6 Air Section, alongside them passing the intelligence on to commanders.

Although it would be a year before the SCUs and SLUs would play their real role, they were to be critical to the future use of *Ultra* intelligence by operational commanders. They were designed to provide the intelligence produced by the codebreakers swiftly and securely to commanders in the field. The SCUs were the communications experts linking the unit to the codebreaking centres, while the SLUs were made up of intelligence officers provided by MI6, who passed the *Ultra* material on to the commanders. Their role was to control the use of all high-grade signals intelligence, not just Enigma material, strictly to ensure that only those who had been indoctrinated knew of its existence. They also had to enforce the regulations on its use, making sure that it was never acted upon without a secondary source being available, to prevent any German suspicion that Enigma had been broken, and to liaise with the codebreakers on any queries from commanders.

The SLU officer was responsible for personally delivering the *Ultra* message to the commander or to a member of his staff designated to receive it. All messages were to be recovered by the SLU officer as soon as they were read and understood. They were then destroyed. No *Ultra* recipient was allowed to transmit or repeat an *Ultra* signal. Any action taken by a commander on the information given him by *Ultra* was to be by way of an operation order or command or instruction which in no way referred to the *Ultra* signal and could not lead the enemy to believe his signals were being read. No recipient of *Ultra* could voluntarily place himself in a position where he could be captured by the enemy.

The procedures used within Hut 3 were also altered in the light of lessons learned during the Battle of France. The amount of material coming in had strained its resources to the limit. Hut 3 itself became more organised and the number of staff increased with four reporters on each watch and with one officer from each of the Air and Military Sections of MI6 sat on each watch as Air or Army advisers, significantly upgrading the basic two-man watches that were clearly not sufficient during the fighting in Norway and France. 'Hut 3 and Hut 6 were side by side,' said Ralph Bennett, one of the watch intelligence reporters. 'They were linked by a small square wooden tunnel through which a pile of currently available decodes were pushed, as I remember by a broom handle, in a cardboard box, so primitive were things in those days.'

The messages arrived through the wooden tunnel from Hut 6 in batches of between fifteen and twenty and were immediately sorted into different degrees of urgency by the Watch No. 2, or Sorter. They were split into four separate piles. Pile 1, by which the Hut 3 priorities would remain known throughout the war, was the most urgent messages. Pile 2 was less urgent but still needed to be processed and turned into agent reports within four to eight hours and Pile 3 needed to be reported but could be safely sent to MI6 headquarters at Broadway Buildings in London by overnight bag. The fourth pile was nicknamed the *Quatsch* pile after the German word for rubbish and did not need to be processed at all, although they were kept on file for future research.

'Skimming the incoming material to assess urgency and importance remained the most responsible and tricky job,' recalled Lucas.

> It would have been sufficiently troublesome, even if all decodes had arrived in an easily readable state (as a small proportion did throughout), since the pure intelligence problems involved were often extremely difficult to solve on the spur of the moment – a difficulty which became even worse later on, as our work grew more complicated. But since a high proportion of decodes were corrupt, sometimes very corrupt, it was often impossible, on a necessarily cursory reading, to assess the importance, or even the simple sense, of a message. Thus, in times when there was much material (and in Hut 3 we usually had too much to do or else, though rarely, too little) the Sorter had a heavy responsibility, since by a simple mistake he could cause an obscure but urgent message to be laid aside for hours or even days.

Hut 3 was set up like a miniature factory with the Watch Room at its centre. The Watch sat around a circular or horseshoe-shaped table, with the Watch No. 1 at the head of the table, while the air and military advisers sat at a rectangular table to one side. There were up to half-a-dozen men on the Watch, each of whom had to deal with a message taken from the highest priority pile in which there were messages, first of all 'emending' them, i.e. filling in any gaps left because of radio interference or garbled letters, a process that had similarities to solving a cross-word puzzle. They then compiled an alleged agent's report based on the message, working from the original German, rather than translating it first, in order to guard against the introduction of errors.

'The watchkeepers were a mixture of civilians and serving officers, Army and RAF,' said William Millward, an RAF officer who worked in Hut 3 as an air adviser.

> I cannot remember any women involved in this part of the operation, presumably because it was still thought to be wrong for a woman to work on the night shift or because it was thought to be a man's job. At the rectangular table sat serving officers, Army and RAF, one or two of each. These were the Advisers. Behind the head of Watch was a door communicating with a small room where the Duty Officer sat. Elsewhere in the Hut were one large room housing the Index and a number of small rooms for the various supporting parties, the back rooms.

Once the watchkeeper had written the report it was checked by the Watch No. 1, who then passed it to either a military or an air adviser depending on the content. The adviser's job was to ensure it made military sense and to add any comments on what was previously known about the unit before passing it back to the Watch No. 1 so that it could be teleprinted to London.

'Material came in from Hut 6 in more-or-less cablese German and a lot of it corrupt,' said Jim Rose, another of the air advisers.

> Urgent messages were sent direct to Commanders-in-Chief. All messages went up to the service ministries. If the air adviser or the military adviser had anything to comment he was allowed to do so and then next morning we would send deeper comment to the Commander-in-Chief. Some of the information was tactically immediate, some of it was strategic and some of it was a build-up of order-of-battle, strength, weaknesses, supplies and so on, which most generals don't know about their enemy. So it was very important in so many ways.

Meanwhile, Nigel de Grey was put in charge of an 'Intelligence Exchange' Section, Hut 3a, to work on long-term intelligence analysis and reporting. 'There was an inevitable tendency for us to concentrate on the more urgent and spectacular aspects of our information,' Lucas said, 'to try to send out intentions and front lines, battle HQs and tactics with all possible speed, while ignoring by comparison matters of more lasting interest such as organisation, strength, habits of the *Luftwaffe* and the German Army and so on.' De Grey's role was to remedy that by setting up a group of backroom analysts and reporters. One of their first tasks was to set about acquiring more detailed maps than the Baedeker tourist guides the Hut 3 Watchkeepers had been forced to work with during the campaigns in Norway and France. They also looked at the various terms used by the Germans, many of which had completely baffled academics more used to translating Goethe than Guderian; and, most importantly of all, began to build up a detailed picture of the structure of the German armed forces.

The fall of France cast a dark shadow over everyone at Bletchley Park, but the French liaison officers from 'Mission

Richard' were clearly worst affected. 'I remember seeing several of the Frenchmen who were attached to the French Mission here clustered around the wireless set with their ears almost glued to it,' said Phoebe Senyard. 'They were listening to very faint announcements made by the BBC, or getting on to a French station and becoming more and more dejected and downcast with every fresh announcement.'

Mavis Lever was eating her dinner in the mansion dining hall when the news that Paris had fallen was announced. 'We had some Frenchmen working with us at the time and I was sitting next to one of them and he burst into tears,' she said. 'I simply did not know what to do. So, I went on eating my sausages. I mean we weren't going to get any more and it seemed to me there was nothing really I could do if other people were going to burst into tears. I'd got a night shift to work on, so on with the sausages.'

Following the German invasion, Bertrand and the Poles set up a new station on a country estate, the Château de Fouzes at Uzès in Provence, working with the Vichy French government's *Groupement des Controles Radioélectriques*. This was supposed to be monitoring British communications with the underground resistance movement but in fact assisted Bertrand and the Poles by intercepting Enigma traffic and allowing them to continue to do their work on Enigma. Bertrand also managed to make contact with Bletchley Park, via MI6. They remained there until the Germans occupied the whole of France in October 1942 when they escaped to the UK.

Hut 6 was at this stage still breaking Enigma keys by hand using the Cillies and Herivelismus and waiting for Turing's Bombes to help them. The first of the Bombes, known with misplaced optimism as Victory, had been produced in the space of three months and had come on stream in March 1940. It was a fast running electrical machine in a bronze cabinet six-and-a-half feet high, more than seven feet wide and two-and-a-half feet deep, containing a series of thirty rotating drums equating to the wheels of ten Enigma machines, although later versions simulated the action of twelve machines. It contained around ten miles of wire and about a million soldered connections.

The Bombe was a remarkable piece of technology for its time. It was designed to run through all the various possibilities – of wheel choice, order, ring position and machine settings – at high speed in order to test that the Cillies or cribs suspected by the codebreakers were actually in use. The codebreakers provided the operators with a 'menu' suggesting possible equations of clear letters to encyphered letters which was fed into the Bombe. Each time the machine found a possible match, it stopped and was quickly tested by the operator on a British Type-X cypher machine rigged up to work like an Enigma machine to see if it produced German text.

If it did, the operator was able to declare: 'The job's up' and pass it back for decryption. If it was just garbled letters, as was frequently the case, the process continued until the Bombe had found the right combination or exhausted all the possibilities, in which case the codebreakers' suspected crib or Cilli didn't work and a new one had to be found. But Victory kept making 'false stops' and took far too long to test a single 'menu' so it was only used on Naval Enigma, which was not yet being broken on a regular basis. Welchman suggested a solution of a diagonal board to cure the 'false stops' and Turing immediately agreed this would correct the problem. It was not until August 1940 that the first of the Bombes with the diagonal board, *Agnus Dei*, later corrupted to Agnes or even Aggie, was introduced, assisting Hut 6 in its breaks into the Enigma cyphers.

With the end to fighting in France and Norway, the Germans turned their attention towards Britain. Concerns over the possibility of an imminent invasion pervaded the atmosphere at Bletchley Park. 'The sinister covername for an *Operation Sea Lion* began to appear in the *Luftwaffe* traffic,' said de Grey. 'It did not require much ingenuity to identify this name with the preparations for invasion which continued unabated through-out the late summer and early autumn.'

Neville Chamberlain's association with appeasement and the inadequate response to the German attack on Norway had led, at the beginning of May, to his resignation and replacement by Winston Churchill, the man who had ordered Room 40 to be set up. The new Prime Minister soon became obsessed with Bletchley Park, treasuring the intercepts delivered to him each day by Stewart Menzies, the Chief of MI6 and Director of Bletchley Park, in a battered old wooden dispatch box covered in fading yellow leather.

With Hitler's next move expected to be an attack on Britain itself, Churchill made a series of speeches aimed at building up 'the bulldog spirit'. They were epitomised by his 'finest hour' address to the House of Commons and his warning that the British would defend their island on the beaches. Detachments of Home Guards were set up around the country and Bletchley was no exception. Some of the codebreakers were enthusiastic recruits. Malcolm Kennedy recorded in his diary that there had been a wireless appeal 'for volunteers between seventeen and sixty-five to form local defence units against parachutists. I sent in my name to join the detachment which is to be formed at Bletchley, so I may yet have a chance to take a smack at Brother Boche once more!'

One of the more surprising members of the Bletchley Home Guard was Alan Turing. But in typically eccentric fashion he did it solely on his own terms, joining only in order to learn how to fire a rifle, said Peter Twinn. 'They told him to fill this form in and Turing thought to himself: "I don't see why I should sign this, it won't do me any good and it might be a bit inconvenient." So when he'd learned how to fire a rifle and done as much as he thought was of value to him, he thought: "Well, I've got everything I can out of this, I'll just give up going to the Home Guard." When the officer in charge said he would do what he was told because he had agreed to be subject to military discipline, Turing replied, and I can hear him saying it: "Well, you had better look at my form. You'll see I didn't sign that bit".'

Ann Harding, a colleague of both 'Prof' Turing and Peter Twinn in the German Naval Section Hut 4, recalled that the men taking part in the Home Guard were known as 'parashots' since they were expected to shoot the German paratroopers as they tried to land. 'Most of the men had become parashots,' Harding recalled. 'One day Prof had an awful thought. "Peter, what do we do if they land in the maze? There would be the most awful muddle, Peter, with us and them getting lost." This was quite a thought as it was a large maze. The threat of invasion was very real. Many people had heavy sticks or, in the case of farms, pitchforks hidden behind their doors, ready to attack.'

Noel Currer-Briggs, an Intelligence Corps officer, recalled that at one point a mixture of the Home Guard and the regular Army marched into Bletchley as part of an Army recruiting campaign. 'There were lots of oddballs there, people from all over Europe with obscure languages, and there was one chap from Eastern Europe in battledress and a bowler hat, much to the dismay of the sergeant who was trying to make us look smart. It made Dad's Army look like the Coldstream Guards.'

Plans were put in place to set up a mobile codebreaking unit to operate behind the defending British troops should the Germans manage to cross the Channel. The codebreakers' records were to be evacuated to Canada and there was even talk of moving GC&CS across the Atlantic as well if need be.

'The war situation was now becoming very grim,' said Phoebe Senyard.

So during the ghastly months of May, June, July and August when the fear of German invasion was greatest, arrangements were made to organise a mobile section of GC&CS. The air was electric with feeling. Those who had been chosen were photographed and supplied with special passports or identifi-

cation cards and were in a sense excited by the project, although
no doubt dismayed by the reason for their evacuation. I was
surprised at the number of people whose feelings were hurt
because they had not been included in the list, while certain
of the more lighthearted and venturesome of the section came
out with suggestions of what we could do should the Germans
come and how we could advance our careers under the German
Herrenvolk. Joking apart, times were very serious and air raid
alarms were continuous night and day. We used to use the slit
trench at the back of Hut 4 until it was declared unsafe. Special
orders were issued about the dispersal of staff should Bletchley
Park be attacked and so the gloomy days wore on.

Column BQ, as the mobile unit was to be called, was to
comprise around 500 people: 140 of the codebreakers and 360
wireless operators from the various Y stations. The transport
was to be a mixture of private cars and four ancient Midland
Red buses, hired by the War Office, one of which promptly
split along the length of its roof while the other three continuously broke down. 'I am told that the petrol consumption is
about five miles to the gallon,' complained one of the column's
organisers, 'and I think it questionable if they had to go a long
journey whether they would arrive at their destination with any
degree of certainty.'

Most of the private vehicles were in somewhat better condition, although possibly no less dangerous. One of the cars
volunteered as Column BQ transport was the grey Bentley
driven by Diana Russell Clarke, who had become renowned for
driving it at breakneck speed along the country roads around
Bletchley. 'There was one occasion when I was coming back
from leave going about sixty-five which now we would think
was very slow, and burst a front tyre,' she said.

The car went into a frightful wobble. But eventually I got
it onto a nice wide verge. There was a car coming from the

other direction and the occupant got out to see if I was alright. It turned out to be Commander Travis. He said: 'My God, I might have realised it would be you, Diana.' I'd obviously frightened him to death; he thought I was going to go straight into him.

Fortunately, the invasion never came and neither the Bentley nor the buses were ever needed. The codebreakers were able to remain at Bletchley Park where it was not simply a question of breaking Enigma. Hitler and his generals realised that if they were to invade Britain they would need to control the skies otherwise the RAF and the Royal Navy would cause major, probably critical, damage to their forces as they tried to land. So on 10 July 1940, the *Luftwaffe* launched a series of attacks on coastal ports, and subsequently on RAF airfields and aircraft factories, that was to become known as the Battle of Britain. The name of the battle came from a speech made by Churchill in the House of Commons on 18 June in which he said that the Battle of France was over and the 'Battle of Britain' was about to begin.

Upon this battle depends the survival of Christian civilisation. Upon it depends our own British life, and the long continuity of our institutions and our Empire... Let us therefore brace ourselves to our duty, and so bear ourselves that if the British Empire and its Commonwealth last for a thousand years, men will still say, 'This was their finest hour.'

The role of Bletchley Park and signals intelligence in tracking the German bombers and fighters attacking the UK is not widely known but the Air Section, which had a dual role as a GC&CS section and as a section of Air Intelligence, AI4f, was able to break the low-level codes used by the *Luftwaffe* to control the German bombers flying from their airfields in France to attack the UK. 'Exploitation of this material for intelligence purposes should have been a moderately straightforward process,' said Bill Bonsall, a member of the Air Section who would later go on to become the head of its post-war successor GCHQ.

> No great brainpower and no special machinery were needed. It was essentially a pencil and paper operation. But in practice unnecessary obstacles had to be overcome before it reached its full potential, the main one being the Air Ministry's view that the role of GC&CS should be confined to codebreaking. It maintained this view for the first half of the war.

Bonsall was recruited to Bletchley by Martin Charlesworth, one of the dons who had been inculcated in the work of GC&CS at the start of the war but had stayed as President of St John's College, Cambridge, to talent-spot potential codebreakers. He and another candidate were invited to Charlesworth's rooms where Denniston and Tiltman were waiting to interview him. 'They asked us if we were interested in confidential war work,' Bonsall recalled.

> We both said yes and were told that we would be hearing further from them. After a delay of some weeks, I received a letter instructing me to Bletchley Junction, telling nobody, not even my parents, where I was going. I was duly met and taken to the Mansion, where I signed a copy of the Official Secrets Act and was given the address of a billet in the Buckingham Road. When I reported back the following morning, I was taken round to Hut 4 and introduced to Joshua Cooper who said I was going to be working on the radio communications of the German Air Force. Within minutes, I was seated at a trestle table copying out coded messages onto large sheets of paper.

Given the RAF's approach to the codebreakers, which was epitomised by Blandy's initial insistence that Cheadle should not get involved in producing 'stuff for people at Bletchley to fool about with', the refusal to allow the Bletchley Park Air Section to send out intelligence reports was perhaps less of a surprise than it should have been, but Josh Cooper found a way round the problem. He attached his own people to each of the wireless intercept shifts at Cheadle to break the basic *Luftwaffe* codes alongside the operators with Air Intelligence, agreeing that they could provide intelligence rather than the raw signals. These would have otherwise been largely unintelligible to their recipients, who included RAF Fighter Command at Bentley Priory north of London, from where the fighter defences were controlled. 'I applied to the Air Ministry for a number of Computor Clerks,' Cooper said. 'This curious title had nothing to do with electronic computers, which had not yet been invented, but was an echo of an old War Office covername for cryptanalysts – Signal Computor. A successful Computor Clerk watchkeeper was going to need considerable initiative, and would have to fit in with the special world of Cheadle radio operators.' The 'Computors', as they were known, were trained up at Bletchley before being sent to Cheadle and the move proved highly successful, said Bonsall.

> Arriving shortly before the Germans invaded Western Europe the 'Computors' soon achieved their primary task of breaking the air/ground codes completely and quickly enough to derive current intelligence from them. The original three-letter codes were replaced in 1941 by three-figure codes. These codes were harder to break but the 'Computors' developed techniques which resulted in their being broken quickly and completely enough to yield intelligence. To begin with, the 'Computors' worked in the main set-room, with the result that their raw material reached them quickly and the operators could see that their intercepts were eagerly awaited.

The *Luftwaffe* low-level communications between the aircraft and ground controllers were intercepted by Cheadle and, increasingly as the *Luftwaffe* communications switched to

VHF, by a network of small RAF mobile and fixed Home Defence Units based along the eastern and southern coasts at Peterhead and Fifeness in Scotland, Blyth in Northumberland, Scarborough, Skegness, Gorleston, Harwich, Fairness, South Foreland, Hawkinge, Beachy Head, Portsdown Hill, Portland Bill, Strete (near Dartmouth), Coverack and Hartland Point. This network, which was coordinated by RAF West Kingsdown in Kent, provided vital tactical intelligence on the preparations of the German bombers and their fighter escorts. Bletchley gave advance notice of the planned times of raids, the intended targets and the numbers of aircraft involved.

The introduction of the 'Computor Clerks' to Cheadle had allowed Cooper to find a way around the RAF chiefs' perverse view that one of their own intelligence branches should not be allowed to produce intelligence. Under his direction, the Bletchley Air Section had complete mastery of all the *Luftwaffe* low-grade codes and cyphers. 'Its cryptanalytic achievement was formidable,' said Birch. 'With far more lower grade German material to deal with than the other Service sections, it could claim at the end of 1940 that all known *Luftwaffe* non-machine cyphers were readable; of meteorological cyphers, four German, five Russian and two Italian had been read.' Cooper was an extraordinarily astute man whose career in signals intelligence, or Sigint as it is known in the jargon of the codebreaker, went on to span the inter-war period, the Second World War and the Cold War, but he became known to many who arrived at Bletchley during the war as one of the more unusual of the senior staff.

Ann Lavell, who arrived at Bletchley in July 1940 as an 18-year-old WAAF, became Cooper's PA. She recalled that he had a distinctively nervous habit of putting his right hand behind the back of his head and stroking his left shoulder. She found his eccentricity difficult to deal with. 'He was absolutely mad, frightening really,' she said.

At first I didn't like him at all. I thought he was horrible. But when I got to know him I got quite fond of him. But he was not really one of us. He was on another plane, I think. He'd get awfully embarrassed and worried when he felt he wasn't acting like an ordinary human being. There was one time when he kicked over a fire extinguisher and it started foaming and he didn't know what to do and he picked it up, rushed to and fro, and a friend of mine went and took it from him and put it out of the window. He wasn't very practical but once you knew him and got over the slightly forbidding exterior he was very nice and very kind. I've got a rather delightful caricature of him, doing this very familiar gesture of right hand behind head and scratching left ear.

Once they were standing beside the lake and Cooper was drinking a cup of coffee. When he finished he stood there with the empty cup and was clearly slightly embarrassed by having it in his hand. 'So he just threw it in the lake,' Lavell said.

R. V. Jones recalled that Cooper was frequently asked to take part in interrogations of pilots. The first time he did this, he and two other interrogators were sat behind a trestle table when the captured *Luftwaffe* pilot, wearing perfectly pressed Nazi uniform and highly polished jackboots, was marched in and halted in front of them. 'He clicked his heels together and gave a very smart Nazi salute,' said Jones.

The panel was unprepared for this, none more so than Josh who stood up as smartly, gave the Nazi salute and repeated the prisoner's '*Heil Hitler*'. Then realising that he had done the wrong thing, he looked in embarassment at his colleagues and sat down with such a speed that he missed his chair and disappeared completely under the table.

Gwen Davies, another member of the Air Section, remembered Cooper as being 'a very, very strange man, who would burst into the watch sometimes and shriek something absolutely unintelligible and burst out again'. Most of the junior members of staff had difficulty understanding what he was saying, but there was no doubting his brilliance.

> There was a great degree of tolerance at Bletchley for eccentricities. There had to be because so many of the people were very, very eccentric indeed. At least half of the people there were absolutely mad. They were geniuses, no doubt many of them were extremely, extremely clever, but my goodness they were strange in ordinary life.

As the number of messages on the *Red* cypher dropped due to the decline in German offensive operations, Hut 6 had much less work but on 2 September 1940, a new Enigma key, *Brown*, was broken with the aid of Cillies and the newly introduced Bombe *Agnus Dei*. The messages in the *Brown* Enigma had risen during the late summer of 1940, when the Battle of Britain was in full swing and the RAF Hurricanes and Spitfires were fighting off the *Luftwaffe* daytime bombing raids, said Stuart Milner-Barry. 'Nobody knew what its contents would be and the most extravagant hypotheses were entertained.' The *Brown* traffic was found to be communications between a number of *Luftwaffe* stations in France which were directing wireless beams across Britain to guide the German bombers to their targets. It was a critical moment and the timing of the break could not have been more opportune. Having lost the Battle of Britain, the *Luftwaffe* was about to switch to the period of night-time bombing that would become known as the *Blitz*. The breaking of the *Brown* Enigma was to give Bletchley the first of a number of major contributions to the war effort.

'It proved a delightful and a most entertaining key cryptographically,' said Milner-Barry,

> because although the traffic was small, the density of cribs and of Cillies was phenomenal. Never before or since have so many

and such gross breaches of the most elementary rules of cypher and procedural security been committed as by the specialists in beam bombing. They never learned and the German signals officers apparently were powerless to intervene. It was also extremely exciting because of course the object of the exercise was to discover the target before it was too late to be of use to the Air Ministry. The handling of *Brown*, moreover, gave us our first insight into the necessity of close liaison between intelligence and cryptography.

After the famous 'Few' had swept the skies of Britain clear by day, Hut 6 played its part in rendering the skies as hazardous by night. As most raids took place in the early evening, just after dark, the time factor was constantly on the thoughts of the cryptographer and a sense of urgency, such as was never felt again, permeated the whole Hut. For, never again, was the battle so close that the results of one's work had an immediate personal interest, when the difference of an hour in breaking time might mean the difference between life and death for some inhabitants of this embattled island.

R. V. Jones was already convinced that there was a system of German wireless beams criss-crossing the UK to guide the *Luftwaffe* bombers onto their targets. These had been mentioned by captured German prisoners-of-war and a piece of paper salvaged from a Heinkel bomber shot down in March 1940 referred to '*Funkfeuer Knickebein*', or in English 'Radio Beacon Dog-Leg'. The word *Knickebein* recurred on a low-level coded message intercepted by Cheadle. Jones recalled getting a call from Professor Frederick 'Bimbo' Norman, the pre-war Professor of German at King's College, London, and one of the Hut 3 reporters, in the early hours of the morning one day at the beginning of September 1940.

'Two or three nights before the bombing of London started on 7 September, my sleep was interrupted by an event which made more impression on my memory than any bomb ever did,' Jones said.

> The cryptographers had broken a new line of Enigma traffic. There was mention of beams, including one which said that the beam width was eight to ten seconds of arc, or an angle of one in twenty thousand, which would imply that the beam was no wider than twenty yards at two hundred miles. I asked Bletchley to put every possible effort into making further breaks into the new line of traffic. If only we could decode the Enigma messages in time, we could find where and when the German bombers were going to attack and so counter them by having fighters waiting and by having our jamming ready on the right frequencies. This would make great demands on the codebreakers, for the orders did not go out to the beam stations until the afternoon, giving only two or three hours to make the break, but for such a prize they strained every resource of human intelligence and endurance; and it was a great day, late in October, when they achieved this fantastic feat for the first time.

Despite the codebreakers' frequent ability to break the *Brown*, providing 'vital intelligence' that allowed the RAF fighters to lie in wait for the German bombers, it was occasionally impossible. This was sadly the case with one of the most devastating bombing raids carried out by the Germans, against Coventry on 14 November 1940. Enigma had revealed that there was to be a major operation against the UK on that day and that it was codenamed *Moonlight Sonata*, but the only clue to what it might be was the vague mention of a codeword *Korn* (the German for corn). There was no indication as to what it meant but it later transpired that it was an alliterative code for Coventry which the Germans spelt with a K. On the day itself, the *Brown* Enigma could not be decyphered. The raid on Coventry destroyed 4,000 homes, three-quarters of the city's industry and killed as many as 600 people, injuring more than a thousand others. After the secret of the breaking of the Enigma cyphers emerged in the 1970s, a myth grew up that Churchill had insisted that the RAF should not attempt to stop the raid going ahead in order to prevent the Germans realising that Enigma had been broken. It was certainly the case that there was concern that the way in which the RAF fighters were waiting for the Germans and the air raid precautions put in place in the target areas might lead the Germans to suspect that Enigma was being broken but this played no role in the Coventry raids and the initial concerns over the effect on Enigma were not at any event raised until some time after the Coventry raid.

The simple truth is that the keys for that day were not broken until after the raid had taken place. Keith Batey, one of the Hut 6 codebreakers working on the *Brown* cypher, said he had

a clear recollection of our saddest failure: although messages in early November 1940 had given notice of a special operation codenamed *Mond[licht]*, we did not know more and to our dismay did not break any key for several days before 14 November: the result was the unhindered and disastrous bombing of Coventry. The missing keys were later broken and we could not explain the earlier failure.

A week after the Coventry raid, Bletchley Park itself was bombed. 'On arriving at office this morning, found it had been bombed in the night,' Malcolm Kennedy recorded in his diary.

Typists' room and telephone exchange in our building blown to bits by a direct hit and the vicarage next door damaged by another bomb which landed in the garden. A third exploded in the road outside, while two more landed over at the Park, one of them bursting a bare half-dozen paces from Hut 4. By great good fortune there were no casualties. We, however, have had to give up our room to the typists and have been moved to the room used by the South American Section who, in turn, have been transferred to the Park.

Gradually, there was more cooperation between the RAF intelligence and signals chiefs and Bletchley Park, who thanks to the reports from Cooper's 'Computors' and the *Brown* Enigma were beginning to appreciate the value of the intelligence the codebreakers could provide. They set up a new RAF intercept site at Chicksands Priory in Bedfordshire, which took some of the burden of the Enigma traffic from the Army operators at Chatham, but it was not until early 1942, when the Bletchley Park Air Section challenged the very low Air Intelligence assessments of the number of *Luftwaffe* fighter aircraft – an argument borne out by Bomber Command's lack of preparation for the German fighter defences it faced during the bombing of Germany – that it was finally allowed to issue its own daily reports to RAF customers on *Luftwaffe* command and control and tactics.

CHAPTER 5

BREAKING NAVAL ENIGMA

While the attacks on Army and air force Enigma had produced fairly rapid results once the fighting began, the German Navy Enigma was recognised as a far more difficult nut to crack. Frank Birch recalled being told by Denniston at the start of the war that 'all German codes were unbreakable'. There was no point in 'putting pundits onto them' because nothing they could do would work, Denniston said. This was particularly true of Naval Enigma. According to Hugh Alexander, who was to become the head of the Naval Enigma section, 'when the war started probably only two people thought that the Naval Enigma could be broken – Birch, the Head of German Naval Section, and Turing, one of the leading Cambridge mathematicians who joined GC&CS. Birch thought it could be broken because it had to be broken and Turing thought it could be broken because it would be so interesting to break it. Whether or not these reasons were logically satisfactory they imbued those who held them with a determination that the problem should be solved and it is to the pertinacity and force that, in utterly different ways, both of them showed that success was ultimately due.'

Turing himself admitted that his main reason for working on Naval Enigma rather than any other problem was because 'no one else was doing anything about it and I could have it to myself'. He started where the Poles left off and for the first three months of the war concentrated on trying to work out the complex indicating system which was one of the factors that made Naval Enigma so much more difficult to break. He succeeded in December 1939 in solving the indicating system using Polish decrypts for the first week of May 1937, but could not make any progress against wartime Naval Enigma without a 'pinch', the capture of original German cypher keys or settings.

Harry Hinsley had arrived at Bletchley in October 1939 aged just twenty, having been interviewed by Tiltman and Denniston in Charlesworth's rooms at St John's College, Cambridge, along with Bill Bonsall. 'I was formally invited to join GC&CS about four days later,' Hinsley recalled. 'It was all done with minimum fuss and maximum dispatch.' He was sent to Hut 4 and put in the care of Phoebe Senyard, who ensured he toured the Naval Section, learning what everyone was doing. Unlike many of the dons, Hinsley did not have a privileged background. He was a grammar school boy from Walsall, in the Black Country. His father was a wagoner who drove a horse and cart between the local ironworks and the railway station and Hinsley had won a scholarship to St John's. A slight, bespectacled young man with wavy hair, he began working on traffic analysis of naval signals, putting together intelligence from the way in which the naval networks operated, where the individual stations or ships were located by direction-finding (DF), and the plain text messages that they passed. Following the original rehearsal, which the Naval Intelligence Division did not regard as having gone well, the Admiralty insisted that the GC&CS traffic analysts must work in the Operational Intelligence Centre (OIC) in London, which coordinated all naval intelligence. But the intelligence available from 'log-reading' or traffic analysis might be vital to finding cribs that would help Turing and Twinn, so Birch decided Hinsley must fill the gap together with a female intelligence analyst, 23-year-old Jocelyn Bostock, who was already working on the problem. The young and enthusiastic Hinsley was an immediate hit with Senyard.

'I can remember quite well showing Harry some of the sorting and how delighted he seemed when he began to recognise the different types of signals,' she said.

He joined up with Miss Bostock, who was working on frequencies and callsigns. I then had to pass to Harry any strange, new or unknown signals, break of routine, or change of procedure which I noticed, for by that time one of my duties was the recognition of all German naval signals. No one was allowed to pass any cypher message out of the section except via me. This order of Mr Birch's was very definite as we were on the lookout for any changes or new types of code, or for any slip up on the part of the Germans, and I was able, by long use, to identify German naval procedure and to tie new methods with old, passing them immediately to Harry who was on the lookout for these things too. Those were very enjoyable days indeed. We were all very happy and cheerful, working in close cooperation with each other. If I was in difficulty, I knew I could go to Harry. It was a pleasure because he was always interested in everything and took great pains to find out what it was and why.

Relations between Hut 4 and the Admiralty were however far from cordial. While Hut 3 worked to the War Office and the Air Ministry via MI6, the Naval Section was officially NID12, part of the Naval Intelligence Division, and in direct contact with the OIC. But whenever any of the codebreakers attempted to talk to the intelligence officers in the Admiralty, their advice was virtually ignored.

'Communication with the Admiralty was distinctly primitive,' Hinsley recalled.

I used a direct telephone line which I had to activate by turning a handle energetically before speaking. On this I spoke, a disembodied voice, to people who had never met me. They rarely took the initiative in turning the handle to speak to me and they showed little interest in what I said to them.

In the second half of May 1940, Hinsley began to report evidence that a number of German warships were about to break out of the Baltic. The OIC ignored his warnings.

This was to lead to one of the Royal Navy's worst disasters of the Second World War, the sinking of the aircraft carrier HMS *Glorious*.

'For about a fortnight beforehand, I pretty well rang the OIC once or twice a day and said: "Look you ought surely to pass a signal out on this. Can you possibly pass a signal out?".', Hinsley recalled. 'They showed some interest. But were not sufficiently convinced to send a warning to the Home Fleet.'

On 7 June 1940, the *Glorious* and her two escort destroyers were spotted by a German flotilla which included the pocket battleships the *Gneisenau* and the *Scharnhorst*, Hinsley said.

On that day more than ever, I was saying to the duty officer: 'For goodness sakes, can't you just persuade them to send an alert or even "It may be the case".' He said: 'I can't because first of all my traffic analysis group doesn't agree with your interpretation. It doesn't see the point, doesn't see there's any evidence and secondly my boss, the chief of the OIC, will not go to the operational chaps and say send this kind of signal out on your kind of information'.

The next day HMS *Glorious* and her two escort destroyers, HMS *Acasta* and HMS *Ardent*, were sunk with the loss of 1,500 men.

'The *Glorious* was capable of making a limited torpedo strike and could have flown defensive patrols if she had received even a qualified warning,' Hinsley said.

But the OIC, for all that it included these indications in its daily bulletin, resisted Bletchley's suggestion that such a warning should be sent to ships at sea. It was not prepared to accept inferences drawn from an untried technique by civilians as yet unknown to its staff.

Bletchley Park's warnings to the Admiralty were the subject of a sustained cover-up. Even today, and despite the fact that Hinsley detailed the advice given to the Admiralty in the official history of British Intelligence in the Second World War, the Ministry of Defence still claims that 'British intelligence sources failed to discover that the German force had sailed.'

After the sinking of the *Glorious*, the OIC began to take more interest in what Bletchley Park said, and the GC&CS traffic analysts who had been detached to the Admiralty were sent back to the Naval Section. 'Steps were taken not only to improve the working relations between the operational and the intelligence staffs in the Admiralty, but also to bring the OIC and the Naval Section at GC&CS closer together,' Hinsley said. 'It was as a direct result of the loss of the *Glorious* that regular visits between the two groups were instituted and that the OIC recognised that it had to rely on Naval Section's greater familiarity with the German naval wireless system and to co-operate with the Naval Section in relating this knowledge to other operational information. It did so with a will.' Nevertheless, it was clear that some naval intelligence officers clearly resented its very existence. 'There was more than a suspicion of professional jealousy,' noted Charles Morgan, who served in Naval Intelligence. 'It was almost a point of honour to find the answer from our own records, even if a trifle incomplete, rather than have recourse to a BP telephone extension.'

Reviewing what happened after the event, Birch had a more dispassionate view of the situation, identifying the problem as being more a case of the OIC not being persuaded of the reliability of the traffic analysis process. 'Admiralty was by no means convinced of its reliability,' Birch said,

> and there were good grounds for scepticism, for this inferential technique, which called for the severest mental discipline, seemed to have a fatal attraction for the romantically minded with more flair than judgement. Enthusiasts made extravagant claims; critics dismissed the whole subject as crystal-gazing.

In an apparent effort to heal the rift, Hinsley was called down to the Admiralty and even sent to visit the Home Fleet at Scapa Flow. This caused some minor problems since, like many of the civilians at Bletchley, Hinsley wore only casual clothes, corduroy trousers and jumpers, and had no presentable clothes. 'Scrounger' Green said he was called in by Birch and told 'to produce a suit of clothes – a hat he would not wear – for a shining light who was summoned to the Admiralty and who had nothing else to wear but a pair of corduroys and a Fair Isle pullover'.

The new liaison had a limited effect, Hinsley recalled. 'They began to realise that in spite of the fact that we were scruffy and young, and civilian, we had something to contribute. They took great pains thereafter always to be in close touch and always to argue and listen to us, taking the trouble to appoint a liaison officer to Bletchley to whom we could always show the facts.' But despite the closer liaison, the difficulties continued. A few months later, Alec Dakin, an Egyptologist from Brasenose College who had been newly recruited into Hut 4, visited the Admiralty and was aghast to discover that the OIC appeared to be deliberately 'obstructive and dismissive' of Bletchley Park. Asked by Birch and Travis what was behind the problem, Hinsley blamed it on 'a competitive spirit which instead of being of a healthy type is obviously personal. It couches itself in a show of independence and an air of obstruction. It appears to be based on personal opposition to Bletchley Park. I suspect that another reason for their inadequacy is incapacity pure and simple.'

Turing and Twinn were working on the German Navy's 'Home Waters' cypher, which they dubbed *Dolphin*. 'There were at the time only two (daily-changing) Naval Enigma keys – for home and foreign waters respectively,' Birch said. 'As the latter never carried enough traffic for cryptanalysts to work on, the Home Waters key was, in effect, the only objective.'

The Naval Enigma Section would eventually be housed in Hut 8 but at the beginning it was set up in a small corner of Hut 4, the Naval Section's base to the left of the mansion, Senyard said

> Around about the beginning of April 1940, Mr Birch sent around a circular to the effect that there would be a new cryptographic section formed and that we should probably be very uncomfortable for about a fortnight or more in the endeavours to house them.
>
> We put our backs into it in order to welcome the newcomers, by tidying up our files and papers, binding and storing into cupboards all signals and books such as not in current use. Everyone who could be spared temporarily from their jobs was pressed into service and room was made for it, but it was a tight squeeze. We almost felt as if we ought to all breathe in together.

The move to Hut 4 was followed by a key pinch. Two of the new wartime wheels for the Naval Enigma had been captured in February when the U33 was sunk while trying to lay mines in the Firth of Clyde, then on 26 April 1940, HMS *Griffin* captured a German Navy patrol boat, a converted trawler, off the Norwegian coast and towed her into the Orkneys. Unfortunately, after the German ship arrived at the naval base of Lyness, it was looted by British sailors looking for trophies. But some cypher tables and some sheets of signal pad on which encyphering had been carried out were recovered and these allowed Turing to confirm how the indicating system worked as well as providing him with letter for letter cribs for messages encyphered on the 25 and 26 April. The information on the relatively few pieces of paper that could be retrieved led to the breaking of six days' worth of traffic, Birch said. 'In fact, special intelligence from Naval Enigma might have been continuously forthcoming from then on – a whole year earlier than in the event – if the German trawler had not been looted before examination.' Even with the captured material, the keys for 26 April were difficult to get out. Since the first Bombe, nicknamed *Victory*, had been introduced in March 1940, it was used to find the solution. It was a measure of the difficulties involved both in breaking Naval Enigma and with the first Bombe that it took a fortnight before it finally came up with the answer, scarcely a practical solution to solving Naval Enigma. Welchman's clever modification to the Bombe, known as the diagonal board, would make it much more efficient, but the Bombes fitted with the diagonal board would not be introduced until August.

The frustration felt by Hut 8 and in the Naval Section was exacerbated by the fact that the entire second half of 1940 'produced depressingly few results', while the German submarines, the U-Boats, began to cut into the vital Atlantic convoys bringing food, machinery and oil to the UK. The Fall of France had given the U-Boats new bases on the French Atlantic coast that allowed them much easier access to the Allied convoys in what was effectively the beginning of the Battle of the Atlantic. The U-Boats used the *Rudeltaktik*, or 'wolf pack' tactic, devised by their commander Admiral Karl Dönitz while he was a prisoner of the British during the First World War. The German Navy had broken the British Merchant Navy Code and was reading many Royal Navy operational messages so the wolf packs knew the routes to be taken by the convoys and could lie in wait.

They lined up north to south across the shipping routes. Once contact was made with a convoy, the closest U-Boats shadowed it, sending out homing signals to draw in the other members of the pack. When all the U-Boats were assembled, they pounced *en masse*. This would peel the Royal Navy escorts away as they chased off individual U-Boats, allowing the rest of the pack to attack with impunity. In the immediate aftermath of the Fall of France, the U-Boats made hay against the convoys and although they did not start to use the wolf pack tactic routinely until September 1940, from June onwards, they were sinking increasing numbers of convoys, eating into Britain's

vital supplies, making it imperative that the U-Boat Enigma
was cracked as soon as possible.

It was the job of the Admiralty's Operational Intelligence
Centre (OIC) to re-route the convoys around the U-Boats and
to do this it needed Bletchley Park to report where the U-Boats
were. Turing and Twinn had moved into Hut 8 in June 1940
and had been bolstered by the addition of Tony Kendrick and
Joan Clarke, who would at one point become briefly engaged to
Turing, despite his homosexuality.

Clarke had been one of Welchman's students at Cambridge.
'I arrived at Bletchley Park on 17 June,' she said.

> After the routine administrative matters I was collected by
> Alan Turing, to work on Naval Enigma in Hut 8, instead of
> with Welchman in Hut 6. In my first week, they put an extra
> table in for me in the room occupied by Turing, Kendrick
> and Twinn. I think it was Kendrick who said, 'Welcome to
> the sahibs' room' – the only time that I met that term for it.
> Kendrick, exceptionally, never progressed beyond calling me
> Miss Clarke, and himself was known only by his surname.
> Another exception to the general use of Christian names was
> Turing, but this was not because of any need of formality with
> the Head of Hut 8; he was widely known by his nickname,
> Prof, even during the short time when an actual university
> professor was working with us.

Unlike Turing, Kendrick remains one of the unrecognised great
codebreakers of Bletchley Park. 'He was a member of Hut 8
from early 1940 until July 1942,' said Rolf Noskwith, one of the
mathematicians who joined the section.

> It was said that any new suggestion had already been proposed
> by Kendrick at some earlier date. Severely crippled by polio,
> he was a very private man, but he was courteous and kind,
> and he had a fine sense of humour. He was even shabbier

dressed than the rest of us; strips of tattered lining were seen
to protrude from his threadbare suit. It was believed that this
was his protest, as a career civil servant, against the abandon-
ment of pinstriped trousers after GC&CS moved to Bletchley.
Sometime after the war, I met him at a concert; he was working at the Ministry of Defence. 'England is safe then,' I said.
'Yes,' he replied. 'I don't interfere too much'.

Like Clarke, Noskwith never knew Kendrick's Christian name
when they were serving together at Bletchley and didn't in fact
learn that it was Tony until the early 1990s, long after Kendrick
himself was dead.

The Hut 8 codebreakers had little hope of making a breakthrough without a pinch that at least gave them the new bigram
tables used by the German naval operators to encypher the
Enigma keys. Without a break into the *Dolphin* cypher used
by the U-Boats, the OIC could not locate them and was forced
to watch helplessly as the Allied merchant ships with their vital
supplies were sent to the bottom of the Atlantic. During the
period from June to October 1940 the U-Boats sank several
hundred Allied ships, with U-Boat commanders lauded like 'air
ace' fighter pilots at home, and the U-Boat crews nicknamed
those months *Die Glücklicke Zeit,* the Happy Time. By the
summer of 1940, with attacks on Allied shipping mounting
rapidly, the need to find a sustained break into the U-Boat
cypher had become imperative.

Galvanised by Birch's determination to help Turing and
Twinn make a breakthrough, and by Hinsley's youthful enthu-
siasm, Naval Section kept producing what they saw as potential cribs with no real understanding of how useless they were
without the bigram tables. It got to the point where 'Hinsley's
"certain cribs" became a standing joke'. In late August of 1940,
the tensions boiled over. Frustrated by the continued insistence
of Turing and Twinn that they must have 'pinches' of more
German material if they were to make a breakthrough and that

cribs alone were not enough, Birch complained to Travis over
the lack of progress.

> I'm worried about Naval Enigma. I've been worried for a long
> time, but haven't liked to say as much. Turing and Twinn are
> like people waiting for a miracle, without believing in mira-
> cles... I'm not concerned with the cryptographic problem of
> Enigma. Pinches are beyond my control, but the cribs are
> ours. We supply them, we know the degree of reliability, the
> alternative letterings, etc. and I am confident if they were tried
> out systematically, they would work. Turing and Twinn are
> brilliant, but like many brilliant people, they are not practical.
> They are untidy, they lose things, they can't copy out right, and
> they dither between theory and cribbing. Nor have they the
> determination of practical men.

Despite his initial suspicion of the new young mathematicians,
Dilly Knox was undoubtedly very fond of Turing and believed
in his codebreaking abilities, but even he despaired of him at
times. 'Turing is very difficult to anchor down,' Knox told
Denniston in late 1939. 'He is very clever but quite irresponsible
and throws out a mass of suggestions of all degrees of merit. I
have just, but only just, enough authority and ability to keep
him and his ideas in some sort of order and discipline. But he is
very nice about it all.'

Turing and Twinn were to become quite close. 'He was a
genius,' Twinn said.

> He was easily the brightest chap in the place. But he would
> occasionally come round to my digs and play chess and I
> should think that out of five games, he would win three and I
> would win two. But I knew very little about chess apart from
> the rules. I knew absolutely nothing about the tactics or strat-
> egy. It always seemed to me extraordinary that this brilliant
> chap was absolutely no good at chess at all. It was only because

he hadn't given it his attention of course, but it was a rather curious phenomenon. The other thing about Turing is that everyone says he had a stutter. I spent nine months with him in the same room. What I would say is that when he was asked a question which he thought was interesting, he would get very excited. It wasn't stuttering, he was just having difficulty getting everything he wanted to say out.

Turing's eccentricities were legion. He cycled into work wearing a gas mask to stop the pollen sparking off his hayfever, chained his coffee mug to a radiator and buried his life savings as insurance against a collapse of the pound. 'He had all kind of crackpot notions based on the fact that he didn't think the currency would stand up to a substantial war,' Twinn said.

He wanted to keep something of value and he put a lot of money into silver bars. Having extracted them from his bank with the utmost difficulty, he went and buried them somewhere. He had a very elaborate set of instructions for how to find them after the war. But he never did find them. What he'd neglected to think about was that someone might build a new town over the site.

The Naval Intelligence Division was now so desperate to break into Enigma that Rear-Admiral John Godfrey, the Director of Naval Intelligence, informed Birch that he was 'setting up an organisation to arrange "pinches" and I think the solution will be found in a combined committee of talent in your department and mine who can think up cunning schemes'.

The main member of this 'committee of talent', so far as Godfrey was concerned, was a 32-year-old Ian Fleming, later the creator of James Bond. Like the hero of his spy thrillers Fleming was a Lieutenant-Commander, although unlike Bond he was not in MI6. He was in fact serving in the Naval Intelligence Division and was Godfrey's personal assistant with special responsibility for liaising with MI6 and Bletchley. Fleming devised an elaborate plan to 'pinch' a set of keys from a German ship with the aid of a captured *Luftwaffe* bomber. 'I suggest we obtain the loot by the following means,' he wrote before outlining a plan that has all the feel of a first, tentative blueprint for the fictional hero who was to make him famous. Those taking part in *Operation Ruthless* should each be 'tough, a bachelor, able to swim', he wrote, pencilling in his own name in brackets alongside one of the positions. 'Pick a tough crew of five, including a pilot, wireless operator and word-perfect German speaker (Fleming). Dress them in German Air Force uniform, add blood and bandages to suit.'

These men would then wait until the next German air raid on London and, as the bombers returned home, take off and hide among the other aircraft. On the French side of the Channel the bomber would send out an SOS. It would then switch off one engine, lose height fast, 'with smoke pouring from a candle in the tail', and ditch in the sea. The team would then put off in a rubber dinghy, having ensured that the bomber sank before the Germans could identify it, and wait to be rescued by the German Navy. Fleming's plan continued: 'Once aboard rescue boat, shoot German crew, dump overboard, bring boat back to English port.'

Frank Birch, ever with an eye for the theatrical, gave enthusiastic backing to the 'very ingenious plot'. Fleming duly obtained a captured bomber and took his team to Dover to wait for the next big raid. But reconnaissance flights failed to find any suitable German vessels in the Channel and *Operation Ruthless* had to be called off, causing immense disappointment at Bletchley Park. 'Turing and Twinn came to me like undertakers cheated of a nice corpse yesterday, all in a stew about the cancellation of *Ruthless*,' Birch told Fleming.

The burden of their song was the importance of a pinch. Did the authorities not realise that there was very little hope, if any, of their deciphering current, or even approximately current, Enigma for months and months and months – if ever.

Contrariwise, if they got a pinch – even enough to give a clue to deciphering one day's material, they could be pretty sure, after an initial delay, of keeping going from day to day from then on; nearly up-to-date if not quite, because the level of traffic now is so much higher and because the machinery has been so much improved. The 'initial delay' would be in proportion to the pinch. If the whole bag of tricks was pinched, there'd be no delay at all. They asked me to add – what is self-evident – that they couldn't guarantee that at some future date, near or remote, the Germans mightn't muck their machine about again and necessitate another pinch. There are alternative operations possible. I put up one suggestion myself, and there are probably lots better. Is there anything in the wind? I feel there ought to be.

The second half of Birch's memo catches well the air of desperation that now existed. The two new Bombes fitted with the diagonal board came on stream in August and September 1940 but given that there was little chance of them breaking Naval Enigma in 'real time' without bigram tables and guaranteed cribs, they were largely used for the *Red* Enigma for Hut 6, which would give a guaranteed product within hours. Birch complained that Naval Enigma was 'not getting fair does' but in reality, there could be no complaint over how little time Hut 8 got on the Bombes.

The Navy was doing what it could to find the pinch that would help the codebreakers and there was a significant move forward in early March 1941 when British commandos captured the *Dolphin* key tables for February 1941 from the German armed trawler, the *Krebs*, off Norway's Lofoten Islands. As a result, Hut 8 was able to read Naval Enigma messages for most of February and for part of April although not in the 'real time' that could have led to the production of useful intelligence.

What it did do though was allow them to reconstruct the bigram tables then in use.

One problem the naval codebreakers faced with the 'pinches' was that when captured naval signals documents came in they were frequently saturated with water and in danger of falling apart. Fortunately, Lieutenant-Commander Geoffrey Tandy, who was in his early forties and in charge of captured documents in Birch's Naval Section, was a former curator at the Natural History Museum and had access to special materials used in the preservation of old documents. His presence was doubly fortunate. He had been sent to Bletchley Park because he was an expert in cryptogams, not – as the recruiting officer clearly assumed – encyphered messages, but mosses, ferns, algae, lichens and fungi.

The RAF also lent a hand in the deliberate generation of genuine cribs that might help, dropping mines into the sea at certain points where the Germans would discover them and report them. In a process known as 'gardening', the mines were dropped in locations where the coordinates gave the most chance of providing a break into the Enigma traffic. 'The RAF dropped mines in specific positions in the North Sea so that they would produce warning messages that would give us a crib,' said Noskwith.

The positions were carefully chosen so that the German naval grid references contained no numbers, especially 0 and 5, for which the Germans used more than one spelling. One day, while on duty in the morning, I was told by intelligence that it was very important for us to read the next day's messages as quickly as possible. 'Would gardening improve the chances of an early break?' I thought about it and gave the answer 'Yes'. That night was stormy and I lay in bed worrying whether my judgment had been correct or whether I had needlessly endangered the lives of the air crews. I was extremely relieved when I heard the next day that there had been no flying because of all the bad weather.

Around the same time as the Lofoten Islands 'pinch', the codebreakers discovered that messages sent on Enigma were also being sent using a lower level hand cypher, known by the Germans as the *Werftschlüssel,* the Dockyard Key, providing a potentially useful source of cribs. The *Dolphin* 'Home Waters' Naval Enigma traffic, sent in four-letter groups, was now teleprinted direct to Hut 8 from the Royal Navy intercept site at Scarborough. But there was still no continuous break. The search went on for a 'cunning scheme' that would find the crucial 'pinch' to help Turing and his team, now strengthened by the arrival of Hugh Alexander from Hut 6 with Hut 8 moving on to a 24-hour shift system in an indication of the growing belief that the vital breakthrough was not far away.

It came when Hinsley found messages to and from German weather ships among the Enigma traffic. The Germans encoded the weather messages using the *Wetterkurzschlüssel,* or short weather key, and they were then sent as short weather signals. They were made as short as possible to cut down the amount of time spent transmitting and make it more difficult for the British DF sites to locate the ships sending the weather messages. These weather ships, stationed in two places, north of Iceland and in the mid-Atlantic, would need to have exactly the same equipment and keys as any other ship using Enigma but would be far more vulnerable to raids designed to furnish a 'pinch'. Just as importantly, the same encoded short weather messages were then being encyphered using the Naval Enigma when they were sent on to other ships, providing a rich source of potential cribs.

The German weather-ship the *München* was captured in early May, providing the settings for June. A few days later, more material was captured when the *U-110* was forced to surface off Iceland. A second weather-ship, the *Lauenberg,* captured at the end of June gave Hut 8 the settings for July. Turing and his team read through June and July using the captured cyphers. From the beginning of August they were on their own. But as a result of the continuity established over the previous two months they had built up a library of cribs that, together with those provided by the weather messages, gardening, and a process known as Banburismus, allowed them to decypher *Dolphin* with only a few days missing in August and September and from 20 September 1941 every day until the end of the war.

The break into *Dolphin* was followed by success against the *Offizier* system, which allowed Naval Enigma cyphers to be double-encyphered by officers for confidential messages. Leslie Yoxall, another mathematician from Sidney Sussex, Cambridge, devised a way of breaking the *Offizier* cyphers. Alexander recalled that Yoxall 'caused a considerable sensation in breaking an "example" that had been set him on a length of eighty letters. This was particularly striking as it happened about a day after Turing – rightly recognised by all of us as the authority on any theoretical matter connected with the machine – had stated his opinion that 200 letters constituted a theoretical minimum. Yoxall must indeed have been inspired on this occasion as none of us ever succeeded in after days on a length of under 100 letters without some sort of crib.' The system for breaking *Offizier* became known as Yoxallismus.

Initially, Banburismus was absolutely vital to the breaking of Naval Enigma. Its name derived from the fact that it involved the use of long strips of paper, which were known to the codebreakers as 'Banburies' for the simple reason that they were printed in Banbury. It was devised by Turing as a means of cutting down the number of possibilities of wheel orders in order to cut the amount of time the Bombes would need to find the wheel order. The Bombe could test all the 17,576 possible positions on a single wheel order in about twenty minutes. So to test all 336 possible wheel orders would have taken one Bombe 112 hours, or nearly five days. Even if five Bombes were put to work on the problem it would take a full twenty-four hours. Banburismus aimed to cut the possible wheel orders to around twenty, which reduced the time for a single Bombe to a more manageable six hours and forty minutes. With so few Bombes in existence at this stage, the reduction in wheel orders obtained from Banburismus was extremely important. Noskwith said:

> The aim was to identify the right-hand and middle wheels because you could locate the turnover point of the wheel. Most wheels had different turnover points, so if you could show that the middle wheel turned over between E and F that would be, I think, wheel two. Identifying the right-hand and middle wheels meant you had to try fewer combinations on the Bombes.

A Banburismus section was set up in Hut 8 to look for messages containing similar streams of letters which had been sent with the wheel positions relatively close to each other giving streams of the same letters. These coinciding streams of letters were known as 'fits', said Patrick Mahon, another of the Hut 8 codebreakers.

> Banburismus aims first of all at setting messages in depth with the help of 'fits' and of a repeat rate much higher than the random expectation. The idea behind Banburismus is based on the fact that if two rows of letters of the alphabet, selected at random, are placed on top of each other the repeat rate between them will be one in twenty-six, while if two stretches of German Naval plain language are compared in the same way the repeat rate will be one in seventeen. Cypher texts of Enigma signals are in effect a selection of random letters and if compared in this way the repeat rate will be one in twenty-six but if, by any chance, both cypher texts were enciphered at the same position of the machine and then written level under each other, the repeat rate will be one in seventeen because, wherever there was a plain language repeat, there will also be a cypher repeat. Two messages thus aligned are said to be set in depth.

The initial searches for 'fits' were done using tabulating machines which picked up coincidental streams of four or more letters, Mahon said. 'At the same time messages were punched by hand onto Banburies, long strips of paper with alphabets printed vertically, so that any two messages could be compared together and the number of repeats be recorded by counting the number of holes showing through both Banburies.'

The Banbury sheets were about ten inches wide and several feet long. They had columns of alphabets printed vertically on them, giving horizontal lines of As, Bs, Cs, etc. Clerks punched holes into the paper to correspond with the encyphered messages, thus with a message beginning JKFTU, the J of the first column would be punched out, the K in the second column, the F in the third column and so on. They then aligned the sheets of paper over each other on top of a dark-coloured table and moved them to the left or right looking for repeats where the holes coincided and the table showed through.

The aim was to find points in a number of messages where a sequence of the machine coincided. If there were two messages with the indicators equating, for example, to the starting points XYK and XYM, then the second message would start two spaces on. So if the initial letter of the second message was moved to a position over the third letter of the first message then the letters in each column would be encoded in the same position. This would show up in an unusual number of repeats. The more repeats there were the more likelihood there was of the two sequences having been encyphered in the same position.

'If you're lucky and you're lucky pretty frequently, you might come across a four- or five-letter repeat,' said Peter Twinn.

You would say to yourself, 'A five-letter repeat, it's greatly against the odds, there must be a reason for it, what is it?' and the answer is that it represents the re-encodement of the same German word in both messages and you might be able to make a reasonable guess at what it was, having seen some German messages encyphered in the past. So that would give you a little start and then you would try and fit a third message on and you might find with a bit of luck that, when you staggered it off with both of them, this third message had two trigrams. One clicked with one of your messages and another trigram clicked with three in a quite different place on the first message. I'm leaving out a lot of the difficulties, but you gradually build up a selection of twelve or fifteen messages out of the day's traffic which if you make some other guesses and, if you're very, very lucky, you can do one of a number of three things. You can, for a start, cut down the number of wheel orders the Bombes need to check. But you can also either find out the wiring of a brand new wheel or you can work out with a reasonable degree of accuracy what these messages might be saying.

The Hollerith tabulating machines, mechanical digital data processors, which made the initial searches for the Banburismus 'fits', were provided by the British Tabulating Machine Company (BTM) based at Letchworth. They were controlled by a BTM expert called Frederic Freeborn, who ran the central index in Hut 7, which initially housed the automated Hollerith punch-card sorters. Under Freeborn's direction, female clerks not only carried out searches of the Enigma traffic for features that might assist the codebreakers, they cross-referenced every piece of information passing through Bletchley onto punch cards. A request for details of a radio station, unit, codeword, covername or indeed any type of activity would swiftly produce every card containing any previous mention or occurrence.

Marjorie Halcrow, a 22-year-old graduate from Aberdeen University, was one of those recruited by Freeborn to work in Hut 7. 'The cards were actually punched up on a machine about the size of a typewriter,' she said.

There was a room containing about twenty or thirty of them called the punch room where girls copied the coded messages onto these punch cards. The main room contained much larger machines, about the size of a small piano, called the sorting machines which could read the cards and sort the hundreds of thousands of messages into different categories. There were loads of sorters and there were collating machines that were even larger. The whole department was filled with machinery. It was a very noisy place, all banging on all night and day long.

Eventually there were so many Hollerith machines in use that they were operated at four separate outstations clustered around Bletchley. This frequently forgotten part of Britain's wartime codebreaking operations was not always used as efficiently as it might have been. Welchman recalled:

> The cryptanalytical sections would have had a better service if they had simply discussed their needs with Freeborn instead of dictating to him. This would have given him the chance to programme the overall use of his equipment and staff in a way that would have been advantageous not only for each individual problem solution, but for the overall service he was providing.

Hut 8 was now divided into four sections. The registration room, where the traffic arrived and was sorted; the 'Banburismus Room', where codebreakers tried to break the keys using Banburismus; the 'Crib Room', where the codebreakers tried out cribs; and 'the Big Room' where female clerks punched up the messages on the Banbury sheets and decyphered messages on Type-X machines once the wheel order, settings and keys had been recovered.

The codebreakers themselves rarely read the decrypts. Peter Twinn recalled having very little interest in what they were actually saying. 'I would have to confess I don't think I really understood the full significance of it,' he said.

> I think I'd have to excuse myself by saying that we lived at that

time in a very narrow little world. Remember that I was an inexperienced lad of twenty-four or twenty-five and I'd come into it straight from university, I don't think I had a real grasp of what a major war was all about and we did work very much in a rather monastical way. I don't recall ever having decoded a message from start to finish to see what it said. I was much more interested in the methodology for getting German out of a coded message.

The decyphered messages were passed via Z Watch, the Naval Section's equivalent of Hut 3, over a newly installed teleprinter link that allowed the Hut 8 decrypts to be sent direct to the OIC, giving prior warning of the wolf-pack patrol lines and allowing the convoys to be routed away from danger. The OIC was fully indoctrinated into Enigma so there was no need for the agent's disguise required for Hut 6 German Army and *Luftwaffe* decrypts. The result was truly dramatic. Between March and June 1941, the U-Boats had sunk 282,000 tons of shipping a month. From July, the figure dropped to 120,000 tons a month and by November, when the wolf packs were temporarily withdrawn from the Atlantic, to 62,000 tons.

The breaking of the Naval Enigma was one of the main reasons for this drop in the fortunes of the U-Boats, providing the British with a welcome respite during which the vital supplies had a much greater chance of getting through, Harry Hinsley said.

It has been calculated that, allowing for the increased number of U-Boats at sea, about one-and-a-half million tons of shipping (350) ships were saved. This intermission was invaluable for the level of British supplies, the building of new shipping and the development of anti-submarine defences.

Despite the brilliance of men like Turing and Alexander, the Naval Enigma could not have been broken without the

Bombes. Larger improved versions known as Jumbos because of their size had been introduced and in order to protect them from German air raids they were dispersed to new outstations at nearby Wavendon and Adstock. At the same time, the Bletchley Bombes were moved out of the back room in Hut 1 and into Hut 11, acquiring a number of new operators.

The eight Wrens who arrived on 24 March 1941 were a trial measure. Previously the Bombes had been operated by soldiers, airmen and sailors who before being called up had worked for BTM, which built the Bombes. But male servicemen were at a premium and the number of Bombes was being constantly increased to cope with the need to keep the breaks of keys going, so it was decided to try the Wrens out as 'an experiment'.

Morag Maclennan had followed her brother into the Royal Navy at the age of seventeen and was very disappointed to discover that she was being sent to Bletchley rather than Portsmouth or Plymouth.

> We got off at the station and somebody met us and we went up a little gravel path, straight into Hut 11. There were all these machines and you were given a thing called a menu with this strange pattern of letters and figures on it. You had to plait up this machine at the back with these great big leads which had to be plugged into different bits.
>
> Then at the front, you had this rack with rows and rows of drums marked up by colour and you were told what combination of colours you were to put on. You would set them all, press a button and the whole row went round once and then moved the next one on. It took about fifteen minutes for the whole run, stopping at different times, and you recorded the stop and phoned it through and, with any luck, sometimes it was the right one and the code was broken.
>
> It was very smelly with the machine oil and really quite noisy. The machine kept clanking around and unless you were very lucky your eight-hour watch would not necessarily

produce a good stop that broke a code. Sometimes you might have a good day and two of the jobs you were working on would break a code and that was a great feeling, particularly if it was a naval code. Obviously, we hoped to do it for everybody. But there was an extra little surge of pride if it was a navy one.

Initially, the Wrens were not trusted with any details of what they were doing and it was a boring, frustrating task, she said.

The job itself was pretty dull. You were just working the machines the entire time. Because if all the bread and butter codes were broken, there were always ones that had got missed from a few days before or trying out more experimental ones. So the Bombes were never idle. But after a bit I think it was thought that it would be useful for our morale to know a little bit more of what the codes were dealing with, what areas they covered and of course the odd successes. Some weren't all that dramatic. They weren't necessarily operational, but they were building up the picture of exactly what air force squadrons and tank units were where, or where ships were and what they were doing. But when we were breaking the U-Boat ones in particular, we were told about the U-Boat sinkings and convoy protection, so we felt good about that.

By the end of the war, there were just under 2,000 Bombe operators, of whom 1,676 were Wrens, at six different locations around the country. They had their own unit, HMS *Pembroke V*, and Wrens had gone on to take up a number of other roles in GC&CS, including codebreaking itself. They were billeted together at a number of beautiful old country homes, including Woburn Abbey, which became known as the Wrenneries. But they never allowed themselves to forget that they were part of the Royal Navy, calling their living quarters, fo'c'sles; their dormitories, cabins; and saluting the areas in front of the country houses in which they were billeted as the quarterdeck.

Their arrival improved the social life and the Wrenneries became renowned for their dances. Barbara Quirk lived in a Tudor mansion called Crawley Grange, an hour's drive away from Bletchley.

> I remember our watch was having a dance in the most glorious ballroom in Crawley Grange, beautiful oak panelling from floor to ceiling, and we were told by our chief officer, who didn't work at Bletchley, that we couldn't have any drink. So we got some of the men who were coming from one of the camps around, they might have been Americans, they might have been British, I can't remember now, to bring some beer. They brought a mobile bar on a jeep and parked it outside the Wrennery and when the chief officer found out, we were all gated for a month.

Joan Baily was billeted first at Crawley Grange and then at Gayhurst Manor, although she actually worked at Bletchley itself.

> I found the atmosphere rather exciting because we had to try to break these codes and if we didn't get the codes up we knew that somebody had had it. If we were on night shift, we had to sleep during the day of course and I remember they had problems with an RAF aircraft flying low over Gayhurst. We found out afterwards it happened to be because my sister was sunbathing on the roof with nothing on.

CHAPTER 6

A CRIME WITHOUT A NAME

The early spring of 1941 saw the German and Italian advance into the Balkans, a move that had been predicted by Bletchley on the basis of *Luftwaffe* preparations showing up in the *Red* Enigma and the heavy movement of German troops and armour south by rail which was reflected in messages encyphered on the German Railway Enigma. It was codenamed *Rocket* by Bletchley and broken by John Tiltman, who had a roving brief, breaking any codes and cyphers that were not being attacked, or could not be broken, by other departments.

Tiltman, the head of Hut 5, the GC&CS Military Section, was arguably one of the best codebreakers working during this period. Born in London on 25 May 1894, he was so obviously brilliant as a child that he was offered a place at Oxford at the remarkably young age of thirteen. He served with the King's Own Scottish Borderers in France during the First World War, winning the Military Cross for bravery, and was seconded to MI1b, the War Office codebreaking unit, shortly before it merged with Room 40 to become GC&CS. A tall, rangy man, who had bad back problems and therefore liked to work standing up at a specially constructed high desk, Tiltman was a leading expert on hand cyphers. He habitually wore his regimental tartan trews, but had an otherwise rather casual approach to military uniform.

William Filby, who worked as a cryptanalyst in Hut 5, recalled their first meeting. 'My arrival was unforgettable,' Filby said.

> As I saluted, I stamped the wooden floor in my Army boots and came to attention with another shattering noise. Tiltman

turned, looked at my feet, and exclaimed: 'I say old boy. Must you wear those damned boots?' I became the only other rank at BP in battledress and white running shoes, much to the disgust of the adjutant.

Hut 6 was by now a much larger operation and it began to expand on the number of different Enigma cyphers it was working on. The reliance on the *Red* and the *Brown* Enigmas might well mean they were missing vital life-saving and war-winning intelligence. It also left the codebreakers vulnerable to German security improvements on the *Luftwaffe* keys. 'All through this year [1941], there persisted, at any rate in my mind, the sensation that it was all much too good to be true,' said Stuart Milner-Barry,

> that any day now the enemy would discover, and that we should wake up one morning to discover, that it was all over. In those days the effects of getting in a jam were much more noticeable because with only two or three keys work simply came to a standstill if nothing broke for a few days and the whole Hut descended rapidly into the darkest abyss of despair.

Welchman, the head of Hut 6, expressed concern that Hut 6's concentration on the *Red* Enigma was putting too many eggs in one basket. In a 'screed' to the members of Hut 6, he said,

> Since we have neither enough intercept sets to cover all E [Enigma] traffic nor enough bombes to deal with all menus that could be produced we must be very careful to use our resources to the best advantage. Although we must concentrate the greater part of our resources on those colours which are high in the scale, it is most important that we ourselves should not lose interest in any type of E traffic. We should retain a clear idea of what is worth doing, even if we cannot at present do as much as we would wish, and our aim should always be to break every key and to take all steps that may possibly

assist future breaking. From the crytographic point of view the breaking of any key may be valuable because key repeats or re-encodements may occur.

Hut 6 broke into *Violet,* the *Luftwaffe* administrative cypher, on Christmas Eve 1940 and *Light Blue,* the *Luftwaffe* cypher for north Africa and the Mediterranean, on the last day of February 1941, an event that led to raucous celebrations. 'This occurred when the first party of American visitors were being shown round Hut 6,' recalled Stuart Milner-Barry, 'and must greatly have astonished any of them who had the idea that the British were a phlegmatic race.'

A lack of MI6 coverage of Italy, highlighted in 1935 by the Abyssinia Crisis and caused in part by the refusal of the British ambassador in Switzerland to allow MI6 to use Switzerland as a base for running agents into Italy and in part by lack of funding, led the then Chief of MI6 Admiral Hugh Sinclair to rely heavily on GC&CS to produce intelligence on Italy. As a result, Bletchley Park had good coverage of Italian codes and cyphers and was able to warn of Italy's entry into the war in June 1940, a month ahead of time. Italian diplomatic and colonial cyphers had been read for several years and the Naval Intelligence Italian section, led by William 'Nobby' Clarke, was completely on top of most Italian naval codes and hand cyphers from about 1937 onwards. Similarly, Bletchley was able to read most Italian air force and Army codes and hand cyphers. The Italian Enigma had been initially broken by Dilly Knox during the Spanish Civil War and was covered by his research section. It was unclear whether it was the same machine until, in September 1940, Mavis Lever, one of Knox's assistants and only nineteen, managed to break the keys proving it was the same machine. She was halfway through a German degree at University College London when the war broke out.

I was concentrating on German romantics and then I realised

the German romantics would soon be overhead and I thought
well, I really ought to do something better for the war effort.
I said I'd train as a nurse and their response was: 'Oh no you
don't. You use your German.' So I thought, great. This is going
to be an interesting job, Mata Hari, seducing Prussian officers.
But I don't think either my legs or my German were good
enough because they sent me to GC&CS.

She initially worked in a section in London perusing the
personal columns of *The Times* for coded spy messages and using
captured codebooks to decode them when Bletchley began to
call for more staff.

I was taken to Dilly Knox's section, in the cottage. It was very
much a research unit. Hut 6 was up and running and operational, but Dilly had been one of the great pioneers of it all. He
was working on things that hadn't been broken. It was a strange
little outfit in the cottage because... well, organisation is not a
word you would associate with Dilly Knox. When I arrived, he
said: 'Oh, hello, we're breaking machines, have you got a pencil?'
That was it. I was never really told what to do. 'Here you are,
here's a whole load of rubbish, get on with it.' I think looking
back on it that was a great precedent in my life, because he taught
me to think that you could do things yourself without always
checking up to see what the book said. That was the way the
cottage worked. We were looking at new traffic all the time or
where the wheels or the wiring had been changed, or at other new
techniques. So you had to work it all out yourself from scratch.

Knox had a unique knack of using his imagination to open up
codes and cyphers. 'He would stuff his pipe with sandwiches
sometimes instead of tobacco he was so woolly-minded,'
Lever said.

But he was brilliant, absolutely brilliant. It just seemed to come naturally to him. He said the most extraordinary things. He was a great admirer of Lewis Carroll, 'Which way does the clock go round?' And if you were stupid enough to say clockwise, he'd just say: 'Oh, no it doesn't, not if you're the clock, it's the opposite way.' And that's sometimes how you had to think about the machines. Not just to look at them how you saw them but what was going on inside. That was the only way in which one was really trained. But trained is a bad word because that was the one thing you mustn't be. You have got to look at each thing afresh and wonder how you could approach it.

The need to look at codes and cyphers from different perspectives was drummed into Knox's assistants and served both Lever and the Royal Navy well when she spotted one missing element in a long Italian Naval Enigma message.

The one snag with the Enigma of course is the fact that if you press A, you can get every other letter but A. I picked up this message and – one was so used to looking at things and making instant decisions – I thought: 'Something's gone. What has this chap done. There is not a single L in this message.' My chap had been told to send out a dummy message and he had just had a fag and pressed the last key of the middle row of his keyboard, the L. So that was the only letter that didn't come out. We had got the biggest crib we ever had, the encypherment was LLLL right through the message and that gave us the new wiring for the wheel. That's the sort of thing we were trained to do – instinctively look for something that had gone wrong or someone who had done something silly and torn up the rulebook.

The keys she uncovered as a result of the Italian operators' mistake were to provide the Royal Navy with its first major victory of the war. Messages decyphered by Lever provided details of the Italian Navy's plans to attack British ships off the Greek coast and led to a Royal Navy victory at the Battle of Matapan.

'We didn't often know the results of our activities, which messages were important,' Lever said.

> Because you see you might actually break a message which said nothing to report which would give you the settings for the rest of the messages. But the Italian messages were done individually. The first Matapan message was very dramatic stuff: 'Today's the day minus three', just that and nothing else. So of course we knew the Italian Navy was going to do something in three days' time. Why they had to say that I can't imagine. It seems rather daft but they did. So we worked for three days. It was all the nail-biting stuff of keeping up all night working. One kept thinking: 'Well, would one be better at it if one had a little sleep or shall we just go on,' and it did take nearly all of three days.
>
> Then a very, very large message came in which was practically the battle orders for what turned into the Battle of Matapan. How many cruisers there were, and how many submarines were to be there and where they were to be at such and such a time, absolutely incredible that they should spell it all out. It was rushed out to Cunningham and the marvellous thing about him was that he played it extremely cool. He knew that they were going to go out and confront the Italian fleet at Matapan but he did a real Drake on them.

The Italian intention was to intercept British convoys en route from Egypt to Greece. Such was the Royal Navy's superiority over the Italians that Cunningham initially did not believe the Italians would dare to carry out these plans, but pressure was applied from the Admiralty to ensure that he did believe it. Knowing that the Japanese Consul in Alexandria, who was reporting on the movement of the Mediterranean Fleet, was a keen golfer, the British admiral ostentatiously visited the club house with his clubs and an overnight bag. 'He pretended he was just going to have the weekend off and made sure the Japanese spy would pass it all back,' Lever recalled. 'Then under cover of the night, they went out and confronted the Italians.'

In a series of running battles over 27 and 28 March 1941, Cunningham's ships attacked the Italian flotilla sinking an entire Italian cruiser squadron of three Italian heavy cruisers and two Italian destroyers with the loss of 3,000 Italian sailors. Without radar, the Italians were caught completely by surprise, Lever recalled.

> It was very exciting stuff. There was a great deal of jubilation in the cottage and then Cunningham himself came to visit us with Admiral Godfrey to congratulate us in person. We rushed down to the Eight Bells at the end of the road to get some bottles of wine and if it was not up to the standard the Commander-in-Chief Mediterranean was used to he didn't show it. The cottage wall had just been whitewashed. Now this just shows how silly and young and giggly we were. We thought it would be jolly funny if we could talk to Admiral Cunningham and get him to lean against the wet whitewash and go away with a white stern. So that's what we did. It's rather terrible, isn't it? On the one hand, everything was so very organised and on the other these silly young things are trying to snare the admiral. We tried not to giggle when he left. He had shaken us all warmly by the hand and we thought that was the end of Matapan. It was in fact practically the last we would hear of the Italian fleet, which only made one more appearance before surrendering to Admiral Cunningham in 1943.

Despite the British victory at Matapan, German troops, supported by the *Luftwaffe*, executed yet another *Blitzkrieg* through Yugoslavia and into Greece. British and Greek troops facing insuperable odds were forced to retreat. But the campaign was the first in which the intelligence unearthed by the Bletchley Park codebreakers could be passed on to the commanders in the field direct from Bletchley Park itself rather than through MI6, as had occurred in Norway and France.

A direct 'Special Signals Link' had been set up between Bletchley Park and Cairo in early 1941 to feed the *Ultra* intelligence to the British forces in the Middle East and it was extended to the British headquarters in Athens shortly before the German invasion. The *Red Luftwaffe* key provided comprehensive details of the discussions of the German *Fliegerverbindungsoffiziere* or *Flivos*, the air liaison officers who coordinated air and ground operations, and although this had to be passed on in a highly sanitised fashion, it ensured that the British could make an orderly retreat.

It also gave early warning that German airborne forces were moving to the Balkans in preparation for the invasion of Crete. A series of messages beginning in late March provided the British with every detail of the operation, from the preparations to the complete plan of the airborne assault, and the day, 20 May, on which it was to be launched. The problem was to find a plausible way of camouflaging the source of all this intelligence so as to ensure the Germans did not realise that Enigma had been broken.

On Churchill's orders, Hut 3 produced a detailed report purporting to be a complete dossier of the German plans obtained by an MI6 agent inside the German GHQ in Athens. This was sent to Cairo over the special Middle East link and then passed to General Bernard Freyberg, the New Zealand Commander in Crete, encyphered in the virtually unbreakable 'one-time pad' cypher system. Although Freyberg did not have the resources to fight off a sustained attack, the knowledge garnered from the 'German documents' robbed the Germans of any element of surprise – Freyberg allegedly looked at his watch when the German paradrop began and said: 'Right on time.' Alerted by the codebreakers, his men were able to pick off the enemy paratroopers at will, causing carnage and considerably delaying the inevitable defeat.

'Crete was an example of how knowing a great deal, through the *Red*, didn't necessarily lead to the correct results,' said John Herivel.

> All the German plans, the details for the invasion of Crete were known through Hut 6 decodes on the *Red*. We all knew about the German plans for the airborne assault on Crete – because there was no attempt to stop the people in Hut 6 from knowing what was in the decodes – and therefore we felt very confident that we would defeat it. But in fact we didn't. What did happen was that they had such enormous difficulty in taking Crete and suffered such enormous losses that Hitler decided he wouldn't try a parachute descent in that strength again.

The tendency of the Admiralty's Operational Intelligence Centre (OIC) to ignore much of what Bletchley Park Naval Section said reappeared in April and May of 1941 during an event that was to have a dramatic effect on morale at Bletchley Park – the sinking of the *Bismarck*. The battleship, the showpiece of the German navy, had been in the Baltic since her completion the previous September. The Admiralty was watching and waiting for her to break out into the Atlantic to attack the Allied convoys bringing supplies to Britain.

Early indications that the *Bismarck* was about to leave the Baltic came in decrypts of the *Red* Enigma which showed that the *Luftwaffe* was mounting a close watch on the activities of the British Home Fleet anchored in Scapa Flow. An MI6 agent was dispatched to monitor the passage of ships through the Kattegat, the narrow strip of water separating Denmark from Sweden, and, on 20 May, he reported that two large German warships had left the Baltic bound for the North Sea. The sighting was confirmed by photographic reconnaissance and a few isolated breaks into the main Naval Enigma cypher showed that the *Bismarck*, accompanied by the new cruiser the *Prinz Eugen*, was about to attack Britain's transatlantic trade routes.

A British naval squadron was dispatched to hunt the *Bismarck* down. She was sighted on the evening of 23 May and next morning was engaged by the *Hood* and the *Prince of Wales*. The *Hood* was sunk and the *Prince of Wales* hit but not without the *Bismarck* herself sustaining some damage. She parted company with the *Prinz Eugen* and the Royal Navy ships lost contact with her. Throughout the following day there was confusion as to what direction the *Bismarck* was travelling in. The repeated insistence by Bletchley's Naval Section that the *Bismarck* was heading for the safety of a French port was ignored. Hinsley had telephoned the OIC following the engagement to tell the duty officer that radio control of the *Bismarck* had switched from Wilhelmshaven to Paris, a clear sign that she was sailing south towards France. It was not until the early evening of 25 May, following yet another heated telephone conversation between Hinsley and the OIC, that this reasoning was finally accepted.

The manner and speed of its confirmation were to become a part of the Bletchley folklore. Just minutes after Hinsley's angry exchange with the Admiralty, Hut 6 decyphered a message on the *Red* Enigma from General Hans Jeschonnek, the *Luftwaffe* Chief of Staff, who was concerned over the fate of a relative, a member of the *Bismarck*'s crew. He was told that the battleship was making for the safety of Brest. Armed with this news, Royal Navy ships of both the Mediterranean and Home Fleets closed in on her. When aircraft from the *Ark Royal* succeeded in jamming her rudder on the evening of 26 May, her fate was sealed. In messages only decrypted after she had been sunk, Admiral Lutjens, the officer commanding the *Bismarck*, signalled: 'Ship unmanageable. We shall fight to the last shell. Long live the *Führer*.'

The success against the *Brown* Enigma, which prepared the RAF fighter aircraft to take on German bombers during the *Blitz*, was highly secret and not known to many of the staff, whereas the sinking of the *Bismarck* had involved not only Hut 6 and Hut 3, but also the Naval Section Hut 4, using intelligence that didn't come from Enigma. So for most of those working at Bletchley this was the first time they had seen tangible evidence of the effect they could have on the war. News of the codebreakers' role in the affair swiftly got around the Park raising morale and giving them a real feeling of making a contribution to the war effort. Malcolm Kennedy was in the dining room in the mansion at Bletchley Park when the news came through on the one o'clock news that she had been sunk. 'Spontaneous cheering and clapping broke out from those at lunch when the announcement was made,' he said, 'though some of us had heard the good news slightly before. To give the devil his due, *Bismarck* put up a very good show.'

Years later, Mavis Lever took her son to see the film *Sink the Bismarck*.

> I saw it go down and suddenly I really did feel quite sick. I put my head down and my son said to me after a while: 'It's alright Mummy, it's gone down.' He didn't know. But I was thinking how awful it was that one's breaking of a message could send so many people to the bottom. But that was war and that was the way we had to play it. If we thought about it too much we should never have been able to cope.

Throughout the campaign in the Balkans, Railway Enigma had been indicating a series of movements, named after famous actors and film stars, heading north and east towards Poland. During March, April and May, message after message on links using the *Red* cypher pointed to a major concentration of German troops and air support converging on an assembly point at Oderberg, near Krakow. While much of the movement could have reflected a German attempt to intimidate Moscow, as many in Whitehall were inclined to believe, the inclusion of a prisoner-of-war interrogation unit and the urgency with which units were being pulled out of the Balkans convinced the codebreakers that the Germans were about to turn on their Russian allies.

'It becomes harder than ever to doubt that the object of these large movements of the German Army and air force is Russia,' said one long-term report issued by the Hut 3 research section in early May.

> From rail movements towards Moldavia in the south to ship movements towards Varanger fjord in the far north there is everywhere the same steady eastward trend. Either the purpose is blackmail or it is war. No doubt Hitler would prefer a blood-less surrender. But the quiet move, for instance, of a prisoner-of-war cage to Tarnow looks more like business than bluff.

It was not until 10 June, when the Japanese diplomatic section translated a message to Tokyo from the Japanese ambassador in Berlin confirming that the invasion was imminent, that Whitehall finally accepted, amid a welter of evidence from *Ultra* decrypts emanating from Hut 6, that the codebreakers had got it right. Twelve days later, Hitler launched the aptly named *Operation Barbarossa*, the invasion of the Soviet Union. It was to bring some of the most distressing decrypts the code-breakers were to handle at any point of the war.

The messages of the SS and the *Ordnungspolizei*, the ordi-nary uniformed German police, who were mopping up behind the German lines during *Operation Barbarossa* make chilling reading, providing details of the systematic murder by the advancing German forces of thousands of Jews. The first news of these killings was read at Bletchley Park. On 18 July 1941, Army intercept operators based temporarily at Chicksands picked up a message from *Obergruppenführer* Erich von dem Bach-Zelewski, *Ordnungspolizei* commander in the Soviet republic of Belorussia, to Kurt Daluege, head of the *Ordnungspolizei*, and Heinrich Himmler, the *Reichsführer-SS*, or head of the SS.

The cypher in use was a basic double transposition cypher. In a transposition cypher, the letters that make up the text of the message are shuffled in some pre-determined way. As the name suggests, in a double transposition system, the order of letters produced by the initial process is shuffled a second time. It was broken relatively easily by Bletchley Park, originally by Tiltman, but thereafter in routine fashion in Hut 5.

Von dem Bach-Zelewski's message read: 'In yesterday's cleansing action in Slonim, carried out by Police Regiment Centre, 1,153 Jewish plunderers were shot.' (Slonim is a town in south-west Belorussia, midway between Warsaw and Minsk.)

On 4 August von dem Bach-Zelewski reported that in further mopping-up operations in an area south of the Belorussian town of Pinsk his men had shot dead 'ninety Bolsheviks and Jews'. Later the same day, he reported that his SS Cavalry Brigade was still removing opposition in the region north to north-east of Lake Sporowski. 'As at the evening of 3 August the SS Cavalry Brigade had liquidated 3,274 Partisans and Jewish Bolsheviks. Police Battalion 306 has shot dead 260 guerrillas,' he said. Three days later von dem Bach-Zelewski reported that the SS Cavalry Brigade was now pushing further forwards. 'By midday today a further 3,600 had been executed, so that the complete total for those executed by the brigade is now 7,819. This brings the total in my area to more than 30,000.' His apparent determination to make as much of the killings as possible was such that one Bletchley Park analyst noted: 'The tone of this message suggests that word has gone out that a definite decrease in the total population of Russia would be welcome in high quarters and that the leaders of the three sectors stand somewhat in competition with each other as to their scores.'

It is worth noting that the *Ordnungspolizei* were ordinary uniformed police officers, the same police officers who are supposed to protect people against crime and in whom most normal law-abiding people in civilised countries place their trust. There were three main German formations, roughly speaking, mopping up behind the German lines. Von dem Bach-Zelewski's men were the central formation, operating in Belorussia. There was a northern formation designated to carry out mopping-up operations in the Baltic republics, and another through the Ukraine in the south. At the heart of each formation was an *Einsatzgruppe,* or task force, made up largely of members of the *Gestapo* and *Sicherheitspolizei,* the Security Police, and split into four separate *Einsatzkommando.* It was the *Einsatzgruppe* of each formation that was expected to orchestrate the bulk of the killings. But messages decyphered by Bletchley Park very soon showed that the ordinary police units, as well as of course the SS troops, were heavily involved in the killings.

There had, as yet, been no indication in the messages intercepted at Chicksands that the police units in the north and the south were killing Jews, although there was no doubt that ruthless brutality was being inflicted on the local population throughout the occupied areas of the Soviet Union. On 24 August, clearly angered by the intercepts, Churchill made a BBC broadcast in which he denounced the 'most frightful cruelties' that were being carried out in those parts of the Soviet Union occupied by German forces:

Whole districts are being exterminated. Scores of thousands – literally scores of thousands – of executions in cold blood are perpetrated by the German police troops upon the Russian patriots who defend their native soil. Since the Mongol invasions of Europe, there has never been methodical, merciless butchery on such a scale or approaching such a scale. We are in the presence of a crime without a name.

Churchill did not mention anywhere in his speech that large numbers of those killed were Jews because to do so would have made very clear that the information came from intercepted German police messages.

On 23 August 1941, the day before Churchill made his speech, Bletchley Park decyphered a message from SS *Gruppenführer* Friedrich Jeckeln, commander of the SS and police troops in the south, which confirmed that like von dem Bach Zelewski, he was also busy killing Jews. In a report sent not only to Himmler and Daluege but also to Reinhard Heydrich, head of the Security Police, Jeckeln said 314 Battalion of the Police Regiment South had shot dead 367 Jews in the area around the Ukrainian towns of Belokorovichi and Luginy, south-west of Kiev. This was an important message. It confirmed the analysis of the Bletchley Park intelligence reporter that there was more to the killings of Jews than just von dem Bach-Zelewski misinterpreting his orders, or portraying his actions in a way likely to curry favour with his superiors. It was very clear that Jews were being killed simply because they were Jews. Its content may have been relayed verbally to Churchill by Stewart Menzies, the Chief of MI6. They discussed intelligence matters each morning and the Prime Minister was very clearly interested in the activities of the police troops operating behind the eastern front. It would be strange indeed if Churchill had not discussed them with Menzies prior to making his BBC broadcast.

The first message decyphered by the British on 24 August, the actual day that Churchill made the broadcast, found Jeckeln telling Himmler, Daluege and Heydrich that the 10th Infantry Regiment of the 1st SS Brigade had taken twenty-nine prisoners and shot dead sixty-five 'Bolshevik Jews'. His *Einsatzgruppe* had 'shot dead twelve bandits and guerrillas and seventy Jews'; 314 Battalion of the Police Regiment South had shot dead 294 Jews; 45 Battalion had shot dead sixty-one Jews and the Police Squadron (possibly members of the small police air force accompanying the police troops) had shot dead 113 Jews.

The item was the first to be decoded that day by Bletchley Park's Military Section so it is possible that it was sent on by teleprinter to MI6 in time for Menzies to have discussed it with Churchill before the Prime Minister made his 'crime without a name' broadcast. But the evidence appears to suggest that, at the very least, Churchill had not seen the full details of either of the two Jeckeln messages, because a few days later, on 27 August 1941, Bletchley Park issued the first of a special series of Most Secret reports concerning the activities of the police troops and specifically prepared for Churchill.

These reports, written out on good quality paper, had a very limited circulation. There were just two copies, one of which was kept on file at Bletchley Park, with the other going direct to Menzies, who passed it on to Churchill in his daily bundle of intelligence, singling it out in the covering letter. The way these reports were handled leaves no doubt that they were produced specifically for Churchill and at his request. They are concise and to the point and signed personally by Nigel de Grey, now head of research in Hut 3.

De Grey's first report in this series covers Jeckeln's message of 23 August announcing that his men operating in the Luginy area have shot dead 367 Jews. It was seen by Churchill on 28 August and the Prime Minister circled the figure 367 in red. The second on 30 August began with the words: 'Further light on the use being made of the Police Forces in the back areas on the Russian front is shed by some of the daily reports received.' It went on to recount the details of Jeckeln's message of 24 August and the killing of a total of 603 Jews.

In this second report, de Grey added new information on further killings from another report to Berlin by Jeckeln, this time on 25 August, in which he reported that his men operating south of Kiev had killed 1,625 Jews. The 1st SS Brigade had taken eighty-five prisoners and shot dead 283 Jews while the Police Regiment South had shot dead 1,342 Jews. Churchill circled the latter figure, the largest figure so far for a single massacre. Also on 25 August, von dem Bach-Zelewski broke what for him appears at first sight to have been a period of silence on the killings, to say that the SS Cavalry Brigade, which was operating in the Pripet marshes, had killed ninety-two Russian soldiers and 150 Jews.

By now there were worrying signs that Churchill's speech on a 'crime without a name' had led to tightened radio security measures. The cypher in use was changing twice a day, making it more difficult to break, and there were clear delays in the intelligence being decyphered. This was almost certainly why a message sent by Jeckeln on 26 August 1941 and in which he reports that his units had shot a further 1,246 Jews, was not included in the 30 August report to Churchill. It was issued separately on 1 September and seen by Churchill a day later. Again the Prime Minister circled the figure for the number of Jews shot.

The slaughter was unremitting. Jeckeln reported on 30 August that the Police Regiment South had shot dead forty-five Jews in the central Ukrainian town of Slavuta and von dem Bach-Zelewski reported that his men had shot dead eighty-four Jews in the Belorussian town of Gorodishche. A day later, on 31 August, Jeckeln reported that 911 more Jews had been shot dead in Slavuta and a further 2,200 Jews shot dead in Minkowzky. This was reported to Churchill on 6 September as 'over 3,000 Jews shot by various units'. On 2 September, Jeckeln reported that his men had shot dead a further sixty Jews and fifteen Partisans in the Kaments-Podolsky region of the southern Ukraine. Four days later, on 6 September, they had shot dead 494 Jews and two Partisans. On 11 September, Jeckeln reported that Police Regiment South had liquidated 1,548 Jews 'according to the usage of war'. This euphemism was commonly used. The victims were variously 'disposed of'; 'liquidated'; 'executed'; 'shot dead'; or sometimes simply 'evacuated'. The upshot was, of course, always the same.

The next day, 12 September, the German Police changed their cypher, starting with the cyphers in use by the police troops in the occupied areas of the Soviet Union. They switched from the double transposition system to a system known as Double Playfair, a fairly sophisticated substitution system, albeit one that Bletchley Park was able to break again with relative ease.

Also on 12 September, Churchill saw his final report on the killing of Jews during this initial period. There were very clear decryption difficulties with this report. It was only shown to Churchill on 12 September, although it dated back to 27 August, when Jeckeln reported that the 1st SS Brigade had killed sixteen Jews and Partisans; Police Regiment South had shot dead 914 Jews; and the 'Special Handling Staff with 320 Police Battalion had shot dead 4,200 Jews. At the bottom of the report, de Grey noted: 'The fact that the Police are killing all Jews that fall into their hands should by now be sufficiently appreciated. It is not therefore proposed to continue reporting these butcheries specially, unless so requested.'

But the messages dried up anyway. A few weeks after Churchill's speech, Daluege warned his commanders that the British might be listening and told them to send details of all future 'executions' to Berlin by courier.

The killings that followed the invasion of the Soviet Union are now recognised as the beginning of the Holocaust. It has been claimed that Churchill covered up the evidence from Bletchley Park of the Holocaust killings. Nothing could be farther from the truth. He not only broadcast to the world, denouncing the German mass murders as a 'crime without a name', he had Foreign Office lawyers collect evidence of the killings for use in future war trials.

One of those involved in decyphering the plethora of messages coming out of eastern Europe was Charles Cunningham who had been called up into the Army as a private.

I had read classics, Latin and Greek, at Glasgow. By way of ancillary to that I had taken a short course in German mainly because many of the best texts and commentaries on the Latin and Greek classics are in German. As a result of that very minimal knowledge the Army posted me to Bletchley Park. On my first day there, I saluted this captain and he turned to me and said: 'Excuse me' – which is not the language normally used by captains to privates – 'Excuse me,' he said. 'What is that noise?' To which I replied: 'That is the air raid siren, sir.' That gives you some kind of an impression of what kind of place Bletchley was; mad people on all sides.

Cunningham was immediately promoted to lance-corporal and put to work on police communications. 'I was a cryptana-lyst working on what was called German police but in fact it included all the security services,' Cunningham said. 'They used a lovely hand cypher system, which was called Double Playfair, named after a British admiral in the mid-nineteenth century who devised it.'

Admiral Playfair's system required the message that was to be encyphered to be split into bigrams so the sentence 'Report to headquarters at once' would be rendered:

RE PO RT TO HE AD QU AR TE RS AT ON CE

The cypher was built in a five by five square around a keyword. If we were to take 'Phoenix' as the key word, it would be written into the square with the remaining letters of the alphabet filling the rest of the square, omitting J which when encyphering was always taken to be I. A Playfair cypher using Phoenix as the keyword would therefore appear thus:

P	H	O	E	N
I	X	A	B	C
D	F	G	K	L
M	Q	R	S	T
U	V	W	Y	Z

Each bigram of the divided message is then replaced by a pair of letters from within the square according to pre-set rules. If the letters appear at a diagonal to each other they are replaced by the letters at the other point of a rectangle so formed. In the case of our message, the first bigram RE becomes OS. Bigrams with letters in the same horizontal or vertical line are replaced by the next letter on, making the second bigram of the above message PO become HE. Letters at the end of the line jump to the next one. So the third bigram RT would be rendered SU. The entire encyphered message would then be written in five letter groups, in this case using four randomly chosen fillers at the end:

OSHES UNRON GIVMG WNSST RCEIN BCVYU

The Germans, having broken this cypher early on in the First World War, decided to adapt it for their own use. They introduced a second square from which the second letter of each bigram was selected and dispensed with the keyword, placing the letters in random order. This complication obviously made it much more difficult to crack. But since the Germans spelt everything, including numbers, out in full, the codebreakers often got plenty of depth. The German fondness for proforma traffic in which everything always stayed in its set place also helped to ensure that the Double Playfair system, used as a medium-grade cypher not just by the German police but also by the Army and air force, was regularly broken.

Proforma messages inevitably required each part of the message to be preceded by a sequential number, the first part being 1, the second 2, and so on. Since these had to be spelt out, EINS, the German word for one, was immediately recoverable and easy cribs were available for the rest of the message. The fact that, when spelt out, the German numbers one to twelve contain all but eight of the letters in the Double Playfair squares made proforma traffic relatively easy to break. But while the actual process of breaking the police cypher was an enjoyable and intensely rewarding task for the codebreakers, the results of their labour were often horrific.

'When you're an individual cryptanalyst just working on the intercepts of the day before, you don't have any real overall picture,' said Cunningham.

You only see the bits of paper in front of you and try to break the cypher and having broken it you pass it on to someone else who does the decoding. The business of the cryptanalyst is simply to get the key. When he's done that, he goes on to another batch. But there was concern over the concentration camps, which was of course a very inadequate term, and one was aware in the case of stuff coming from these camps that very nasty things indeed were going on. They were run by the SS and they made regular returns of the intake and what the output was and you can guess what the intake was and what the output was. You soon got to have a fairly good idea of what you were dealing with. The ironic thing was that these terrible returns, sort of day-to-day status reports, were stereotyped and that is a very good way of getting into that kind of cypher. They provided an excellent crib, which I always thought of as a distinctly unfortunate thing but I suppose it is a kind of way of turning evil into good.

The SS decrypts also revealed the existence of a special SS battalion which, under the guidance of Joachim von Ribbentrop, the German foreign minister, was plundering works of art and sending them back to Berlin. The battalion was attached to Army groups in all the countries invaded by Germany and in Russia made a particular target of the palaces of the former Tsar in Leningrad, suggesting that it may have been behind the disappearance of the legendary Amber Room, a gold and amber encrusted hall in the Winter Palace. The decrypts showed the battalion becoming involved in a wrangle between von Ribbentrop and Alfred Rosenberg, Minister for Occupied Territories, over what should happen to various works of art looted from Russian palaces, museums and monasteries, most of which made their way into the villas of leading Nazi party bosses.

CHAPTER 7

ACTION THIS DAY

Churchill's obsession with the increasing amount of high-grade intelligence the codebreakers were producing hidden away at a secret location in the heart of the British countryside meant it was inevitable that he should want to visit Bletchley Park in person to see them at work. He arrived on the morning of 6 September 1941, his visit kept secret from the bulk of the codebreakers.

The decrypts delivered by Menzies had most recently included the reports on the German killings of the Jews on the Eastern Front and the preparations by German U-Boats to attack Allied shipping in the Atlantic, while Hut 6, having proved its worth in the Balkans, with its warnings over the invasion of Russia and as the place where Enigma was being broken most regularly, was one of the highlights of Churchill's visit.

'Travis took him on a tour of the many Bletchley Park activities,' Welchman recalled.

> The tour was to include a visit to my office and I had been told to prepare a speech of a certain length, say ten minutes. When the party turned up, a bit behind schedule, Travis whispered, somewhat loudly, 'Five minutes, Welchman.' I started with my prepared opening gambit, which was 'I would like to make three points,' and then proceeded to make the first two points more hurriedly than I had planned. Travis then said, 'That's enough, Welchman,' whereupon Winston, who was enjoying himself, gave me a grand schoolboy wink and said, 'I think there was a third point, Welchman.'

The three-rotor Enigma cypher machine used by the *Wehrmacht* with the lid open and the plugboard, or steckerboard, visible at the front of the machine. The three rotors or wheels can be seen at the top of the picture. The letters on the side of each wheel were used to indicate its precise starting position.

The Polish codebreaker Marian Rejewski (TOP LEFT) was the first man to break the 'steckered' Enigma machine. The Poles were assisted by information provided by Hans Thilo Schmidt (TOP RIGHT), codenamed *Asche*, a French spy inside the German Defence Ministry, who sold Enigma manuals and key settings to the French intelligence service. Gustave Bertrand (BELOW with wife Mary), the head of the French Cypher Bureau, later passed them to the British.

The codebreakers arrive at Bletchley Park in August 1939 (TOP). They include Dilly Knox (BOTTOM RIGHT), the only British codebreaker at this stage to have broken Enigma cyphers, and Alan Turing (BOTTOM LEFT), who was to play a key role in the breaking of the German Navy's Enigma cyphers. Knox subsequently broke the German intelligence service Enigma cypher. That break was crucial to the Double Cross deception operations that helped ensure the success of D-Day.

Alastair Denniston (TOP LEFT) was the first head of Bletchley Park. Professor E. R. P. 'Vinca' Vincent (TOP CENTRE) worked on Italian naval cyphers. John Tiltman (TOP RIGHT) was the chief cryptographer from early 1942, breaking numerous codes and cyphers. Hugh Alexander (LEFT) another of the leading codebreakers and head of the Naval Enigma section Hut 8.

RIGHT: A rare photograph of German operators using the Enigma machine.

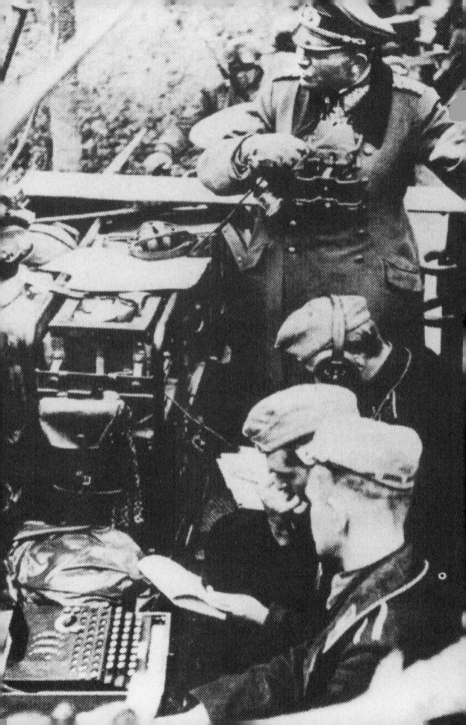

Photographs of the codebreakers working inside the Bletchley Park mansion before the moves to the wooden huts are very rare. Leslie Lambert (TOP), who worked in the Air Section, was better known as the popular BBC radio personality A. J. Alan. Joan Wingfield (RIGHT) was a 24-year-old Italian linguist who had joined GC&CS in 1937.

BELOW: Codebreakers watching a game of rounders. Standing (LEFT TO RIGHT): Captain William Ridley, MI6 Chief Administrative Officer; John Barns, Naval Section; George McVittie, Head of Meteorological Cyphers in Air Section; Marjorie de Haan, Diplomatic Section; Alastair Denniston, Head of Bletchley Park. Seated (LEFT TO RIGHT): Edward Smith, Hut 3; Edmund 'Scrounger' Green, Naval Section; Barbara Abernethy, Denniston's PA; Patrick Wilkinson, Naval Section; Alan Bradshaw, GC&CS Chief Administrative Officer.

TOP: Two thirds of the people working at Bletchley Park were women. They included around 2,000 members of the Women's Royal Naval Service, or Wrens, most of whom operated the Bombes (shown here) testing possible solutions of the Enigma wheel orders and key settings.

BELOW: Women worked in a wide variety of roles, including codebreaking. These woman are working on the Enigma cyphers in Hut 6. There is an Enigma machine on the table to test solutions.

Welchman took the Prime Minister on a tour of Hut 6, introducing him to John Herivel as the man responsible for beginning the continuous break into the vitally important *Red* key. 'Churchill didn't say anything,' Herivel recalled.

> He just gave me a deep penetrating look, not a very friendly look, rather a scowl, and then he went on. Later that day, we were told the Prime Minister wanted to see us. There was a little pile of material which the builders had conveniently left near the end of Hut 6 and Churchill stood up on it and in just a few words, with deep emotion, he said how grateful he was to us for all the good work we were doing in the war effort. So that was our finest hour.

Churchill would later laud the codebreakers as 'the geese that laid the golden eggs and never cackled' but was reputedly so startled by the eccentricity of some of the codebreakers that he turned to Menzies, who was visiting with him, and said: 'I know I told you to leave no stone unturned to get staff, but I didn't expect you to take me literally.'

Malcolm Kennedy recorded the visit in his diary entry for 6 September 1941.

> The PM paid us a surprise visit this morning and after inspecting some of the work of BP gave a short talk thanking us for what we have done and stressing the great value of our work. Sir Dudley Pound, the First Sea Lord, paid a similar visit of thanks at the time of the '*Bismarck*' show. Very decent of these old boys to come down in person to thank us when they themselves must be terribly loaded down with their own work and vast responsibilities. Instructions issued to keep Churchill's visit a secret, but all Bletchley seems to know about it.

Only a few of the codebreakers were able to hear what Churchill said but there was an immense feeling of pride that the Prime

Minister had visited them and disappointment among those, like Anne Lavell, who were not there to hear him speak. 'I was terribly cross,' she said. 'I was on four to midnight shift that day and when I came up the place was buzzing like an ant-heap, and I'd missed it all, he'd been and gone.'

Churchill's visit was timely given Denniston's inability to get anyone in Whitehall to provide the new recruits and the equipment the codebreakers needed. He was doing what he could but since so few people were allowed to know the *Ultra* secret Denniston was unable to make clear the importance of the work being done at Bletchley Park. He was seen in Whitehall as the head of an obscure Foreign Office department that could not possibly be allowed to compete with the needs of the forces who were fighting the war and he did not wield the necessary power or weight of personality to force the issue. The requests for more resources were getting nowhere.

It was clear to the leading members of Hut 6 and Hut 8 that Denniston's old-fashioned approach, while perfectly well suited to keeping the varied, often difficult characters who inhabited the inter-war GC&CS happy, was not adequate to running the increasingly mechanised Bletchley Park codebreaking operation. The German military operations in North Africa, the Mediterranean, the Balkans and on the Eastern Front were now generating a massive amount of work for the codebreakers. There was far too much to do and too few people, and equipment, particularly Bombes and radio sets, to do it.

Welchman, Milner-Barry, Turing and Alexander, 'the wicked uncles' as they were known among their junior staff, decided to go straight to the top. On 21 October, 1941, they wrote a letter to Churchill reminding him of his visit and his praise for their work.

> We think, however, that you should know that this work is being held up, and in some cases not being done at all, principally because we cannot get sufficient staff to deal with it.

> Our reason for writing to you direct is that for months we
> have done everything that we possibly can through the normal
> channels and that we despair of any early improvement with-
> out your intervention.

They emphasised that they had written the letter entirely on
their own initiative and were careful to stress that the problem lay with the Foreign Office and the service ministries who
seemed not to understand 'the importance of what is done here
or the urgent necessity of dealing promptly with our requests.
No doubt in the long run these particular requirements will be
met, but meanwhile still more precious months will have been
wasted. If we are to do our job as well as it could and should
be done, it is absolutely vital that our wants, small as they are,
should be promptly attended to.'

Fearing that if the letter were sent through Denniston or
Menzies it would never reach Churchill, they decided that
Milner-Barry should go to Downing St himself to deliver it. He
would later remember his own 'incredulity at hearing my own
voice say "10, Downing Street" to a taxi driver at Blackfriars and
arriving unopposed – the first and no doubt the last time that I
shall find myself inside those doors.' While he was unopposed
in his attempt to get to Number 10, it was a different matter
once he was inside. Brigadier George Harvie-Watt, Churchill's
principal private secretary, insisted that no one saw the Prime
Minister without an appointment and demanded more details of
this matter of supposed great national importance. Milner-Barry,
who had not thought to bring any official identification with him,
was equally insistent that he could not discuss it with anyone
who was not authorised to know about it. Eventually, Harvie-
Watt agreed to pass the letter on to Churchill, whose immediate
response was a minute to General 'Pug' Ismay, his chief military
assistant. 'Make sure they have all they want extreme priority and
report to me that this has been done,' Churchill wrote, scrawling
across the minute the ominous warning: 'Action this day.'

From that point on, resources began to flow into Bletchley Park. A comprehensive building programme was put in place in anticipation of a staff of around 3,000 – at the time, with the number of staff still some way short of 1,000, a highly optimistic figure. The first priority was a canteen to replace the old dining hall in the mansion which was now far too small, leading to long queues at mealtimes. There were also to be a number of custom-built brick blocks to house the necessary expansion. The Ministry of Labour was ordered to hold a meeting with Denniston and Menzies at which the needs of the codebreakers were to be considered favourably. The service chiefs were instructed to provide more clever young men and to enlarge the Y services immediately to provide the coverage that Welchman, Milner-Barry, Turing and Alexander demanded. Expensive new orders for many more bigger Bombes – the Jumbos – were placed with the British Tabulating Machine Company and the Royal Navy agreed to supply additional Wrens to operate them.

Tiltman set up a training school for cryptanalysts in order to give the new entrants a basic grounding in codebreaking. It was called the Inter-Service Special Intelligence School and was housed briefly in an RAF depot in Buckingham before moving into the gas company showrooms in Ardour House, Albany Rd, Bedford, where it swiftly became known to locals as 'the Spy School'.

The military resorted to unusual methods to bring in the right type of recruit to Bletchley Park. Stanley Sedgewick's job as a managing clerk with a firm of city accountants was classified as a reserved occupation which meant that call-up was deferred for six months at a time. Every day, he travelled into London by train. 'I became quite good at solving the crossword puzzles appearing in the *Daily Telegraph*,' Sedgewick said.

Towards the end of 1941, the appearance of a crossword marking a milestone in the history of the *Telegraph* inspired several letters from readers claiming they had never missed them, or never failed to solve them, or never took more than so many minutes to solve them.

A Mr Gavin, Chairman of the Eccentrics Club, wrote saying he would donate £100 to the Minesweepers Fund if it could be demonstrated under controlled conditions that anyone could solve the *Daily Telegraph* puzzle in less than twelve minutes. This prompted the editor to invite readers wishing to take up this challenge to present themselves at the newspaper's offices in Fleet St on a Saturday afternoon. I went along to find about thirty other would-be fast solvers. We sat at individual tables in front of a platform of invigilators including the editor, Mr Gavin, and a timekeeper. The editor then selected a sealed envelope out of a stack of seven, each containing the puzzles due to appear the following week.

Four of those present completed the puzzle correctly in 7 minutes 57.5 seconds; 9 minutes 3.5 seconds; 9 minutes 52.5 seconds; and 10 minutes 38.5 seconds. I was one word short when the twelve-minute bell rang, which was disappointing as I had completed that day's puzzle in the train to Waterloo in under twelve minutes. We were then given tea in the chairman's dining-room and dispersed with the memory of a pleasant way of spending a Saturday afternoon. Imagine my surprise when several weeks later I received a letter marked 'Confidential' inviting me, as a consequence of taking part in 'the *Daily Telegraph* Crossword Time Test', to make an appointment to see Colonel Nicholls of the General Staff who 'would very much like to see you on a matter of national importance'.

Colonel Freddie Nicholls was in fact the head of MI8, the military intelligence department concerned with Bletchley Park and the Army's radio interception or 'Y' Service. 'I arranged to attend at Devonshire House in Piccadilly, the headquarters of MI8, and found myself among a few others who had been contacted in the same circumstances,' Sedgewick said.

> I think I was told, though not so primitively, that chaps with twisted brains like mine might be suitable for a particular type of work as a contribution to the war effort. Thus it was that I reported to 'the Spy School' at 1, Albany Rd, Bedford. On completion of the course I received a letter offering me an appointment as a 'Temporary Junior Assistant' at the Government Communications Centre and started at BP.

Sedgewick worked in Hut 10, Josh Cooper's Air Section, on German weather codes. 'The results were used – usually currently – to permit weather forecasts to be made for operational use by Bomber Command,' Sedgewick said. He was unaware until long after the end of the war that they were also used as crucial cribs for the Naval Enigma.

The Y service was to be gradually expanded by around 1,000 wireless sets and, since these were to be manned twenty-four hours a day, seven days a week, more than 4,000 operators. As a result of Chatham's vulnerability to German air raids, new Army stations had been built at Harpenden, in Hertfordshire, and at Beaumanor, near Loughborough in Leicestershire, where from October 1941 – when the Army operators from Chatham moved there – most of the Enigma traffic was taken. The RAF intercept site at Chicksands Priory was now expanding rapidly and a new General Post Office (GPO) site to augment the work of Sandridge was opened in a rambling eighteenth-century rectory at Whitchurch in Shropshire.

There were also a number of Y Service interception stations abroad in Palestine, Egypt, Malta, Gibraltar, India and South Africa as well as the Far East Combined Bureau, based in Singapore until the Japanese invasion when it moved to Ceylon. There were now 155 radio sets concentrating solely on different types of Enigma traffic, 132 of them in the UK and the others at various points around the world with all the material pouring into Hut 6 Registry by teleprinter.

By the end of the war the Y Service had grown to an astonishing size. 'The Y Service was an amazing organisation,' said Joan Nicholls.

> It began with a few people before the war and ended up with thousands of us. Wherever the Germans were we were listening. Berlin, Essen, anywhere in Germany, anywhere in Russia, all over the continent, Holland and so on. At Beaumanor there were 900 female ATS intercept operators and 300 civilian intercept operators, the men, so there were 1,200 of us manning four set-rooms twenty-four hours a day and that was only one station.

Hundreds of Wrens were drafted into Bletchley, not just to look after the new Bombes, but also to work in a number of other codebreaking and intelligence roles. They were allocated their own trade, 'Special Duties X', and a new Bombe outstation was opened up at Gayhurst Manor, north of Bletchley. The increase in numbers of people arriving put strain on the administration, which had to find billets for them all. 'Many more service people came in, many more Wrens,' said Mavis Lever, one of the civilian codebreakers. 'The more people came, the further you had to go out to villages, right over beyond Woburn and into Bedfordshire and around Buckinghamshire and a vast system of taking people in and out and so on, whereas before we were all very locally billeted.'

When the shifts changed over at 9am, 4pm and midnight, swarms of people descended from a variety of vehicles, many of them driven by young female Motor Transport Corps (MTC) volunteers, young debutantes who had no need to be paid for their war work. 'The MTC drivers were really very attractive girls,' said Barbara Abernethy. 'They were usually quite wealthy and they had to buy their own uniforms, which were beautifully cut, and they were all pretty. But they worked very, very hard.' The staff coming on shift had been brought in from various billets all over the surrounding countryside and those going off shift were taken home in the same fashion.

'We would do eight-hour shifts,' said Morag Maclennan, a Wren working in the Hut 11 Bombe section.

> You would come out of your transport, buses or shooting brakes. They were the great things, shooting brakes dashing all over the villages of Buckinghamshire bringing people in. Huts were being built all the time and extra pieces of equipment being installed. Things were going on in the far reaches of the park that I didn't know very much about.

Some of the vehicles were extremely old and unreliable, said Julie Lydekker, a junior assistant in the Air Section.

> They laid on extraordinary old seaside char-a-bancs, with doors all down the side. One of the people who used to come on this char-a-banc was A. J. Alan. He used to be in the Hunt Hotel, Lindslade, and when the buses broke down he would take us in and give us ginger wine. He was always very amusing.

In an attempt to relieve the pressure for new billets, the servicemen and women were moved into military camps, recalled Ann Lavell.

> We were hauled out of our billets, many of us wailing and screaming mightily, and by this time we were all dressed up as flight sergeants. A flight sergeant is really quite somebody in an ordinary RAF station but we were nobodies. We were put into these frightful huts that took about twenty-four people and had these dangerous cast-iron stoves in them that got red hot and sent out smoke everywhere. There was a terrible feeling

between the camp authorities and the Bletchley Park people. They couldn't bear it because they didn't know what we did and because we could get in past the sentries. The guards actually said: 'Halt, who goes there?' If you arrived at night, they did the bit about 'friend or foe' and you said, 'Friend' and they said, 'Advance friend and be recognised'. The camp people absolutely hated not knowing what was going on and some of the officers tried to bully out of the junior people what they were doing.

By now most people, apart from the dons, wore uniform. 'There was a period when the hierarchy, such as it was, was completely chaotic,' said John Prestwich, one of the Hut 3 intelligence reporters.

Some people were group-captains, some people were lieutenants and so on. So for a longish period we all wore civilian clothes and we were perfectly happy about it, uniforms were uncomfortable. Then some wretched admiral came down and said: 'Where are my Wrens?' and there were these girls in skirts and jumpers and he said: 'It's disgraceful. My Wrens should be jumping up, hands down seams of skirts.' So we were all made to wear uniform.

A branch of the Corps of Military Police known as the Vital Points Wardens (VPWs) mounted guard on the camp. The VPWs wore a distinctive blue cap cover rather than the standard Military Police red cap until somebody pointed out that this gave away the fact that Bletchley Park was a 'vital point' and the blue cap covers were removed.

Despite the increase in military control, man management remained relaxed and in keeping with the attitude encouraged by Denniston from the start. Stuart Milner-Barry, then deputy head of Hut 6, recalled that formal orders were rarely given out.

Orders were nearly always given in the form of requests and

accompanied by explanations. The reasons are partly historical. When we began there was in any one room no hierarchy;
the people doing the job were all on the same level. As things
became more complicated, it was obviously impossible to
maintain this agreeable anarchy; somebody had to be responsible if administration was to be carried on at all. So the system of
heads of shift grew up, an innovation looked at askance in the
early days – chiefly because those appointed, particularly in the
girls' rooms, were extremely reluctant to appear to push themselves forward or to assume any kind of authority over their
friends. So any kind of authority there was, was dependent on
leadership and personality and not on any kind of sanctions.

Ann Lavell recalled that the atmosphere at Bletchley Park, even
after the military tried to impose themselves on the members
of the armed forces working there, was unlike any other and
encouraged informality.

You did have this rather happy atmosphere of tolerance. Very
eccentric behaviour was accepted fairly affectionately and I
think people worked and lived there who couldn't possibly
have worked and lived anywhere else. People who would obviously have been very, very ill at ease in a normal air force camp
with its very strict modes of behaviour and discipline were very
happy, very at ease in Bletchley.

ℰℬ

On 7 December 1941, Japan entered the war, attacking Malaya
and Pearl Harbor within the space of a few hours and bringing America into the war.* Bletchley had been warning of the

---

*   The attack on Malaya took place first in 'real time' even though it
     occurred on 8 December; the difference being due to the fact that Pearl
     Harbor was the other side of the international dateline.

build-up to war from the messages passing between the Japanese ambassador in Berlin, General Oshima Hiroshi, and Tokyo. The newly introduced Japanese military super-encyphered codes, in which the message was first encoded using a code book to produce a series of five-figure groups and then had random streams of figures added to it to encypher it, had been broken by John Tiltman in late 1938. A similar high-grade naval super-encyphered code was introduced by the Imperial Japanese Navy in June 1939; within weeks Tiltman had also broken that. At this stage of the war, most Japanese military and naval codes were broken at outstations with the Wireless Experimental Centre, which concentrated on Japanese military codes based at Anand Parbat, just outside the Indian capital Delhi, and the Far East Combined Bureau (FECB), which worked on Japanese naval codes based in Singapore. Shortly before Singapore fell, the FECB moved to Colombo in Ceylon.

The British and the Americans had already prepared for the latter's entry into the war with the British first approaching the US Navy with an offer to exchange cryptographic information in June 1940. They were rebuffed by Captain Laurance Safford, the commander of the US Navy's codebreaking operation Op-20-G, who was very much opposed to any major exchange of information. A direct approach to President Franklin D. Roosevelt succeeded in winning his backing for an exchange of technical information on Japanese, German and Italian code and cypher systems

This made complete sense. The US Army's Signal Intelligence Service (SIS) had broken the main Japanese diplomatic machine cypher, which the Americans codenamed *Purple*, but had not broken Enigma. The British had broken Enigma but not *Purple*. A cryptographic exchange agreement was agreed by senior US and British representatives in Washington in December 1940. The following month, nearly a year before the Japanese attack on Pearl Harbor brought the Americans into the war, a four-man American delegation – comprising two US Army officers, Captain Abraham Sinkov and Lieutenant Leo Rosen, and two US Navy officers, Lieutenant Robert Weeks and Ensign Prescott Currier – set sail for Britain carrying 'certain packages'. The presence in the party of Rosen, the technical expert who had reverse engineered the *Purple* cypher machine, was significant. At least one of the 'packages' the Americans brought with them to Bletchley was a *Purple* machine.

'It was early in 1941,' said Barbara Abernethy, who was then working as Denniston's personal assistant.

> Commander Denniston told me he had something important to tell me. 'There are going to be four Americans who are coming to see me at 12 o'clock tonight,' he said. 'I require you to come in with the sherry. You are not to tell anybody who they are or what they will be doing.'

Currier described landing at Sheerness dockyard on the afternoon of 8 February, and being met by a small delegation from Bletchley Park which included Tiltman. The crates containing the precious Top Secret 'packages' were loaded onto lorries and the convoy headed west towards London en route for Bletchley.

> It soon became dark and the countryside was pitch black with rarely a light showing except for the faint glow emanating from a small hole scraped in the blacked-out headlight lens of the cars. When we arrived at BP, the large brick mansion was barely visible; not a glimmer of light showed through the blackout curtains. We were led through the main doors, and after passing through a blacked-out vestibule, into a dimly lit hallway, then into the office of Commander Denniston RN, chief of GC&CS. Denniston and his senior staff were standing in a semi-circle around his desk and we were introduced to and greeted by each in turn. It was truly a memorable moment for me.

Barbara Abernethy served each of the American guests with a

glass of sherry. 'It came from the Army & Navy Stores and was in a great big cask which I could hardly lift,' she said.

> But Denniston rang the bell and I struggled in and somehow managed to pour glasses of sherry for these poor Americans, who I kept looking at. I'd never seen Americans before, except in the films. I just plied them with sherry. I hadn't the faintest idea what they were doing there, I wasn't told. But it was very exciting and hushed voices. I couldn't hear anything of what was said but I was told not to tell anybody about it. I guess it wasn't general knowledge that the Americans had got any liaison with Bletchley. It was before Pearl Harbor, you see, and presumably Roosevelt was not telling everybody there was going to be any liaison at that stage.

The British kept to the precise letter of the agreement, providing detailed information on how they had broken the Enigma cypher and on their work on a number of other codes and cyphers, including Tiltman's studies of the main Japanese Army system. But in line with the Washington discussions, no details were provided of any of the actual messages they had intercepted. Even if this had not been an American condition, it seems likely that the British would have raised it since they were concerned over the Americans' lack of a secure system for the dissemination of the 'Special Intelligence'.

Denniston told Menzies that Currier and his colleagues had been 'informed of the progress made on the Enigma machine'. The Americans were given 'a paper model of the Enigma machine, detailing its internal wiring and how it worked, together with details of the Bombes. This was as much as, if not more than, the Americans provided.

Without a shadow of a doubt, the most significant contribution on the American side had been the ability to break *Purple*, provided generously from the outset by the US Army codebreakers. The British were again able to read all of the

'State Secret' communiques passing between the main Japanese embassies and Tokyo, and in particular Oshima's reports from Berlin on the intentions of the Nazi leadership and the German High Command.

Safford complained at what the Americans received in return, horrifying the British, and doing nothing to assuage their concerns over US security, by writing an unclassified letter to demand that the Americans be given an Enigma Machine. Safford later claimed that the British reneged on their side of the deal and had 'double-crossed us'.

> The US Navy sent the British all the Comint [communications intelligence] it had on the Japanese Navy in early 1941 and got nothing in return. For several months, US Navy personnel thought they had been double-crossed by the British and were reluctant to go ahead with collaboration in direction-finding and other matters which were greatly to England's advantage throughout 1941. The US Army got German and Italian diplomatic systems from the British and were very happy with the deal.

The false perception that the British were holding back on the exchange deal, largely the result of the US Navy codebreakers, failure to understand the 'paper Enigma machine' the British had handed over, was to become endemic among a number of senior US Navy officers. Yet at the cutting edge, US codebreakers said there was nothing the British held back. Currier recalled an atmosphere of 'complete cooperation' and said the members of the American delegation were shown everything they wanted to see.

> All of us were permitted to come and go freely and to visit and talk with anyone in any area that interested us. We watched the entire operation and had all the techniques explained in great detail. We were thoroughly briefed on the latest techniques applied to the solution of Enigma and in the operation of the

Bombes. We had ample opportunity to take as many notes as we wanted and to watch first hand all operations involved. Furnishings were sparse: a desk with a chair for each of us, a pad of paper and a few pencils. The rooms were a bit cold and uncarpeted and a bit dusty but we soon found out that this was a condition common to all work spaces, including the Director's.

The British codebreakers also did everything they could to make the Americans feel at home, Currier recalled.

During lunch hour on one of the many days at BP, we were introduced to 'rounders', a game resembling baseball played with a broomstick and a tennis ball. It was a relatively simple game with few complicated rules; just hit and run and deep running. It was not long before I could hit 'home runs' almost at will and soon wore myself out running around the bases. Many of our evenings were spent at the home of one or another of our British colleagues. Food and liquor were both rationed, especially liquor, and it was not easy for them to entertain. Whisky and gin were generally unavailable in the pubs and most people had to be satisfied with sherry.

The Americans were also taken to a number of intercept sites and to London where they were put up in the Savoy and introduced to Menzies, Currier said.

I remember standing in a doorway while a few bombs went off, none close, and walking up a narrow stairway to a little reception room with comfortable chairs and a fireplace in which a coal fire was burning. We were served tea and talked briefly about our mission. I was not clear at the time just what role the head of the British Secret Intelligence Service played in the Sigint business nor precisely why we were talking to him. I recall having the impression that he thought we knew a lot more than we did since he spent some time telling us of the difficulty of running agents and collecting intelligence from enemy territory.

We were taken by one of the Royal Navy officers to the Cafe de Paris, an underground London night club on Leicester Square. It was a favourite with Londoners for the very reason that it was underground and relatively safe during a bombing raid. On the evening we were there it was very crowded and noisy, filled with men in uniform dancing to the music of 'Snake Hips' Johnson, a West Indian band leader. The only thing I remember particularly about that evening is a tricycle race across the dance floor between the actor David Niven and some of his fellow officers. The following night, a delayed action bomb crashed through the four or five floors of the building over the club and exploded on the dance floor, killing most of the dancers together with 'Snake Hips' and his band.

Despite subsequent claims that the mission was not as successful as the Americans had hoped, the only real threat to transatlantic cooperation appears to have come during a visit to the Marconi factory at Chelmsford in Essex. 'We were stopped at a road block in a small village,' Currier recalled.

When the local constable saw two men in civilian clothes, obviously not British, riding in a War Department staff car, he reacted quickly and asked if we would 'mind getting out and accompanying him to the police station'. This infuriated our diminutive Scottish driver, who jumped out and confronted the policeman: 'Ye can nae do this, they're Americans on a secret mission.' This had no discernible effect on the constable and it took us the better part of an hour to convince our captors it was alright to let us proceed.

Joe Eachus, a young US naval lieutenant, was sent to Bletchley in early 1942 by Op-20-G, the US naval codebreaking unit, to find out more about the British codebreakers and what they were doing. 'My nominal task was to tell Washington what was happening at Bletchley Park,' he said. 'In that role I got around to see more of Bletchley Park than a lot of the people who were part of it.' There was continuing mistrust on both sides. 'As a liaison officer I was occasionally asked to get specific stuff and on one occasion I was asked by Washington for an organisational chart of Bletchley Park,' Eachus said. 'I went to the man in charge and said could I have a chart of the organisation. He paused and said, "I don't believe we have one." I didn't pursue this with him, but I was never quite certain whether he meant we don't have a chart, or we don't have an organisation.'

Eachus found that the fact that he had his own rations and was happy to share them with the British helped to ease the mistrust. Although there were only two US naval officers, they were officially designated as 'a detached unit' and entitled to their own supplies, Joe Eachus recalled. 'A detached unit covers a multitude of sins, from an individual to a ship,' he said. 'So when I went to London I got my supplies from the same place that ships did, sugar in one hundred pound bags and coffee in twenty-five pound cans. So my office was always very well supplied with sugar. Consequently when I would go to some other office to ask them to tell me about what they were doing, I would take a cup of sugar with me, which made me a good deal more welcome than I might otherwise have been.'

Bletchley Park was now playing a critical role in a large number of different military operations around the world. One of the most neglected of these is the codebreakers' role in what was by any measure one of the most successful intelligence operations in history. The Double Cross System originated with a suggestion at the start of the war by a young MI5 officer, Dick White, that captured German agents should be 'turned' to work as double agents for British intelligence. At this stage, the idea was simply to find out from the questions the Germans asked what they did and did not know. One of the earliest opportunities to turn a German agent came at the start of the war with the

arrest of Arthur Owens, a former MI6 agent who did a lot of
business in Germany and who claimed to have been recruited as
the main agent in Britain of the German intelligence service, the
Abwehr. But when MI5 intercepted his correspondence with his
German controller they realised he was playing the two services
off against each other. Owens agreed to work as a double agent
under the covername of *Snow*. His controller was Lieutenant-
Colonel Tommy 'Tar' Robertson of MI5, who was to become the
effective head of the Double Cross system. *Snow* had been given
a radio transmitter and a very primitive cypher by the Germans.
This was used by MI5 to send false 'reports' from *Snow* to his
German controller, and was sent to Bletchley Park for evalua-
tion. The MI5 radio operator sending the messages noticed that
the control station was working to other stations using different
cyphers and the messages were sent to Bletchley for analysis.
But the codebreaker who looked at them expressed 'considerable disbelief' that they were of any importance. Despite the
codebreaker's scepticism, the radio messages were monitored by
the Radio Security Service (RSS), which employed Post Office
intercept operators and a small army of volunteers, most of them
radio 'hams', who scanned the shortwave frequencies looking for
German agent traffic. Major E. W. B. Gill, now head of the RSS,
and a colleague, Captain Hugh Trevor-Roper (later Lord Dacre),
broke one of the cyphers in use and proved the other messages
were indeed *Abwehr* agent traffic. This caused considerable and
understandable embarrassment at Bletchley and the row over
the significance of the traffic went on for some time with Trevor-
Roper becoming increasingly unpopular with the professional
codebreakers. Eventually, though, Bletchley had to accept that
Gill and Trevor-Roper were right and a new section was set up at
Bletchley, in Elmer's School, to decypher the various messages. It
was headed by Oliver Strachey and both the section and its product became known as ISOS, standing for Illicit Services Oliver
Strachey, although the 'Illicit' was frequently and understandably rendered as 'Intelligence'. By December 1940, Strachey had

broken the main hand cypher in use on the *Abwehr* networks. The resultant ISOS decrypts enabled MI5 to keep track of the messages of the double agents and spot any other German spies arriving in the UK. It also meant that the agents' reports could be designed to allow the codebreakers to follow them through the *Abwehr* radio networks. Hopefully, this would help them break the keys for the Enigma cypher that the German controllers were using to pass the reports on to Hamburg.

By the end of 1940, Robertson had a dozen double agents under his control. A special committee was set up to decide what information should be fed back to the Germans. It included representatives of MI5, MI6, naval, military, and air intelligence, HQ Home Forces, and the Home Defence Executive, which was in charge of civil defence. The committee was called the Double Cross Committee. It met every Wednesday in the MI5 headquarters at 58, St James's Street, in the heart of London's clubland. Initially, with the threat of a German invasion dominating the atmosphere in London, it was decided that the 'intelligence' provided by the double agents should be used to give an impression of how strong Britain's defences were. But by the beginning of 1941, it was clear that more could be done with the double agents. They could be used to deceive the Germans, to provide them with misleading information that would give Allied forces an advantage in the field.

Much of the material passed to the Germans was 'chickenfeed', unimportant information that would give the *Abwehr* a feel that its agents were doing something and had access to real intelligence without telling them anything really harmful. But mixed among this were key pieces of specious or misleading information designed to build up a false picture of what the British were doing. While the response of the *Abwehr* controllers to the double agents' reports helped the Double Cross Committee to work out where the gaps in the Germans' knowledge lay, it did not tell them whether or not the misleading intelligence picture they were attempting to build up was believed in Berlin. The only way of finding this out was by decyphering the messages passed between the *Abwehr* outstations in Paris, Madrid, Lisbon and their headquarters. But these links all used the *Abwehr* Enigma machine, which was completely different to those used by the other German services.

Hut 6 had looked at the *Abwehr* Enigma early in 1941 but had not seen any way to break it so it was handed over to Knox's research section in the Cottage behind the Mansion at Bletchley. By this stage, the changes to GC&CS introduced to process the main Enigma cyphers had left Knox feeling disconcerted and unhappy. Although Knox's research section carried out a great deal of vital work that helped the codebreakers of Hut 6 and Hut 8, he felt sidelined and remained angry that the pre-war GC&CS was being turned into a production line by the young mathematicians that Denniston had insisted on bringing in. While the mathematicians were only interested in obtaining the keys to a cypher before moving on to the next problem, Knox was frustrated by his inability to see the decyphering process through to the end. This, combined with the effects of stomach cancer, which would eventually prove terminal, made him increasingly irascible. Lever recalled tensions between Knox and Welchman over the way in which the latter had wrested control of the codebreaking operation away from him.

Dilly was usually at loggerheads with somebody or other. He rather resented, I think, that other people were having all these operational units and felt he could have done it. But then of course he wouldn't have been able to cope. So I think it was best as it was. Dilly was a Greek scholar and an Egyptologist, looking at papyri and hieroglyphics and things. He didn't go in for technology at all. In fact, he absolutely turned his nose up at all these young men who were coming in from Cambridge, one of them being my husband-to-be, because he said they really didn't know what they were doing. As far as he was concerned, it was all a question of having an imaginative approach. Of course, imagination would not have got him the whole way and he knew that.

Knox was typically tetchy when Denniston objected, on the grounds of security, to his talking to Strachey about the *Abwehr* radio networks.

'Dilly spent some time over at the School with his friend Oliver Strachey (the brother of his good Cambridge days friend Lytton) learning about the organisation of the *Abwehr*,' said Mavis Lever.

> First of all the many different spy networks had to be sorted out covering Madrid, Portugal, the Balkans and Turkey to see how the ISOS hand cypher messages related to Dilly's *Abwehr* Enigma messages sent on from the neutral capitals to Berlin after December 1939. It was hoped that there would be good cribs from the back cypher traffic, which Dilly studied carefully. 'Need to know' restrictions were strictly enforced, but it is difficult to understand why Denniston considered that Dilly had no 'need to know' about ISOS, which was obviously so relevant to his work.

Knox sent Denniston a furious note, typically threatening, yet again, to resign, and insisting, rightly, that he needed to see the ISOS material and any other evidence relevant to the *Abwehr* communications, not least for the provision of 'cribs', if he were to be able to break the *Abwehr* Enigma. He also insisted that he should be the person reporting any material to London rather than Strachey's ISOS section of Hut 3, an illustration of how irritated he was by the way in which everything at Bletchley was becoming like an intelligence factory.

My Dear Denniston
As I think you are aware I have decided to attempt a scheme for

the reconstitution of one or more outlying German enigmas. Before proceeding further in the matter there are one or two points, relevant either to the matter itself or to my examination of points of attack, on which I must press for your assurances, and failing these, for your acceptance of my resignation...

In the event of success the whole traffic must be handled in 'The Cottage' or by your nominees. This is a fundamental point in all research of an academic nature. Research, in fact, does not end till the person responsible has affixed his imprimatur on the last proof sheet...

We still have far too many intelligence sections, appearing to the casual observer as mangy curs fighting over whatever bones are tossed to them, and (as far as circulation goes) burying their booty in grimy and schismatic indexes. Yet what they get is the material which assists the cryptographer in his researches and this he is wholly unable to see. Occasionally someone may hand him a slip of paper with references to a buried file, but this is not wanted. As in Broadway, he wants the documents, all the documents, and nothing but the documents...

These burials of essential documents are, I believe, made in accordance with your policy of 'hush-hush' or concealment from workers in Bletchley Park of the results of their colleagues. Against this I protest on several grounds... Such action cripples the activities of the cryptographer who depends on 'cribs'... Such action wholly destroys any liaison or pride in the success of colleagues...

Knox's belief that he should have control over the way the material he deciphered was reported and his rage at the 'monstrous' way in which Bletchley Park material was passed on to London by intelligence reporters who ignored vital nuances or 'corrected' things without consultation were recurring themes of his letters to Denniston. Knox was a classics scholar of some repute; not the least among his cryptographic achievements had been his completion of the work of Walter Headlam, his tutor at Cambridge, in reconstructing the Mimes of the Greek poet Herodas from the worm-eaten papyri found in 1889 in the ruins of an ancient Egyptian city 100 miles south of Cairo. He had turned down the post of Professor of Classics at Leeds University during the inter-war years in order to continue codebreaking.

> As a scholar, for of all Bletchley Park I am by breeding, education, profession and general recognition almost the foremost scholar, to concede your monstrous theory of collecting material for others is impossible. By profession in all his contacts a scholar is bound to see his research through from the raw material to the final text. From 1920–1936, I was always able to proceed as a scholar, and I simply cannot understand, nor I imagine can the many other scholars at BP, understand your grocer's theories of 'window dressing'. Had these been applied to art scholarship, science, and philosophy, had the inventor no right to the development and publication of his discourses, we would still be in the Dark Ages.

Knox followed this rant with yet another threat of resignation before ending his letter with the words: 'a small grouse…. Yours ever, A. D. Knox.'

Denniston was himself unwell during this period, but his response to Knox's somewhat pompous claims to a superior position due to his ability as 'a scholar' belies a reputation as a poor man-manager.

> My dear Dilly,
> Thank you for your letter. I am glad that you are frank and open with me. I know we disagree fundamentally as to how this show should be run but I am convinced that my way is better than yours and likely to have wider and more effective results. If you do design a super Rolls-Royce that is no reason why you should yourself drive the thing up to the house, especially if you are not a very good driver... Do you

want to be the inventor and the car-driver? You are Knox, a scholar with a European reputation, who knows more about the inside of a machine than anybody else. The exigencies of war need that latter gift of yours, though few people are aware of it. The exploitation of your results can be left to others so long as there are new fields for you to explore.

Within days of that exchange, Knox had made a major break-through, working out the internal mechanisms of the *Abwehr* Enigma and reading a message that had been sent on it.

'Knox has again justified his reputation as our most original investigator of Enigma problems,' Denniston said in a letter to Menzies.

He has started on the reconstruction of the machine used by the German agents and possibly other German authorities. He read one message on 8 December. He attributes the success to two young girl members of his staff, Miss Rock and Miss Lever, and he gives them all the credit. He is of course the leader, but no doubt has selected and trained his staff to assist him in his somewhat unusual methods. You should understand that it will be some weeks, possibly months, before there will be a regular stream of these ISOS machine telegrams.

The first of the messages, known as ISK for Illicit Services Knox, was issued on Christmas Day 1941. The value of the ISK messages to the Double Cross system is impossible to overstate. They alone gave the Double Cross Committee the absolute certainty that the Germans believed the false intelligence they were being fed and showed whether or not individual double agents were trusted or under suspicion, in which case steps could be taken to remedy the situation. Two months later, Mavis Lever solved a separate *Abwehr* Enigma machine, known as GGG, which was used near the Spanish border. By the spring of 1942, the information collected from the Bletchley Park decrypts had built up such a good picture of *Abwehr* operations in the UK that Robertson was able to state categorically that MI5 now controlled all the German agents operating in Britain. The Double Cross Committee was able to watch the Germans making arrangements to send agents to Britain and discussing the value of their reports, Robertson wrote. 'In two or three cases we have been able to observe the action (which has been rapid and extensive) taken by the Germans upon the basis of these agents' reports.'

The breaking of the *Abwehr* Enigma was to be the last of Knox's many codebreaking achievements. Although he occasionally came into work, for the most part he worked from home until his death from cancer on 27 February 1943. Shortly before his death, he was made a Companion of the Order of St Michael and St George (CMG), the award normally made to those whose achievements on behalf of their country cannot be made public. He was probably the only codebreaker in any country to make a successful transition from the hand cyphers and book codes of the First World War to the breaking of the complex machine cyphers like Enigma of the Second World War and his work on the Herodas *Mimiambi* suggests an even greater span of ability. But Knox was far more than that. At his funeral, his great friend from school days at Eton and his studies at Cambridge, John Maynard Keynes, described him as being 'sceptical of most things except those that really matter, that is affection and reason'.

CHAPTER 8

THE *SHARK* BLACKOUT

Denniston was being overtaken by a new world inhabited by younger men whose undoubted skills combined gifts for political manoeuvring that matched their ability as codebreakers. These men saw Denniston as weak and regarded the direct, more forthright approach adopted by Travis as much more likely to obtain the vital equipment and personnel they would need to break Enigma during the sustained fighting that was inevitable once Allied forces invaded Europe.

The differences in approach between Denniston and Travis are well illustrated in an exchange between the two men early on in the war when Knox's great friend Oliver Strachey organised a petition of complaint over the messing arrangements. Travis appears to have regarded the organisation of the petition as akin to mutiny. Denniston's response was to admonish Strachey but he also wrote a memo to Travis urging him to accept that there was no need for rigid naval discipline among the codebreakers at Bletchley Park. Denniston promised that he would talk to all those who had signed the petition, but added:

> I do not however think that the morale of GC&CS is in any way affected by Strachey's present action. So far as I'm aware the attitude of all the staff is keener than it has ever been. All know that they are assisting to the best of their ability in an effort that is bearing fruit on nearly every branch. I cannot agree with your suggestion that Strachey had any intention of encouraging discontent.

After twenty years' experience in GC&CS, I think I may say to you that one does not expect to find the rigid discipline of a battleship among the collection of somewhat unusual civilians who form GC&CS. To endeavour to impose it would be a mistake in my mind and would not assist our war effort, we must take them as they are and try to get the best out of them. They do very stupid things, as in the present case, but they are producing what the authorities require.

The American gift of the Japanese *Purple* machine led Denniston to set up a new Japanese section in Hut 7, which was vacant because Freeborn's Hollerith machinery had been moved to larger accommodation. Hugh Foss, the head of the new section, was a pre-war machine specialist who had broken the previous Japanese diplomatic machine cypher known as *Red* and had until now been assisting the naval codebreakers in Hut 8, where he'd made a notable temporary break into *Shark*. Denniston appears to have assumed that the section would cover Japanese diplomatic, Army, Air and Naval cyphers but, in all probability because the Army and Air cyphers were covered by the Wireless Experimental Centre just outside Delhi, Hut 7 only covered Japanese diplomatic and naval cyphers, and initially concentrated solely on the *Purple* and *Red* Japanese diplomatic machine cyphers.

Hugh Foss was undoubtedly a brilliant codebreaker but he had many eccentricities both at work and at home. He wore a red beard and sandals, leading the Americans to nickname him affectionately 'Lease-Lend Jesus'. His cousin Elizabeth Browning, who was now also working in the Naval Section, was a regular visitor to his home. 'I saw a lot of Hugh and Alison Foss,' she said.

They lived in a bungalow at Aspley Guise with their two small children, one of whom was my goddaughter. The house was always chaotic, as Hugh's wife was a darling but almost totally

incompetent domestically. Hugh went home pretty well every
day at 4.30 in order to put the children to bed, get supper, and
do what he could to organise things. An example of their *modus
vivendi* was the highly complicated arrangement for washing-
up (dreamed up, needless to say, by Hugh). Every article was
supposed to be washed in a particular order – saucers first (as
least polluted by human lips); then teaspoons; then sideplates;
then pudding plates; soup bowls; main course plates; knives;
glasses; cups; forks; pudding and soup spoons; and finally sauce-
pans. As these were usually stacked on the floor the dogs were
a great help. The theory of this procedure in the days before
washing-up machines may have been excellent but in practice
one usually found two or three days' washing up waiting to be
done, with plates and dishes piled around and in the sink. If
one tried to help there would be shrieks of: 'Oh you mustn't do
the cups yet, saucers first'. There was also in theory some weird
arrangement so that things Hugh was supposed to put away
were located at distances appropriate to his great height and long
arms, while Alison, who was small and dumpy, had a shorter
range. But in practice things ended up pretty well anywhere. I
remember having lunch there one day with Hugh's muddy boots
on the table beside me to remind him they needed cleaning.

By the end of 1941, the increase in the numbers of people had
brought a dramatic improvement in the social life. Phoebe
Senyard spent her first Christmas of the war at home. 'I returned
on Boxing Day to find everyone gradually returning to normal
after having spent a riotous time, everyone going out of their
way to make everyone else enjoy themselves.'

The Christmas of 1941 was the last to be held in the old
dining hall in the mansion with a traditional dinner and a fancy
dress dance in the school hall. The highlight of the festive period
was the revue, run by Bill Marchant, a former German master
at Harrow who became deputy head of Hut 3. 'The revues took
place once a year about Christmas or New Year,' said Barbara

Abernethy. 'They were produced by Bill and his wife and they really were excellent because they had good people who wrote the stuff like Patrick Wilkinson and a man called Patrick Barraclough, who was Hinsley's tutor at St John's.'

The revues were not just popular with the staff, recalled Travis's daughter Valerie. Her father would invite senior service officers to Bletchley as a means of improving relations between the codebreakers and Whitehall. 'My father always used to have a tremendous party, inviting all the top brass down from London for the revue and they loved it. The little man who was the caterer for Bletchley Park had a wonderful line in the black market and he used to produce the most sumptuous feasts.'

The quality of the revues was not just the result of the standard of writing, but also the number of professional actors and musicians at Bletchley. Pamela Gibson was a professional actress before Birch recruited her for his Naval Section.

> I spoke German quite well and I had a letter from a rather interfering godmother who said she was sure I was doing splendid work entertaining the troops but she knew a girl who had just gone to a very secret place and was doing fascinating work and they needed people with languages. That made me feel I was fiddling while Rome burnt. So I wrote off to the address they sent me and thought no more about it. I had just been offered a part in a play when I got a telegram from Frank Birch asking me to meet him at the Admiralty. He gave me several tests and said: 'Well, I suppose we could offer you a job' and I said: 'Well, you know about the stage, what would you do if you were me?' He said: 'The stage can wait, the war can't.' So I went to Bletchley.

It was while taking part in one of the revues that she met Jim Rose, her future husband, who worked in Hut 3. Rose recalled writing a sketch in which she was acting.

> We had a brilliant chap called Bill Marchant who was deputy

head of Hut 3 who was a minor C. B. Cochrane and created a revue every Christmas. A lot of very bright people were there and wrote music and lyrics. I wrote a sketch and Pam was acting in it. No one was allowed to go to rehearsals but at that time I was going to Washington just before Christmas so I was allowed in and this glorious vision of loveliness stepped down from the stage and said: 'Your sketch isn't bad.'

The fact that so many clever people were gathered in the one place meant that even if the performances were sometimes not up to professional standards, the scripts were always good, said Christine Brooke-Rose, then a young WAAF officer working in one of the Hut 3 research sections.

There was a sort of hall just outside Bletchley Park itself, a brick hall with a stage with shows once a year at Christmas. There were a lot of people with talent there who wrote bits and there were a few actors doing their bit for the war and a lot of amateurs. It was like a university revue, like Footlights. We thought they were splendid. I've no idea if they really were. The performances may not have been so great but I think the scripts were fairly good because there were a lot of very bright people there. We would go up to London to see a play or a concert. There were people like Peter Calvocoressi who would give musical evenings in their billets. I remember Brin Newton-John, an RAF officer in Hut 3 whose daughter Olivia became a well-known pop star, would sing German *Lieder*. People went cycling around the countryside and there were a lot of love affairs going on.

There were a number of debutantes working in the various indexes or as drivers who determined to liven Bletchley Park up. 'We gave what we thought were splendid parties,' recalled Pamela Gibson, who was head of the naval index where many of the debs worked.

A girl called Maxime Birley, the Comtesse de la Falaise as

she became, was a great beauty and mad about France and I remember her giving a party at which we all had to be very French. People would change partners quite a lot. We were rather contained in a way out place and you could only travel if you managed to get transport so there was a good deal of changing of partners.

Stanley Sedgewick organised twice-weekly dances, many of them fancy-dress, and also provided modern dance lessons. 'This was in the Big Band era of Glenn Miller and I engaged the dance bands of the RAF at nearby Halton and a US Air Force bomber base and demonstrations of jitterbugging.'

On one occasion, a bus-load of the debs and Wrens, including Adrienne Farrell, were invited to a dance in a hanger at a nearby American base where Glenn Miller's Band was playing.

The hangar was crowded and in semi-darkness, lit only by swirling coloured spotlights and resounding with the superb but deafening noise of the band. As each of us entered we were grabbed by one of the waiting line of airmen. After the first dance, I looked eagerly round for my next partner. Alas, we were expected to stay with the same person all evening. I think my partner was as disappointed as I was. On the way home, I noticed with some puzzlement that the bus was half empty.

More erudite tastes were catered for by the Bletchley Park Recreational Club which included a library, a drama group, musical and choral societies as well as bridge, chess, fencing and Scottish dancing sections. Hugh Foss, head of the Japanese section, was in charge of the Scottish dancing in which Denniston himself took part. 'I used to do choral singing and Scottish Country dancing in the evenings which was wonderful exercise,' said Valerie Travis. 'With Hugh Foss, who was a member of the Chelsea Reel School, in command we did it properly. I danced an eight some reel with the 51st Highland

Division at one of the Wrenneries. The Wrens gave marvellous dances out at Woburn.'

Ann Lavell recalled that the choral society was also run by an expert, James Robertson, the conductor.

> There was a little church just behind the Park and they did a little Sunday service for the workers and Julie Lydekker and I sang in that and then, right at the end of things James Robertson ran a choir. He was quite a well-known conductor. He conducted at Sadlers Wells when he escaped from GCHQ. He went to Australia and died there. So it was quite an excitement being in his choir.
>
> Then there was Angus Wilson who was a really quite considerable novelist and was one of the famous homosexuals at Bletchley. He wore a bow tie, which was a bit unusual in those days, and I can picture him in the Beer Hut, where there was a bar and people went for a booze in the evenings or lunchtime, quite a haunt. He had a very funny high voice and I remember hearing this above the hubbub in there. Even then he was known as a novelist [sic] but he became really quite considerable, very well thought of.

The eclectic mix of people based at Station X was an eye-opener for many of the young men and women who found themselves there. Diana Russell Clarke had the time of her life at Bletchley Park.

> We all had a marvellous time, all these young men, not attached. We had a very gay time going out to pubs for supper together when we were free. A lot of romance went on, very definitely a lot of romance. The whole thing was absolutely tremendous fun. It's rather awful in the middle of the war. We had to be there, it was an emergency and I think we all put our hearts into it. But I think we all enjoyed being there.

The increasing success of Bletchley Park in producing vital intelligence, not just from Enigma but also from Oshima's highly detailed messages from Berlin to Tokyo and from lower level naval and *Luftwaffe* codes and cyphers, led to a power struggle within Hut 3 for control of the *Ultra* intelligence reports. The number of Enigma messages had grown from fifty decrypts a day when Hut 3 was first set up to 1,300 a day, making them increasingly important to the service departments and a source of influence that some within MI6 wanted to use for their own purposes. The advisers provided by the Military and Air Sections of MI6 tried to take control of the Hut 3 reporting. The attempted coup was led by Squadron-Leader Robert Humphreys, who had been put into Hut 3 by Frederick Winterbottom, the head of Section IV, the Air Section of MI6. Lucas recalled:

> Humphreys had the highest technical qualifications through his real mastery both of intelligence and of German, but unfortunately he aimed at securing control over the organisation for himself. Moreover, he tried to set up within Hut 3 a semi-independent and almost rival organisation responsible to himself. It cannot be doubted that he made a great contribution to our work and also to getting it taken seriously at the highest levels. Nevertheless, he caused great dissension and disturbance.

An attempt to resolve the situation by giving the military and air advisers a veto over both the circulation of the reports and their content only increased the problems and resulted in an 'imbroglio of conflicting jealousies, intrigue and differing opinions', Nigel de Grey said. The atmosphere in the hut became 'tense and unpleasant' and, with the standard of output being affected, Menzies himself was forced to intervene on a number of occasions. No doubt influenced in part by this and in part by the discontent that had led to the joint letter to Churchill, Menzies decided that Denniston, who had been unwell, was not the right man to control such a rapidly growing organisation. An inquiry put in place by Menzies recommended splitting the organisation in two, with Denniston becoming Deputy Director (Civilian) and limiting his control to the diplomatic and commercial sections, which were to move to London – with the exception of Foss's *Purple* section – while the sections handling German, Italian or Japanese military, air or naval intelligence remained at Bletchley under the control of Travis who was to become Deputy Director (Services). Nigel de Grey was appointed Assistant Director (Services) effectively making him Travis's deputy and Tiltman was made Chief Cryptographer, replacing Dilly Knox who by now was seriously ill with cancer. Denniston was privately 'very bitter' about the way he had been manoeuvred out of control, but took it very well. He moved to very good accommodation in London in March 1942, with the diplomatic sections based in Berkeley St and the commercial sections in Alford House in Park Lane. Change was inevitable, Ralph Bennett said.

> Denniston had spent his life in the time of the Battle of Hastings dealing with hand codes and not much information that you could use militarily. Then he found himself in charge of a huge growing organisation, a lot of us younger and in some ways thinking along different lines, and he got a bit outdated in some ways and was shunted out. It was a bit of bad luck on him because he was a very good chap but he was overtaken by events.

The rows within Hut 3 were removed by putting Squadron-Leader Eric Jones, an air intelligence officer who had taken part in the inquiry, in charge. Jones, a future post-war head of GCHQ, removed all the tension by dint of good man-management.

'There was an inter-service rivalry there and [people] jockeying for position,' said Jim Rose, one of the Hut 3 intelligence officers.

> Jones was just ideal. He had left school at fourteen and had been in the cotton business in Manchester. He was very

intelligent, didn't know German but understood organisation very well. He gave people a free hand. It all became crystal clear. Quite a lot of brainy people had the habit of resigning when they were miffed. We used to keep a graph of when we expected one or two of them to resign but Jones dealt with them.

Jones augmented the Hut 3 system with a team of Duty Officers who would lead each shift, effectively replacing the Watch Number Ones. 'Under his firm but understanding rule, we could concentrate on our work undisturbed by internal conflict,' said Ralph Bennett, who was one of the newly appointed Duty Officers.

The watch received the raw decoded messages straight from Hut 6 with all the corruptions and they translated it into English. Then the translations went to either the air or the Army desk to be put into military sense. These chaps passed it to the duty officer for final vetting and for checking for security. No signal could go out of Hut 3 without the initials of the duty officer.

Bletchley Park's early successes against the U-Boats in the Battle of the Atlantic and the ease with which the Allied shipping convoys were evading the Wolf Packs had led Admiral Karl Dönitz, the admiral in charge of the German U-Boats, to suspect that something was very wrong. Either the British had a very good intelligence network in western France and had managed to infiltrate the U-Boat control system or Enigma had been broken. Dönitz ordered the German codebreakers to look at the Enigma system themselves and demanded to know for sure, was it really impregnable?

'We found ourselves bound to admit that we had not succeeded in finding with our reconnaissance sweeps the convoys for which we had been searching,' Dönitz recalled.

As a result of these failures, we naturally went once more very closely into the question of what knowledge the enemy could possibly have of our U-Boat dispositions. Our cyphers were checked and re-checked to make sure they were unbreakable and on each occasion the head of the naval intelligence service adhered to his opinion that it would be impossible to decypher them.

Nevertheless, when Dönitz was given a chance to make the submarine cypher even more secure he jumped at it. The plan involved a slight internal re-design of the Enigma machine. A new, thinner reflector with different wiring was introduced, leaving space for an extra wheel that, while it did not rotate during encypherment, could be set to different positions, adding a further factor of twenty-six to the number of possible solutions. The German cypher experts were convinced that it would now be impossible for anyone to break.

The first sign of the fourth wheel came in early 1941, in a captured document. In August of that year the *U-570* surfaced south of Iceland only to find that a British Hudson patrol aircraft was directly above her. The pilot, Squadron-Leader J. H. Thompson, dropped four depth charges, two on either side of the U-Boat, causing so much damage that the commander was forced to surrender. Inside the U-Boat was the casing of an Enigma machine with a fourth indicator window.

References to the fourth wheel soon started to appear in decyphered messages and, on occasions, operators used it in error. When the Germans had designed the fourth wheel they had taken into account the fact that anyone using it might have to talk to other stations equipped with only the three-wheel machine. So in one of its twenty-six positions it replicated the action of the old reflector, turning the four-wheel machine into the equivalent of a three-wheel machine. By the end of the year, the wiring of the wheel had been recovered from a number of messages sent first using the fourth wheel and then, after the other operator pointed out the mistake, with just three wheels.

On 1 February 1942, the U-Boats introduced the fourth wheel, creating a new cypher dubbed *Shark* by the Bletchley Park codebreakers. Patrick Mahon, one of the Hut 8 codebreakers, and later the head of Hut 8, recalled:

> This was a depressing period for us as clearly we had lost the most valuable part of the traffic and no form of cryptographic attack was available to us. The effect of a fourth wheel was to multiply by twenty-six the number of possible positions of the machine for each wheel order and also to make Banburismus out of the question. To have obtained sufficient depth on this much improved machine an approximate equivalent increase of traffic would have been necessary.

Hugh Alexander, Turing's deputy and effectively, given Turing's complete lack of interest in administration, the *de facto* head of Hut 8, recalled the next nine months as 'a rather gloomy period' in the Hut's history.

'The change meant that we had to break it quite independently of *Dolphin*,' Alexander said. To make matters worse

> breaking on three-wheel Bombes would be so extremely laborious that unless there was a steady stream of absolutely first class cribs our existing Bombe resources would be quite inadequate. Even given this stream so much Bombe time would be used that the Air and Army keys would suffer very seriously; an average *Shark* job would have taken 50 to 100 times as long as an average Air or Army job so that it would have been a moot point whether it would have been worthwhile even if possible.

While they could continue to break *Dolphin*, which was still being used in the waters of Norway and in the Baltic, they were now unable to do anything with *Shark*. The vital intelligence the Admiralty's Operational Intelligence Centre (OIC) had been using to re-route the Atlantic convoys had disappeared.

'We were dismayed when the fourth wheel appeared,' said Shaun Wylie, the head of the Hut 8 Crib Section.

> We knew it was coming. But it was a grim time. We were very much frustrated; the things that we'd hoped to use went bad on us. We realised that our work meant lives and it ceased to be fun. We did what we could, of course, and we got on with what there was, but we kept an eye out for any possibility on *Shark* that might present itself. There was a lot of pressure and we were trying all we could but we didn't have many opportunities. We had to get *Dolphin* out, but *Shark* was the prime target, the focus of our interest.

The problems caused by the '*Shark* blackout' were exacerbated by an increase in the number of U-Boats in the Atlantic to forty and by the breaking by the *B-Dienst* – the German equivalent of Bletchley Park – of the Royal Navy's Naval Cypher No. 3, which was used for most of the Allied communications about the Atlantic convoys. A week after *Shark* came into force, the OIC's submarine tracking room admitted that it was at a loss to say where the U-Boats were. 'Since the end of January, no Special Information has been available about any U-Boats other than those controlled by Admiral Norway,' it reported. 'Inevitably the picture of the Atlantic dispositions is by now out of focus and little can be said with confidence in estimating the present and future movement of the U-Boats.' A break into *Shark* was desperately needed if the Wolf Packs were not to be given a completely free hand in the North Atlantic.

With a great deal of work, Hut 8 did manage to solve the keys for two days in late February and one day in March. But it took six of the Bombes seventeen days to solve each of those settings. Noskwith recalled that there was a feeling of deep disappointment but while the codebreakers were doing everything they could to solve *Shark*, 'there was an acceptance of the fact that until we had better Bombes, faster Bombes that could work through the twenty-six times as many permutations, we wouldn't really be able to cope with it'.

The Bombe section had been further expanded with the addition of a new outstation at Stanmore, in Middlesex; increased recruitment of Wrens; and two different development programmes put in place to produce an upgraded Bombe that could cope with the four-wheel Enigma machine. Doc Keen began work on a high-speed machine with an additional row of wheels that could complete a standard three-wheel run in less than two minutes. But the first experimental 'Keen Machine' could not be produced before March 1943.

The other development program was led by Dr Charles Wynn-Williams of the Telecommunications Research Establishment at Malvern, where a team of GPO engineers had started working on a high-speed Bombe. This had a long snake-like attachment to replicate the fourth wheel which led to it being called Cobra. But it could not be brought into operation until early 1943.

The codebreakers' acceptance that their best chance of breaking *Shark* was through bigger and better Bombes led to further conflict with the OIC which, as one naval intelligence officer recalled, was unable to look at the problem with such scientific detachment.

There was a danger of BP's researches being too academic. Their researches though brilliantly conducted were more like a game of chess or the arrangement of the jigsaw puzzle. They set the known against the unknown and proceeded to a dispassionate consideration of deductions. We saw the problem in a different light, for us the merchantmen and motor torpedo boats, the patrol vessels, and the *Sperrbrecher* [specially reinforced escort vessels] lived and moved and had their being in a world vibrant with the noise of battle. It was almost as though with a finger on the enemy pulse we brought a warmth and a sense of reality to our research work which was noticeably lacking from many similar efforts by BP.

The concerns were understandable. A total of 2,452 Allied merchant ships were sunk by the Germans in the Atlantic with more than 30,000 members of the British Merchant Navy killed in often horrific circumstances. Sailors floundering in their life jackets after a U-Boat hit could not be rescued because to do so would put the ship taking them on board at too much risk of being sunk itself. 'I saw it first in HMS *Alaunia* in 1940,' recalled one sailor, whose ship was passing within feet of men who were floating in the water after surviving the sinking of their ship.

> They shout, even cheer, as you approach. The red lights of their life jackets flicker when they are on the crest of a wave and are doused as they slip into the trough. Their cries turn to incredulous despair as you glide by, unheeding, keeping a stoical face as best you can. But the cold logic of war is that these men in the water belong to a ship that has bought it and that a couple of dozen more ships survive and must be protected. Each time was as bad as the first. We never got used to it.

Faced with such tragedy, the logic of the Hut 8 codebreakers must certainly have seemed far removed from reality to the naval officers and other ranks working in the OIC, but just like the orders to the ships in the convoys that they must not stop to pick up sailors, it was the only sensible and logical approach to take.

'I have been asked whether our prolonged inability to break *Shark* gave us a sense of guilt,' Noskwith said.

> While we knew the seriousness of the situation, I cannot say that we felt guilty. First, we genuinely felt that, without more captured material, there was no short-term solution. Secondly, we knew that there was a long-term solution because of plans, in collaboration with the Americans, to build more powerful Bombes capable of breaking the four-wheel machines. Thirdly,

we were still regularly breaking *Dolphin* as well as, from the summer of 1942, a separate key called *Porpoise* used for traffic in the Mediterranean. We did have a sad time in July when we were late breaking a crucial day while the Arctic convoy PQ17 was being slaughtered by U-Boats and aircraft.

Two factors prevented the U-Boats from running riot in the North Atlantic in the spring of 1942. First, the Germans did not believe that the three-wheel Enigma could have been broken and were therefore unaware that the introduction of the fourth wheel had left the OIC unable to route the convoys around the Wolf Packs. Second, they had found a new and much easier target. The U-Boats were enjoying their second 'happy time' off the eastern seaboard of the United States.

America's entry into the war in December 1941 had given the Germans the opportunity to attack Allied supply ships at the point where they ought to have been safest, as they travelled along the coast of the United States. The Atlantic was divided into zones in which either the British, Americans, or Canadians had complete control over all naval and merchant shipping. The eastern seaboard was obviously a US-controlled zone. The Americans declined to accept British advice that escorted convoys were safer than individual ships. The US Navy liked the defensive acceptance that some ships would be sunk but more would get through, preferring to send merchant ships along the coast one by one, protected by an offensive programme of routine patrols designed to frighten off the U-Boats.

The result was predictable to all but the Americans. In an operation codenamed *Drumbeat*, the U-Boats simply avoided the patrols, waiting for them to pass before picking off the supply ships one by one. In the first three months of 1942, U-Boats sank 1.25 million tons of shipping off the US east coast, four times the rate they had been achieving in the North Atlantic in 1941. But by mid-1942, a convoy system had finally been put in place, the US Navy had established its own submarine-tracking room and the Liberty Ships, bigger and faster than the pre-war freighters, were being built at a phenomenal rate. Dönitz decided to pull the U-Boats back into the North Atlantic.

It was doubly fortunate for both Bletchley Park and the British that they had not been there when *Shark* was first introduced, said Harry Hinsley. Not only would the number of Atlantic convoys successfully attacked have been much greater during this period but the Germans might have realised that the three-wheel Enigma had indeed been broken.

> Had the U-Boats continued to give priority to attacks on [North] Atlantic convoys after the Enigma had changed, there would have been such an improvement in their perform-ance against convoys that the U-Boat command might have concluded that earlier difficulties had been due to the fact that the three-wheel Enigma was insecure.

The OIC was not totally blind as to the presence of U-Boats in the North Atlantic. Details of new submarines being built and tested in the Baltic could be had from *Dolphin*, which contin-ued to be used in Norwegian and Baltic waters, and from the medium-grade Dockyard cypher. Bletchley Park usually knew when a U-Boat was leaving the Baltic or the Bay of Biscay on an operational cruise and when it was coming back. But once the U-Boats were in the Atlantic, the only indications of what was going on came from direction-finding and radio-fingerprinting techniques, and knowledge of the U-Boats' typical behaviour, capabilities and endurance, none of which were reliable.

The Wolf Packs resumed their attacks on the Atlantic convoys in August 1942 with eighty-six U-Boats, four times as many as when *Shark* was introduced. One of the first attacks came over five days between August 5 and 10 when the *Gruppe Steinbrinck* Wolf Pack of eighteen U-Boats attacked a convoy of thirty-three Allied ships, sinking eleven, a total of 53,000 tons of shipping.

During August and September 1942, the U-Boats located twenty-one of the sixty-three convoys that sailed, sinking forty-three ships. They destroyed 485,413 tons of shipping in September, and in October, when there were more than a hundred U-Boats at sea, sank 619,417 tons, the first time they had destroyed more than 500,000 tons of merchant shipping in a month. At the same time, the number of U-Boats sunk dropped to just five in August and three in September. It rose to eight in October but, by the third week of November, only two U-Boats had been sunk while the number of Allied ships lost that month was rising steadily toward the one hundred mark.

The Admiralty began to step up the pressure on Bletchley Park to break *Shark*. The OIC urged Hut 8 to pay 'a little more attention' to the U-Boat cypher. In a tersely written memorandum, it complained that the U-Boat campaign was 'the only one campaign which Bletchley Park are not at present influencing to any marked extent and it is the only one in which the war can be lost unless BP do help'.

There was no need to push the codebreakers any harder than they were pushing themselves. Turing and Alexander were obsessed with the *Shark* problem, to the detriment of security, as John Herivel recalled.

I was standing on the platform at Bletchley station one day. Alexander and Turing were standing, not all that close, and I could hear them talking at what seemed to me to be the tops of their voices about some matter in connection with Bletchley Park. But it was a cryptographical matter. So they were probably quite safe because no one would have known what they were talking about. On the other hand, if there had been an intelligent German spy on the platform, he might have twigged that it was something to do with cryptography.

Although Turing was in theory head of Hut 8, he spent a great deal of 1942 working on other matters. The hut was effectively run by Alexander but without the full authority that he would have had as head of the hut. Following the OIC's complaint, Alexander was put in charge of Hut 8. One of his first acts was to institute daily 'U-Boat meetings' with the Naval Section. He also increased pressure for the introduction of the new Bombes designed to cope with the four-wheel Enigma machine.

But the solution to *Shark* was already in place. Two days after the Admiralty memorandum, a pinch of two German 'short signal' codebooks arrived at Bletchley providing new cribs for the U-Boat messages. The books had been recovered from the *U-559*, which had been scuttled by its crew after being attacked by the British destroyer HMS *Petard* off the Egyptian coast on 30 October 1942. The *Petard*'s first officer, Lieutenant Anthony Fasson, and Able-Seaman Colin Grazier swam to the submarine before it sank and managed to recover its signal documents. They were joined by a sixteen-year-old Naafi boy, Tommy Brown, who had lied about his age to get on active service. He succeeded in getting out with the codebooks, but Fasson and Grazier went down with the submarine. They were both awarded the George Cross posthumously. Brown, a civilian, received the George Medal. The medals were well-deserved; their heroism was vital in helping to end the U-Boat blackout.

The documents that they had rescued from the *U-559* included the current *Wetterkurzschlüssel*, the Short Weather Signals codebook, and the *Kurzsignalheft*, the U-Boats' short signal book which was used to report locations of Allied convoys. These would provide Hut 8 with the cribs they needed to break into *Shark*. The two codebooks arrived at Bletchley on 24 November and the Hut 8 codebreakers decided immediately to put all their efforts into breaking *Shark*, Shaun Wylie recalled.

> We knew that we had a good chance and we certainly put a tremendous amount of effort into it, Bombe time and all that sort of thing. Looking back on it I think we might have chanced our arm and hoped to be lucky, but we did decide to give it everything.

One vital flaw with the *Shark* machine offered the codebreakers hope of breaking it now they had access to cribs from the *Wetterkurzschlüssel* and the *Kurzsignalheft*. When the U-Boats communicated with the shore weather stations they had to use the three-wheel set-up, making the keys for the first three wheels relatively easy to break. Once they were broken there were only twenty-six options to try out on all the other messages to find out the setting of the fourth wheel. 'We found that certain types of signals still used three wheels,' Noskwith noted. 'These were certain short signals and weather signals from U-Boats. The time when we found these short signals was a very exciting time.'

Wylie took over the codebreaking shift in Hut 8 at midnight on Saturday 12 December. All night they continued the tedious process of looking for cribs from Hut 10's weather reports that might fit the short U-Boat weather messages. Wylie was in the canteen the next morning when one of his colleagues came running in. They had found a *Shark* message with the fourth wheel in the position that allowed it to operate as a three-wheel Enigma. A Bombe menu was constructed on the basis of a potential crib from the Short Weather Signals. It was tried out on six Bombes and the crib came out.

'I was having breakfast and somebody rushed in and said: "We're back into the U-Boats,"' Wylie recalled.

> I asked which it was and it was the one that meant we were going to be able to go on getting into the U-Boat traffic. That was terrific, it wasn't just a one-off. We were going to be able to do it steadily. It was a great moment. The excitement was terrific, relief too.

Once Wylie had checked it out, he was under instructions to inform Travis immediately. There were celebrations in the Hut and at the Admiralty. 'We were elated,' Wylie said.

> We knew that from then on we had good prospects of keeping

in with it. We knew we were in with a chance. I was told to ring up the boss as soon as it came in and Travis was going to ring up Menzies who would ring Churchill.

Within a few hours, Hut 8 had broken the day's keys and decyphered messages began to arrive in the Submarine Tracking Room where Lieutenant Patrick Beesly was on duty. 'They continued to do so in an unending stream until the early hours of the following morning,' he said. 'It was an exciting and exhausting night.'

Pat Wright was one of the young women working in the Big Room at Hut 8, decyphering the messages. She had been recruited earlier that year.

I was just approaching my eighteenth birthday. I had a letter at home asking me if I would go for an interview at the Foreign Office. There were several other girls there. They told us they wanted us to do something but they couldn't tell us what it was and that we would be hearing from them. So I went home and my mother said: 'What did they want you for?' and I replied: 'Well, I haven't the faintest idea.' Eventually we received a letter and train passes to go to Bletchley. We were taken to the big house and were lectured by a very ferocious-looking security officer and we signed the Official Secrets Act. They said: 'The job we want you to do is decoding.' Well, everybody knows the Foreign Office has codes. It didn't seem very secret. We trailed over to Hut 8 where they said: 'Well, the thing is it's German naval codes, we've broken the codes and we want you to do the decoding' – collapse of several young ladies in a heap. None of us were fluent German speakers.

It was then read out to us in no uncertain terms that on no account were we to tell anybody what we were doing. Nor were we to say we were on secret work. It wasn't secret. We were the evacuated office of the Foreign Office and we were copy typists. It was explained to us that the German codes had been broken by this super machine that had been invented. At the same time every day, the Germans transmitted this weather message beginning exactly the same way. This was of course not anything that we lesser mortals had to worry about. This was the brainy boys' department.

The 'copy typists' in the Big Room operated Type-X machines decyphering the messages that came in. They had to wait for the codebreakers to break the keys first.

Sometimes we had to wait a long time. Sometimes it was done quickly. But there was always a backlog of work, so we were never not having to do anything. There were four wheels out of a box of eight which were put into the machine and then turned to the right letter of the alphabet and then there was a plugboard with plug leads that went everywhere. You started off typing and then with a bit of luck you suddenly saw something you could recognise as German. There were of course very clever interpreters there who, if you got into a real fix, where the German went off into garble, would help you, because not many of the messages were wholly intercepted. Bits were missing or not picked up. So it wasn't a case of just typing straight through. Anybody who works a computer now that has this light touch would be horrified. The keys had to be pressed right down and came up with a clankety bang. It was very, very noisy. It printed out on to a long strip of sticky tape a bit like you used to get on old-fashioned telegrams.

When we finished we took the message and stuck it on the back like an old telegram. Then we would send it through and says: 'Shall we go on with this?' and they would say: 'Yes, keep going,' or 'No, don't bother.'

She and the other women working in the Big Room were well aware of the importance of what they were doing.

Clothing was rationed, soap was rationed, sweets were rationed, and the Atlantic convoys coming across were being sunk quicker than they could take up with thousands of men and we were just told that if they could just keep these messages decoded then they would keep the submarines away from the convoys.

One of those working in Hut 4 was Sarah Norton, who had been promoted from the index to translating German decrypts. She remembered the time of the blackout as a very depressing period.

It was a terrible, terrible time because all our shipping was going. We could have starved, actually, and eventually when they broke it the volume of work was just unbelievable because every signal had to be translated. It might just be a floating mine. It might have been something terribly important like a U-Boat attack somewhere. So it all had to be done and we had to work extremely hard.

A new canteen capable of coping with 1,000 people at a single sitting was completed in the spring of 1942 and the builders began work on the larger concrete blocks which would replace the wooden huts. Throughout 1942, wave after wave of new recruits arrived at Bletchley and as the new purpose-built blocks were finished, in the latter half of 1942 and early part of 1943, there was a mass exodus into the new accommodation, although for security reasons the Hut numbers remained the titles of the various sections. The decyphered messages were sent to Z Watch in Hut 4 via Lampson Tubes, vacuum tubes that distributed papers around the Park and were known to the young girls who used them as the 'spit and suck'.

'We moved from Hut 4 which we loved into a horrible concrete building,' said Sarah Norton, one of the debutantes working in the naval index.

To be totally perverse, we insisted on still calling the new block Hut 4. It had a long wide corridor which ended in a

TOP: Gordon Welchman, the Cambridge mathematician who set up Hut 6 to break the German Army and *Luftwaffe* Enigma cyphers.

BELOW: The Hut 6 Registration Room, where encyphered Enigma messages were logged before decoding.

TOP: The codebreaking exchange deal with the Americans led to a number of US personnel working at Bletchley, in this case a US Army master sergeant.

BELOW: Hut 6 dictated what links they needed the various British intercept stations to monitor via Bletchley Park Control, run by bright young men recruited from the main London banks.

The breaking of the *Abwehr* (German Intelligence) four-rotor Enigma cypher (TOP LEFT) by Dilly Knox was critical to the success of the Double Cross deception operations. Knox died in February 1943 and his role as head of the ISK section breaking Enigma cyphers was taken over by Peter Twinn (TOP RIGHT). Keith Batey (BELOW LEFT) led the breaking of new machines. Security was so tight that his wife Mavis Batey (née Lever) (BELOW RIGHT), who also worked in the ISK section, remained unaware of this work until 2011.

TOP: The cast of one of 'Combine Ops', the Christmas revues that made use of the many professional actors, actresses, musicians and writers working at Bletchley Park.

RIGHT: The Lorenz SZ42 *Schlüsselzusatz* attachment used to encypher German military teleprinter communications.

ABOVE: *Robinson*, the first computer used to help to break the *Tunny* encyphered teleprinter messages.

TOP LEFT: Tommy Flowers, the post office engineer who designed and created the *Colossus* computer.

TOP RIGHT: Bill Tutte who, with the assistance of John Tiltman, broke into the *Tunny* system in a mix of sheer brilliance and good fortune.

BELOW: Two Wrens, Dorothy du Boisson (LEFT) and Elsie Booker (RIGHT), operating the *Colossus* computer.

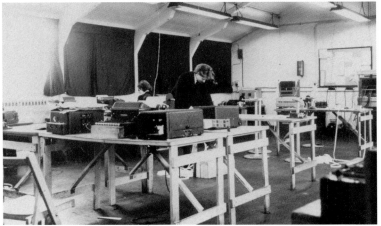

TOP LEFT: Max Newman, who was in charge of the Newmanry and devised the system of using computers to do the initial work on breaking the *Tunny* encyphered teleprinter messages.

TOP RIGHT: Ralph Tester, who was in charge of the Testery, the section that broke the messages by hand after the effect of the chi wheels had been removed by the Newmanry.

BELOW: The Newmanry, where the effect of the chi wheels was removed with the assistance of the *Colossus*, or initially the *Robinson*, computers.

TOP LEFT: Hugh Foss, who broke the Japanese *Red* diplomatic machine cypher before the war and was head of Hut 7, the Japanese section.

TOP RIGHT: Frank Birch, the former actor who was head of Hut 4, the naval codebreaking section.

BELOW: A US Navy WAVE operating one of the US Bombes, which from 1943 provided major support to Bletchley Park's breaking of the Enigma four-rotor cypher machines.

T-junction. One afternoon, we decided to give Jean Campbell-Harris, who later became Baroness Trumpington, a ride in a large laundry basket on wheels that was normally used to move secret files. We launched it down the long corridor where it gathered momentum by the second. To our horror, at the T-junction, Jean suddenly disappeared, basket and all, through some double swing doors crashing to a halt in the men's toilets. A serious reprimand was administered and our watches were changed so we were distributed among a more sober group. But this fortunately did not last long.

Their efforts were rewarded with a dramatic drop in the number of successful U-Boat attacks. But when *Shark* was lost in early March, following the introduction of a new short weather code, it looked as if a new blackout had begun. But by concentrating the increasing number of Bombes on the problem, and with the assistance of the first 'Keen Machine', Hut 8 broke the keys out within ten days.

From that point on, the new-found confidence in Hut 8 and the introduction of the much faster US four-wheel Bombes produced by the National Cash Register (NCR) company in Dayton, Ohio, ensured that Naval Enigma was never as difficult to break again. Relations with Op-20-G were now on a much firmer footing with all the old concerns and complaints removed by the joint interest in cooperating fully to protect the Atlantic convoys. Travis flew to America in October 1942 to meet Capt Carl F. Holden, the US Navy's Director of Communications. They signed the so-called Holden Understanding, which committed both sides to cooperation on the breaking of the German naval cyphers, and in particular *Shark*. The daily keys and any messages that were broken were sent across the Atlantic on US bombers in what became known as 'the Bomber bag'.

Joe Eachus, the US Navy liaison officer, began working in Hut 8 as a naval codebreaker.

My official duty was to report back to Washington what was

happening at BP. But that was not a full-time job, so I under-
took to be a cryptanalyst while I was there. It had been a hobby
of mine before the war. Some of the British had been in the
FO as professional codebreakers for some years, but there were
no US Navy guys who fitted that description. Everybody had
been amateurs before. We were working on German Enigma
and often-times we were reading stuff currently. Other times,
something would happen and we were not and there was
just a feeling of gloom around when we would go for a week
without reading things, very downhearted. Then it got going
again and you would see the smiles in the corridors. That was
very noticeable that people there took a personal interest in
the work. As an officer I was permitted to circulate a good deal
more than most of the people who worked there, I had a good
excuse, and there were a lot of academics there, particularly
from Cambridge. I met professorial types on an equal footing
in a way I would never have otherwise done. They were always
a level or two above me. I found their attitude towards life very
interesting. They were academics primarily and their personal
life was secondary. My view had always been the other way
round, my personal life was the primary thing and my professional life was a way of making a living.

The Americans became so adept at breaking *Shark*, largely due
to the enormous number of four-wheel Bombes they built, that
by the middle of 1944, with Bletchley fully involved in providing intelligence on the invasion of Europe, and with the British
four-wheel Bombes incapable of matching the reliability of their
American counterparts, the US Navy codebreaking organisation
Op-20-G had completely taken over responsibility for breaking *Shark*. The US Navy Bombes were even used to run menus
for Hut 6 during the invasion of Europe, so good had relations
between Op-20-G and Bletchley become. 'In all they produced
well over 100 machines which were of the utmost value to us, not
only on Naval keys but also in Air and Army,' Alexander said.

Indeed considerably more than half the total American Bombe time went on non-naval keys. Their whole hearted cooperation and readiness to use their Bombes for jobs in which they, as an organisation, had no direct interest was always very greatly appreciated by us; a great deal of our success on all keys (Naval, Air and Army) in the last two years of the war was due to their help.

The Allies had been lucky that Dönitz had chosen to concentrate on the eastern seaboard of America for the first part of 1942, Frank Birch said. If he had not, the U-Boats might well have pushed Britain to the brink of starvation.

The only comforting thought about those ten months is that at the time British resources were so meagre that even with all the information in the world only moderate immunity could have been obtained. By March 1943, when Special Intelligence was coming along strong, though not yet at full strength, the Germans had become incapable of reading our stuff and in the great showdown of that month the U-Boats were, as a result of Special Intelligence, driven off the convoy routes for six months.

The break into *Shark* was not the only deciding factor in the Second Battle of the Atlantic; the introduction of the Very Long Range Liberator aircraft, centimetric radar, the Huff-Duff shipborne DF system and new naval support groups, including aircraft carriers, made life altogether too dangerous for the U-Boats. But it was the ability to read the U-Boat messages that allowed the Allies to use these new-found resources to conduct a war of attrition against them, trading the loss of merchant ships for the destruction of a U-Boat, Beesly recalled.

Decisions had to be taken, never lightly, never without due thought, but taken none the less and one had to accept the consequences. We were far removed from the sea but it did not require a great deal of imagination to picture tankers going up in flames, seamen being drowned or maimed, or invaluable cargoes being lost. The only possible way to treat the matter was as though it were a game of chess. Ships or U-Boats were pawns. When one of them was sunk it was removed from the board. One side or the other had gained a point, but the game was not over and one had to turn immediately to consider the next move, to try to save the remainder of one's pieces and to take out some of one's opponents.

Hut 8's ability to read *Shark* also confirmed that the *B-Dienst* had been reading the Naval Cypher No. 3, ensuring that communications security was improved and the Germans were unable to predict the convoys' routes. Nearly a hundred U-Boats were sunk in the first five months of 1943. As the battle swung toward the Allies, Harry Hinsley and the Hut 4 intelligence reporters detected increasing signs of nervousness among the U-Boat commanders. They began to report torpedo failures, made exaggerated claims, and expressed widespread fear of Allied aircraft. By April, their morale appeared to have gone into terminal decline, with the *Shark* decrypts containing 'increasingly frequent references to their fear of air attack and to the efficiency of the Allied surface escorts in following up aircraft sightings'.

By May, the Allied successes against the U-Boats had soared to a level that threatened to wipe them out completely. On May 23, after hearing of the loss of the forty-seventh U-Boat that month, Dönitz ordered the Wolf Packs to be withdrawn from the Atlantic, giving the Allies the respite they needed to get supplies across to Britain in preparation for the invasion of mainland Europe. Bletchley itself was not only involved in the Battle of the Atlantic, it was also heavily involved throughout 1942 in providing intelligence on the fighting in North Africa; playing an important role in operations in the Mediterranean

against the Italian navy; providing information that was critical to the Double Cross System and preparing furiously for
the invasion of mainland Europe. The 110 staff who arrived at
Bletchley Park in August 1939 had swollen to 680 by the end
of 1940 and by the end of 1942 to more than 3,500, of whom
two-thirds were women.

So many of the people working at Bletchley Park were now
women that Edward Travis set up a 'Women's Committee'
to advise him on 'all questions affecting Women at the War
Station' and to ensure 'the promotion of the well-being of all
the women' at Bletchley. The committee included representatives of all three women's services plus Foreign Office civil serv-
ants, and its chairman, a Miss J. V. Wickham, was available at
all times to offer advice and help to 'any civilian woman who is
in difficulty of any kind'.

CHAPTER 9

THE BATTLE FOR NORTH AFRICA

The fighting in North Africa had begun with a sweeping victory over the Italians in early 1941 by General Archibald Wavell, the Commander-in-Chief Middle East. No German troops were in North Africa as yet and the Allied victory was the result of what was virtually an unopposed advance by British and Commonwealth troops against extremely limited resistance. Wavell did receive some assistance from Bletchley from Italian messages decyphered in Josh Cooper's Air Section, with one message leading to the destruction of twenty-five Italian aircraft in a single attack. Bletchley was determined from early on that it should play as large a role as possible in operations in North Africa, arguing that *Ultra* would 'in all probability produce an increasing amount of information of vital operational value'.

The idea of an outpost of GC&CS for the Middle East based in Cairo had first been proposed in July 1938 by the pre-war MI6 Chief and GC&CS Director Hugh Sinclair, but was resisted vehemently by the service intelligence chiefs in Cairo. In early 1940, there was a reluctance at Bletchley to dissipate its resources by sending anyone to Egypt, but by the summer the situation had eased and Bletchley sent a small team of codebreakers out to Cairo in July 1940, reinforcing them a few weeks later with Major Freddie Jacobs, the head of the GC&CS Military Section's Italian codebreaking team, to form a military cryptographic unit called 5 Intelligence School. A 'combined inter-service cryptographic bureau' with the cover title of Combined Bureau Middle East (CBME) was finally set up, in the former Fauna and Flora Museum at Heliopolis and with Jacobs in command, in November 1940.

Denniston arranged for Jacob to be in direct touch with Bletchley via Cuthbert Bowlby, the MI6 regional director in Cairo, for any discussion of cryptographic matters, and asked Jacob to send him a full round-up of what traffic was available there, noting that while the Bureau's ostensible targets were Italian, Arabic and Russian 'some day these may be expanded'.

Almost immediately after the Italians' defeat, an Italian Air Force message referring to *Luftwaffe* escorts for convoys between Naples and Tripoli was decyphered at Bletchley Park. Hut 4 concluded from this that the convoys were carrying Germans and that Hitler must be sending troops to support his beaten ally. The codebreakers' views were dismissed in both the Admiralty and the Air Ministry, and the report did not make its way to Cairo. A few days later, British troops had their first contact with the *Afrika Korps*.

General Erwin Rommel's arrival in North Africa in mid-February 1941 led quickly to the installation of a direct Special Signals Link to Cairo using Type-X cypher machines and on 13 March, the first direct transmission of an *Ultra* report from Bletchley to the CBME. Hut 3 could now send their reports direct to Jacobs who could then brief Wavell. The link had not had time to establish itself before Rommel began a rapid offensive that was difficult to predict.

The available Enigma decrypts appeared contradictory. The *Red* Enigma suggested that Rommel had been told to build up his strength before launching an offensive. But the regional *Luftwaffe* system used by *Fliegerführer Afrika*, broken by Hut 6 at the end of February and designated *Light Blue*, pointed to an immediate advance. Ignoring his orders from Berlin and despite only having a limited force, Rommel attacked immediately and was soon pressing home his advantage against the poorly prepared British troops, taking the Libyan ports of el Agheila and Benghazi before surrounding the Australian garrison at Tobruk. But here he came to a standstill.

The problem for Freddie Jacob, the head of the GC&CS outpost in Cairo, was that only he and George Wallace, the commander of 5 Intelligence School, were allowed to handle the Hut 3 reports coming in from Bletchley, said Henry Dryden, who was originally sent out to Cairo from Bletchley to train codebreakers who had been working on Italian systems to break the German cyphers.

'The first contact between British and German forward troops occurred at the end of February, and on 24 March el Agheila was reoccupied by the enemy,' Dryden said. 'At this point, I was invited by John Tiltman to go out to Heliopolis, "for a month, six weeks at the outside, old boy," to train the Italian experts in breaking German systems.' By the time he eventually got there, Jacob and Wallace were completely bogged down in trying to deal with the flood of *Ultra* messages that was coming in from Hut 3. 'Because of their sensitivity, the messages were shielded from the eyes of the cypher officers by being encoded in a simple substitution before encypherment and dispatch from the United Kingdom,' Dryden said. Jacob and Wallace 'had been taking it in turns, on a twenty-four-hour basis, to decode them before they were sent in a locked box welded to the floor of a special car. As a high proportion of these messages reached Heliopolis during the night, these officers were glad of the 50 per cent reinforcement I provided.'

Given Rommel's maverick disregard for his original orders, General Franz Halder, the Army Chief of Staff, sent his deputy, General Friedrich Paulus, to Tripoli to agree on a strategy, which was then passed back to Berlin, and to Bletchley Park, via the *Red* Enigma. The decrypts also disclosed that the failure to secure the port of Tobruk had stretched Rommel's supply lines and left him desperately short of fuel.

Churchill pushed Wavell to take advantage of this position. But two attempted counter-offensives, forced on Wavell, against his better judgement, by Churchill, failed in the face of the German 88mm anti-aircraft guns, converted by Rommel into an anti-tank role, which had an unrestricted view of their targets across the desert terrain. A single *Ultra* message which ought to have led British intelligence to question why Rommel needed so many armour-piercing rounds for his anti-aircraft guns passed unnoticed on 18 May 1941. The link from Bletchley Park was at any event of little use during this initial period of the war in North Africa, partly because the Hut 3 reporters were still learning their trade, partly because they were relying on *Luftwaffe* messages sent using the *Red* and *Light Blue* Enigma systems, which were the only relevant ones that Hut 6 could break, and partly because of the time it took to carry out the whole process of interception, decryption and the production of an intelligence report.

During fighting, the Bletchley Park reports rarely arrived in Cairo in what the military called 'real time'. All too frequently the land battle had moved on before the intelligence could be given to commanders, said Ralph Bennett, one of the Hut 3 duty officers. 'Very occasionally, the process could be completed in about three hours, but six hours may have been nearer the average.'

A Special Communications Unit (SCU) was sent out to Cairo in April 1941 to assist in the speedy transmission of *Ultra* intelligence to Auchinleck and his commanders in the field. It was the first of the SCUs to be sent on military operations, with many more to follow over the next four years. Based on the units first introduced during the Battle of France, it received *Ultra* reports direct from Hut 3, encyphered using the highly secure One-Time Pad system and sent via the RAF communications centre at Leighton Buzzard. It evolved into two separate organisations: the SCU conducting the communications between Hut 3 and the theatre of operations, and a separate Special Liaison Unit (SLU), providing the intelligence to commanders, ensuring that only those who were cleared to see it saw it, and that it was never used without there being an alternative plausible way in which the information might have been obtained.

> Momentary tactical advantage is not sufficient ground for taking any risk or compromising the source. No action may be taken against specific sea or land targets revealed by *Ultra* unless appropriate air reconnaissance or other suitable camouflage measures have also been taken. If from any document which might fall into his hands, from any message he might intercept, from any word revealed by a prisoner of war, or from any ill-considered action taken upon the basis of such intelligence, the enemy were given cause to believe that his communications are not adequately safe-guarded against interception, he would effect changes which would deprive us of knowledge of his operations on all fronts.

The failure of the second counter-offensive, codenamed *Battleaxe*, led Churchill to transfer Wavell to India, replacing him with Claude Auchinleck, known as 'the Auk'. This coincided with *Ultra*'s first great contribution to the campaign. The *Luftwaffe* provided air escorts for the Italian convoys resupplying Rommel's forces across the Mediterranean and some detail of the convoys was therefore carried on the *Light Blue* cypher. But the information derived from these intercepts was rarely good enough to allow the Royal Navy or the RAF to take action against the convoys.

Then in July 1941, Hut 8 managed to break an Italian Navy machine cypher, the C38m, which provided a flood of detailed information about the convoys. The *Light Blue* cypher gave indications of when a convoy was going to cross the Mediterranean and what it would be carrying while the C38m provided details of vessels involved and the route.

'Between them, the two were mutually complementary sources of news about the convoys' routes and their estimated times of departure and arrival at designated ports,' said Bennett.

'By the late summer of 1941, so many supply ships had been sunk that the Axis operations were severely curtailed and indeed faced complete strangulation.'

Since collating and analysing this information was a job in itself and the information it produced was required by both the Royal Navy and the RAF, it was carried out initially through collaboration between the Hut 4 'Z watch' and the Hut 3 research section now led by Lucas.

'From now until May 1942, longer-term research had to yield place to the more exciting duties of handling operational signals on Axis convoys to Africa,' Lucas said. 'The essential part of the work lay in the identification of covernames, or covernumbers, for turning-points on the routes.' The routes taken by the convoys would have on average half-a-dozen legs on the journey to North Africa. The length of each leg could be worked out from the speed and sailing times specified in the message. The difficulty was in locating the turning points.

> Pins were stuck into a string at distances equal to the lengths of the legs on the map. The string had its ends pinned to the ports of arrival and departure. Any intermediate points already known were also pinned. The rest of the slack was shifted about by trial and error to give the various alternative possibilities until a general shape of route was obtained that made sense and corresponded with our experience of Italian naval habits, for example a respectful detour to the east or west of Malta. Life in the research section was never dull but nothing again ever quite equalled the excitement of angling for Axis convoys with pins and string.

The convoy reports went to Cairo via the Special Signals Link and also to the navy in Alexandria and the RAF in Malta. The protection of the *Ultra* secret was paramount. In accordance with the regulations, no offensive action could be taken unless there was a clear secondary source, overwhelmingly created by aerial reconnaissance. Even this could not be directed solely against the convoy lest the Germans noticed the change in routine reconnaissance patterns. But the material supplied by Bletchley Park allowed the Royal Navy and the RAF to wreak havoc among Rommel's supply convoys.

'*Ultra* was very important in cutting Rommel's supplies,' said Jim Rose, one of the Hut 3 air advisers.

> He was fighting with one hand behind his back because we were getting information about all the convoys from Italy. The RAF were not allowed to attack them unless they sent out reconnaissance and if there was fog of course they couldn't attack them because it would have jeopardised the security of *Ultra*, but in fact most of them were attacked.

By the time Auchinleck launched *Crusader*, a successful counter-offensive which relieved Tobruk in November 1941, the RAF and the Royal Navy were regularly sinking Rommel's supply ships, causing him major problems. The arrival in Malta in late October of Force K, comprising the cruisers HMS *Aurora* and *Penelope* together with two destroyers, heralded a two-month period when supplies to the *Afrika Korps* were brought to a virtual standstill.

The *Luftwaffe* keys had revealed Rommel's own plans for an attack on Tobruk. But the first break into Army Enigma in North Africa confirmed that the failure of supply ships to get through made it unlikely that any attack would take place in the near future. The proliferation of Enigma keys as the Germans sought to improve signals security had led to a change in the nicknames given to them by Bletchley Park. The main keys that had already been broken retained their colour designation. *Luftwaffe* keys were now named after flowers or insects, Army keys after birds and Naval keys after fish.

Chaffinch, as the new Army key was called, was broken after the capture from the headquarters of 16th Panzer Division on 28 November 1941 of the complete keys for November. It provided details of the *Afrika Korps'* shortages of food, fuel and water as well as ammunition for the 88mm 'anti-tank' guns. It also gave Auchinleck full details of how many tanks Rommel had at his disposal and useful information on the German dispositions. The captured documents also assisted in the break into a second *Afrika Korps* Enigma, *Phoenix*, albeit for only a week. These were the first operational German Army keys to be broken in a British Army area of operations and the Hut 6 successes against them were to be the first step of a major turning point in the way *Ultra* was viewed by British Army commanders. Up until that point, all the operational intelligence from Enigma had come either from *Luftwaffe* or German Navy keys, and while the former frequently provided important intelligence for ground forces commanders, it was not regarded as highly by the British Army as it was by the RAF.

Despite the presence of the SLU at the headquarters of the British Eighth Army, the *Crusader* offensive proved beyond doubt that the best use of *Ultra* was in providing the details of enemy strength and dispositions, and often future plans, rather than in tactical information during the heat of the battle. The sheer length of time it took for reports to get from Bletchley to Libya meant that Hut 3 could not compete with the mobile Y Special Wireless Section of Royal Signals and Intelligence Corps personnel in armoured cars who were at the front.

'Despite the amazing speed with which we received *Ultra*, it was of course usually out of date,' recalled Bill Williams, who served as an intelligence officer in North Africa.

This did not mean that we were not glad of its arrival for at best it showed that we were wrong, usually it enabled us to tidy up loose ends, and at worst we tumbled into bed with a smug confirmation. In a planning period between battles its value was more obvious and one had too the opportunity to study it in relation to context so much better than during a fast-moving battle such as desert warfare produced.

Auchinleck's defeat of Rommel forced the *Afrika Korps* back to el Agheila. But within a few months, the Germans had regained much of the ground they had lost and were back in Benghazi. This was at least in part the result of a serious misreading of a decrypt from the Italian C38m cypher which was wrongly seen as suggesting that the *Afrika Korps* did not expect to reach Benghazi. But it was also a result of the failings of the British tactics. Bennett said,

> The troops on the ground on our side were still not used to receiving high-level information. They were also using the wrong tactics. The gunfire was never sufficiently massed to do enough damage to the enemy until Auchinleck managed to change it under pressure in the late summer of 1942.

Although the *Red Luftwaffe* Enigma gave good warning of a German offensive scheduled for the end of May of 1942 and aimed ultimately at regaining Tobruk, Hut 3 was unable to provide any information about Rommel's precise plans, either before or during the Battle of Gazala. By mid-June, Auchinleck had decided to withdraw across the Egyptian border to a stronger position at Alam Halfa, leaving the 2nd South African Division to hold Tobruk as a fortress inside the enemy camp.

Within a week, it had surrendered. Churchill, who was in Washington conferring with Roosevelt, was bitterly disappointed. 'I did not attempt to hide from the President the shock I received,' he would later recall. 'It was a bitter moment. Defeat is one thing; disgrace is another.'

But the tide was about to turn, and as a direct result of a dramatic improvement in the work of the codebreakers at Bletchley Park which included much greater coordination between the codebreaking process and traffic analysis.

During 1940, three teams of officers and mostly female civilians began working on trying to analyse the radio networks and in particular break the German system of daily changing callsigns. They were based at MI8 offices in Caxton St in London, at Harpenden and in Hut 3. This process, subsequently known as 'log-reading' and then later 'traffic analysis', had produced a wealth of usable intelligence during the First World War and had already proved its worth in Hut 4, the Naval Section, where Harry Hinsley was obtaining so much important intelligence. It was not initially regarded by many of the new young code-breakers and intelligence officers working on German Army or *Luftwaffe* traffic in Hut 6 and Hut 3 as likely to produce much intelligence. The reverse soon proved to be the case. Using a variety of information noted down by the 'Y Service' opera-tors on their message logs, including callsigns, locations from direction-finding or identifications from RFP or Tina, and the simple German operator plain language chatter, which when units came under pressure during the battle often contained violations of basic communications security, they were able to build up complete pictures of the units involved and provide fresh intelligence and cribs which would help in the break-ing of Enigma. A new unit, VI Intelligence School, with an establishment of 233 staff, a mix of male members of the Army Intelligence Corps and female ATS soldiers, was set up in March 1941 and based initially at Beaumanor. Even at this stage it was suggested by some in Hut 6, now converted entirely to the idea that 'traffic analysis' was a producer of vital intelligence, that it should be based at Bletchley. It moved there in May of 1942 and was attached to Hut 6, initially as the 'Central Party' but later as Sixta, a title derived from Six Traffic Analysis.

'Our job was to analyse the operator chat,' recalled Jimmy Thirsk, a 27-year-old librarian recruited into the Intelligence Corps to work as a log-reader.

> If you had a section of the *Luftwaffe*, say they were in France with their headquarters in Dijon, and perhaps they had ten outstations round in that area. Every morning they would start up. Each station had a three-letter callsign and they would

change that at midnight according to a pre-set pattern and then
they would call up the outstations just to make contact. Just to
make sure they were all awake and working and they would chat
to each other in clear German. This operator chat was going on
all day long and the intercept operators logged it all down.

Most of the messages were teleprinted from the intercept
stations but the logs used to be brought mainly by motor cycle
dispatch rider. You would be allocated a number of nets. If they
were small ones you might have two or three but you might
have just one. Each day you would plot the radio net. We had
coloured pencils, and you made a circle with a dot in the middle
as the HQ and then the outlying stations were round the circumference of the circle with a line drawn from each of the outstations to the centre and you would note the number of messages
passing on each link. Then at the end of the week you had the
dreaded weekly report and you had to go through your stuff for
the week and compile a report. It was pretty dreary stuff at times.

Their work was assisted by the capture of the *Luftwaffe* callsign
book, the *Rufzeichentafel Ausgabe B*, from a German Army unit
in the North African desert in December 1941. The *Luftwaffe*
was clearly unaware of its capture and continued using the same
system for the next two-and-a-half years.

Longer-term traffic analysis was carried out in the Hut 3
Fusion Room which used all the information produced by various parts of Bletchley Park to build up a complete picture of the
enemy radio networks. Joyce Robinson had a degree in German
and after a brief spell in the Civil Service joined the ATS and was
posted to Bletchley where she was allocated to 'fusion'.

It was really a sort of consolidation of information from a lot
of quarters after material had been dealt with operationally. It
was departmentalised according to networks, or keys, where a
group of one, two or more people considered the behaviour
of certain things so that you knew your network. You were

sometimes able to help Hut 6 when they had difficulties with decoding, with a change in the wheels.

One of her ATS colleagues was Jean Faraday Davies, who was pulled off a German course at the University of London and sent to Bletchley. The Fusion Room coordinated information produced by the log-readers with the intelligence from the deciphered messages, Faraday Davies said. 'Our function was to take these two sources and feed it out in two directions to enable interception to go on or to help decoding.'

The move of the traffic analysts to work alongside Hut 6 had increased the availability of cribs, together with an increased understanding of how the Army Enigmas worked. Up until now the delay in breaking *Chaffinch*, the main *Afrika Korps* Enigma, had been up to a week. From the end of May, they were able to break it daily, albeit with some delay. Another *Panzer* Army Enigma, designated *Phoenix* and broken briefly at the end of 1941 following the capture of three machines and a number of keys, was read continuously from 1 June. A third Army Enigma, *Thrush*, giving details of air supplies, was also broken.

Hut 6 was now able to read all the *Luftwaffe* keys, including the *Red* which had been continuously broken since May 1940; two relatively minor keys called *Locust* and *Gadfly*; and two much more important keys which, in a security blunder by the Germans, were closely linked. *Primrose*, the cypher of the *Luftgau Afrika*, the air formation responsible for administration and supply of the *Luftwaffe* forces in North Africa, was not only an important source in its own right, its keys were also used later by *Scorpion*, the cypher used for communications between the *Flivos* and the ground forces.

During the North Africa campaign, *Primrose* became as high a priority for Hut 6 as the *Red* cypher. 'It was very important,' said Susan Wenham, one of the Hut 6 codebreakers.

Every day the key was changed and about 3 o'clock in the

morning *Primrose* used to send a tuning message through, a very short little message. It was always on the same wavelength and it was always recognisable. So people on the nightshift would watch out for this message and, when they got it, they would tinker about with it and we could quite often break on that message. *Red* had an enormous quantity but it didn't have a nice convenient tuning message that you could find.

Hut 6 was given much more time to get into the Army keys as a result of an extraordinary error by the *Luftwaffe*, Stuart Milner-Barry recalled, describing 1942 as Hut 6's '*annus mirabilis*'. Paradoxically, it was due to an increase in the number of different *Luftwaffe* Enigma keys introduced with a view to making the systems more difficult to crack. It actually achieved the exact opposite, Milner-Barry said.

The Germans suddenly realised that there was no objection, and obviously great advantage in security, in using a large number of different keys for the different major units of the *Luftwaffe*. However, with characteristic blindness the enemy undid much of the good that this step might have done him, for instead of making up entirely separate keys he rehashed old ones on a delightfully simple plan. The effect of this was that, every other month, the majority of Air Force keys were in our hands for the decoding and a tremendous boom ensued which taxed our resources to the utmost.

Since *Scorpion*'s keys were now predictable, Hut 6 decided that it could be decyphered in Heliopolis, making it available to the commanders far quicker than any other material. Because the *Flivos* needed to keep in close contact with the battle in order to coordinate air attacks with the movement on the ground, *Scorpion* provided more details of the fighting, the troop positions and air activity than any of the other cyphers had before.

'It contained much "hot" operational news; it was easy to

break, for the daily settings could be predicted in advance,' said Bennett. 'It was decided to radio them in advance from Hut 6 to Cairo and to send an experienced officer out to compose signals on the spot.'

Meanwhile, during July and August, the number of mobile Y units in North Africa was doubled and they became much better integrated into the command structure. Traffic analysis and direction-finding were improved and the Intelligence Corps and RAF codebreakers attached to the Special Wireless Sections expanded their exploitation of enemy tactical codes and cyphers.

Ultra was now totally in the ascendant. In the first nine months of the Special Signals Link to the Middle East, between March and November 1941, Hut 3 had sent just over 2,000 signals to Cairo. Between November 1941 and July 1942, it had sent five times that figure.

Desperate for a victory and fully aware of the information from *Ultra* that was now available, Churchill decided it was time for change. Auchinleck was a fine general but did not have the necessary killer instinct. He brought in General Harold Alexander as Commander-in-Chief Middle East and appointed General Bernard Montgomery to take command of the Eighth Army.

Within days of his arrival, Montgomery was the beneficiary of a major piece of *Ultra* intelligence that was to change the military's view of the codebreakers. On 15 August, Rommel, newly promoted to Field Marshal, explained to Hitler what he planned to do next. The details of the plans had to go first through his direct commander, Field Marshal Albrecht Kesselring, the German Commander-in-Chief South, and they were transmitted using the *Red* cypher, which Hut 6 had no problems reading.

Two days earlier, Montgomery had outlined what he believed the Desert Fox would do. It matched the signal sent to Kesselring almost to the letter. Rommel intended to attack around the time of the full moon due towards the end of August, swinging south around the end of the British lines before striking north to come up behind the Eighth Army, cutting it off from Cairo. But to do so he would have to cross a major obstacle: the Alam Halfa ridge.

'Monty arrives in the middle of August and is told not to go and take charge until the next morning,' said Ralph Bennett.

> He goes up to Alam Halfa to have a look round, one day before he is going to take over. He sums up the situation and realises that if Rommel is going to attack he will almost certainly do so on a route that will take him through the Alam Halfa ridge.
>
> A few days later, Rommel tells Hitler what he is going to do, which is exactly that. We get this signal and we tell Monty. So there is Monty, the new boy, who has just made a pep talk to his troops, now knowing that his hunch as to what Rommel will do is exactly right. He can't tell anybody about it but when Rommel attacks Monty is ready.

Two other new developments at Bletchley Park also helped Montgomery. Hut 3 had just started receiving reports deciphered from the *Chaffinch* cypher, giving a complete breakdown of the fighting strengths of the *Afrika Korps* and comprehensive returns on the availability of tanks. Meanwhile, its joint operation with Hut 4 to detect the Axis supply lines had been improved, partly by the decision to place Royal Navy advisers inside Hut 3 to track the convoys and, more importantly, by Hut 8's breaking of *Porpoise*, the German Navy's Mediterranean cypher.

Throughout the second half of August, the RAF and the Royal Navy redoubled their attacks on the Axis convoys. Meanwhile, the codebreakers were able to monitor a series of high-level exchanges between the German commanders. Those between Kesselring and Rommel showed the two were barely on speaking terms. They also revealed that the Desert Fox was unwell. Then came the approval, first by Hitler and later by Mussolini, of Rommel's plans.

More importantly perhaps, given the Desert Fox's predilection for ignoring orders, Bletchley and Heliopolis were able to chart the regrouping of the German forces in readiness for the attempt to outflank the Eighth Army as well as the problems and delays to the operation caused by the non-arrival of two of the supply ships. Montgomery had briefed his troops on what Rommel was about to do. Then the supply problems led to a four-day postponement.

'Believing that the confidence of his men was the prerequisite of victory, he told them with remarkable assurance how the enemy was going to be defeated,' said Williams, the Eighth Army commander's chief intelligence officer.

> The enemy attack was delayed and the usual jokes were made about the 'crystal-gazers'. A day or two later everything happened according to plan. The morale emerging from the promise so positively fulfilled formed the psychological background conditioning the victory which was to follow.

After finding his way through the Alam Halfa ridge blocked, Rommel was forced to retreat for lack of fuel. From then on, *Ultra* played a privileged part in Montgomery's plans. He allowed Williams access to his command post day or night with any new information the codebreakers produced.

'Imagine the situation in the desert in the late summer of 1942,' said Ralph Bennett, who was sent out to the Middle East to report from Cairo on the *Scorpion* traffic.

> There is Montgomery. He's got a little truck park with his own command truck and the Army and the Air commanders forming three sides of a little square. Then the fourth one is the wireless truck to receive the *Ultra* signals so that Williams can make immediate contact with Montgomery and the other commanders to give them the urgent *Ultra* information.

Ultra played no significant part in the Battle of el Alamein itself. But Montgomery knew from *Chaffinch* and *Scorpion* the precise numbers of troops and tanks he faced, while the sinking of the supply ships, 50,000 tons in October alone, nearly half of the cargo which left Italy for North Africa, had a crucial influence on the *Afrika Korps'* ability to resist. So tight were its margins of supply that the sinking of an Axis convoy during the battle itself had a direct influence on the fighting.

On the afternoon of 2 November, with Montgomery having punched two holes in the *Panzer* Army's defences and about to force his way through, Bletchley decyphered a message from Rommel to Hitler asking permission to withdraw. '*Panzerarmee ist erschopft*', he said. The Panzer Army was 'exhausted' and had precious little fuel left. The response from Berlin was that Rommel should stand his ground at all costs. He was to 'show no other road to his troops than the road leading to death or victory'.

But in the face of far superior troops, he was forced to retreat along the coast road towards el Agheila. Why he wasn't pursued at speed and destroyed either by intensive RAF bombing raids or Montgomery himself remains a puzzle. *Chaffinch* revealed on 10 and 11 November that one of his *Panzer* divisions had just eleven tanks while the other had none at all. Five days later, with all attempts to resupply the German troops being frustrated with the aid of *Ultra*, the *Red* Enigma carried a special situation report from Rommel to Hitler in which he described his fuel supplies as 'catastrophic'.

Bennett was by now in Cairo as the experienced Hut 3 officer who was to oversee the issuing of reports from the *Luftwaffe* Enigma decyphered in Cairo.

My temporary absence meant that among much else I missed the fierce indignation and dismay felt throughout the Hut at Montgomery's painfully slow advance from Alamein to Tripoli, incomprehensible in the light of the mass of *Ultra* intelligence showing that throughout his retreat Rommel was too weak to withstand serious pressure.

Edward Thomas, who was the Hut 4 liaison officer in Hut 3 during this period, was a first-hand witness to the fury within Hut 3 at Montgomery's inaction even when told, absolutely correctly, that in the aftermath of Alamein, the Desert Fox had only eleven tanks and virtually no fuel.

> After the war, I found my initials at the bottom of the signals giving details of three supremely important tanker movements at the time of el Alamein. Their sinking was largely responsible for Rommel's long and halting retreat westwards. I well remember the frustration that exploded from our Hut 3 colleagues at Montgomery's failure to overtake and destroy him.

Their anger was clearly shared by Churchill. Following the victory at el Alamein, he had said: 'This is not the end. It is not even the beginning of the end. But it is, perhaps, the end of the beginning.' Now he bombarded Alexander with pieces of *Ultra* suggesting that the Eighth Army kill the *Afrika Korps* off for good.

'Presume you have read the *Boniface* numbers QT/7789 and QT/7903 which certainly reveal a condition of weakness and counter-order among the enemy of a very remarkable character,' one signal from the Prime Minister stated with obvious impatience, while another pointed out: '*Boniface* shows the enemy in great anxiety and disarray.'

But Montgomery feared that Rommel's greater mobility might allow him to turn the tables on the British yet again and decided to err on the side of caution, ignoring the repeated suggestions of Churchill, Alexander and Air Marshal Arthur Tedder, the commander of the Middle East Air Force, that the Desert Fox should be pursued and annihilated.

'Unfortunately after Alam Halfa, Monty was inclined to be a bit boastful about having got it right,' said Ralph Bennett.

> He was inclined to think he was right all the time. At el Agheila,

he insisted on being cautious, which of course was Monty's great thing most of the time, although he knew perfectly well, because we had told him over and over and over again, that Rommel had inferior defences and very few tanks.

Within days of the victory at el Alamein, Allied forces landed in Morocco, Algeria and Tunisia as part of *Operation Torch*, the invasion of North Africa – designed to provide a base from which to attack Italy and southern France. British and American troops under General Eisenhower pushed east with the aim of linking up with Montgomery. Meanwhile the Axis forces began pouring troops into Tunis, a reinforcement chronicled in some detail by Hut 3 from the *Luftwaffe* Enigma, the Italian C38m and *Porpoise*, the German Navy's Mediterranean cypher.

Plans were put in place well in advance to keep the *Torch* commanders supplied with *Ultra*. They were agreed at a conference in Broadway attended by Nigel de Grey, representing Travis; Harry Hinsley, on behalf of the Naval Section in Hut 4; and Eric Jones, the head of Hut 3. Four separate Special Liaison Units were set up to pass the material on, one to serve Eisenhower's headquarters, one with the forward elements of the troops pushing eastwards and two others with the occupation forces in Oran and Casablanca.

A number of codebreakers from Bletchley Park, including Noel Currer-Briggs, a member of Tiltman's Military Section, were sent out to reinforce a mobile Y unit, 1 Special Wireless Section. Their role was to help in breaking the Double Playfair hand cypher that was used by the German Army for its medium-grade messages, while Bletchley concentrated on the *Luftwaffe* cyphers and a new Army Enigma introduced for the campaign which Hut 6 designated *Bullfinch*.

The mobile Y unit set up its base in an old Foreign Legion fort at Constantine in eastern Algeria, Currer-Briggs recalled. 'Fort Sid M'Cid was built in true Beau Geste tradition on top of a hill above the astonishing gorge which bisects the city of Constantine,' he said.

> It may have looked romantic, but it was the filthiest dump imaginable. One of my most vivid memories of it is cleaning the primitive latrines, a row of stone holes set in the thickness of the wall over a fifty-foot drop which had to be emptied through an iron door set in the base of the ramparts. It would be a good punishment if somebody had done something wrong but nobody had. So the adjutant and I said: 'Let's get on and do it', and we started shovelling shit. I can still smell it. I recall with more pleasure, reading Virgil on the battlements. Hardly typical of military life but in the true tradition of BP.

The Tunisian campaign was to be dominated by Rommel's last two throws of the dice. In the first, *Ultra* was to demonstrate its potential frailties; partial intelligence turned out to be wrong; German orders that seemed to indicate one option had already been superseded by the time they were decyphered. As a result Rommel trounced the Americans in the Kasserine Pass, a vital communications link through the Atlas mountains, before turning round and heading east with the intention of taking on Montgomery, who had advanced to Medenine in eastern Tunisia.

Ultra gave Montgomery full details of Rommel's plans to throw the whole of the *Afrika Korps* against the Eighth Army positions. Throughout the last week of February and the first week of March, information from Bletchley and from 1 Special Wireless Section, now moved closer to the British commanders, built up a complete picture of Rommel's plans.

'This was a most exciting time for us,' said Currer-Briggs.

> Traffic was coming in thick and fast. We were theoretically working in shifts but there was so much to do that we hardly ever took time off, and frequently worked when we should

have been resting. It was far too exciting to twiddle one's thumbs in idleness.

For the codebreakers in Hut 6 and their intelligence reporting colleagues in Hut 3, this was seen as final payback for Crete. Whereas in Crete they had every detail of the German plans but no way of preventing it happening, now they had every detail of Rommel's plan and the forces ready and waiting to counter it.

By the time Rommel's troops attacked the Eighth Army positions on the morning of 6 March with a total of 160 tanks and 200 guns, they were faced by a solid wall of 470 anti-tank guns, 350 field guns and 400 tanks. Fed by the codebreakers with every detail of his planned assault, the British simply sat and waited for the Desert Fox. By evening, his tanks largely reduced to burning wrecks, Rommel called the battle off. Three days later, he left Africa, never to return.

The fighting in Tunisia continued for two more months but the North African campaign had effectively ended and the British were already making plans for one of the necessary side-effects of victory. The *Ultra*-led attacks on the Axis supply convoys had been carried out with the future need to be able to feed a large number of prisoners in mind, said Edward Thomas. 'While those with cargoes of tanks, fuel and ammunition had been selected for attack, ships known from the decrypts to be carrying rations had been spared.'

Although Montgomery claimed them as his own, it was his victories in North Africa which finally persuaded the British Army and the RAF that *Ultra* was an extremely powerful weapon and one that could win the war. It was one of the main reasons behind the British defeat of the *Afrika Korps*, said Jim Rose. 'If you look at the position at the Fall of Tobruk in July 1942, that's only a few months before el Alamein, Rommel was really in the ascendant. Things looked desperate when Churchill was with Roosevelt and he heard about the fall of Tobruk, but then six months later they had completely changed. That would not have been possible without *Ultra*.'

For the codebreakers themselves, two and a half years of hard slog had enabled them to create an efficient organisation capable of ensuring that, while individual keys might occasionally be lost, the bulk of the German's top secret communications would be read, and that the information they contained could be passed to the men who were able to make best use of it: the commanders in the field. North Africa was where *Ultra* finally proved itself to be the source of intelligence the military could trust. Until then, the RAF and the Royal Navy had derived real benefits from the Enigma decrypts and understood their importance. The Army had placed a lot of trust in its eventual value, providing the bulk of the intercept operators who intercepted Enigma messages and many of those who worked on them at Bletchley, but had been slow to see the tangible value the *Ultra* reports could provide. That changed in North Africa, said Lucas.

From the summer of 1941 until the surrender in Tunisia in May 1943, a very large part of our work was concerned with North Africa, where it may be said without hesitation that 'Source' was decisive. This was because, at long last, efficient arrangements had been made for passing our information to those who could best use it, the operational commands.

Partly in consequence of certain differences in the character of War Office and Air Ministry, partly because of the scantiness of military, as compared with air, intelligence from Hut 3, relations with these two ministries also differed. While Air Ministry looked to BP for their most important source, the War Office received comparatively little. They therefore treated Hut 3 as a very subsidiary source.

It was not until the African campaign that Hut 3 established itself in the eyes of the War Office as a purveyor of goods which were priceless, unobtainable elsewhere, and already well

processed when issued. In the African campaign, every formation, every unit, had been known and placed, no reinforcement could accrue to the enemy across the Mediterranean
without due warning.

More than that, *Ultra* had come of age. The new organisation
sketched out by Welchman and Travis had taken over from the
GC&CS of the inter-war years. The dedication and enthusi-
asm that had characterised the inter-war years remained but
the need to work in new ways to cope with the huge scale of
wartime codebreaking had been fully embraced.

'Until Alam Halfa, we had always been hoping for proper
recognition of our product,' said Ralph Bennett of his return
to Bletchley Park from Egypt in March 1943. 'Now the recognition was a fact of life and we had to go on deserving it. I had
left as one of a group of enthusiastic amateurs. I returned to a
professional organisation with standards and an acknowledged
reputation to maintain.'

The War Office now saw sense in sending potential codebreakers to Bletchley where previously it had felt that it was not
getting enough in return for the effort its intercept operators and
intelligence analysts were putting in. Members of the Army and
the ATS were quartered at Shenley Rd Military Camp, about
half a mile from Bletchley Park. Bernard Keefe, who worked on
Japanese codes, recalled that the camp was commanded by an
infantry officer, Colonel George Fillingham.

> He was quite mad, probably too much even for the Durham
> Light Infantry, who no doubt gladly shot him off to what the
> rest of the Army regarded as a nuthouse. He was not allowed
> into BP and wasn't told what was going on. He took out his
> frustration on us; he hated the sight of long-haired intellectuals
> and used to stop them and give them sixpence to get a haircut.
> He organised boxing – I was put into the ring with someone
> six inches taller and just about survived; then he started cross-

country runs before breakfast. I shall never forget the sight of Staff-Sergeant Asa Briggs, future professor and historian of the BBC, trying to keep up with less portly young blades.

BP was an astonishing community. I was born to a poorish family in Woolwich. My father was a clerk in the local Co-op society, my family descendants of illiterate Irish immigrants who fled the famine in 1849. I shall never forget the impact of arriving in BP; it was a microcosm of the highest intellectual life. I discovered there was a lively opera group run by James Robertson, later Music Director of Sadlers Wells – I sang with orchestra for the first time as the Gardener in *The Marriage of Figaro* and the Constable in Vaughan Williams's *Hugh the Drover*. Soon after I arrived I organised lunch-time concerts in the Assembly Hall outside the main gate. There were many professional musicians – Captain Daniel Jones, the doyen of Welsh composers, Lieutenant Ludovic Stewart, violinist, Jill Medway, a singer, Captain Douglas Jones (later Craig), singer and later company manager at Glyndebourne. There was a choir conducted by Sergeant Herbert Murrill, future Head of Music at the BBC. Working with me on the Army Air codes was Lieutenant Michael Whewell, bassoonist, and later producer in charge of the BBC Symphony Orchestra. There was a great deal of bed-hopping, the odd pregnancy and post-war divorces; all that was much easier for the civilians who lived in outlying villages; we had to make do with the Wrens in whatever nest we could find.

The Allies now turned their attention to the invasion of southern Europe, for which *Operation Torch* had been a necessary precursor. They began by disguising their intentions using a deception plan worked out by the Double Cross Committee which did not involve a double agent at all, but did rely heavily on the codebreakers being able to confirm that the *Abwehr* had been fooled. The most obvious stepping stone to Italy was Sicily, just a short hop across the Mediterranean from Tunisia. The problem was to find a way of giving the Germans the impression that General Dwight Eisenhower and his British colleague General Harold Alexander had other plans, forcing the Germans to reinforce other areas and weakening the defences in Sicily.

Charles Cholmondley, the RAF representative on the Double Cross Committee, devised *Operation Mincemeat*, a plan centred around the known level of collaboration between the Spanish authorities and the Germans. The idea was to drop the body of a dead 'British officer' off the coast of Spain, close enough to ensure it would be washed up on the beach, with the intention of making it look as if it had come from a crashed aircraft. He would be carrying documents indicating that the main thrust of the Allied attack would be somewhere other than Sicily. The Spanish were neutral but their sympathies lay with the Nazis and they would undoubtedly pass these on to the Germans, who would reinforce their garrisons in the suggested targets at the expense of the real one.

Ewen Montagu, the Royal Navy representative, took charge of the operation, acquiring the body of a dead tramp from a London hospital and giving it the identity of Major William Martin, Royal Marines, an official courier. Attached to Martin's wrist by a chain was a briefcase containing a number of documents, including a letter from one senior British general to another discussing planned assaults on Greece and an unspecified location in the western Mediterranean, for which Sicily was to be a cover. A further letter from Lord Mountbatten, the Chief of Combined Operations, referred jocularly to sardines, which was rightly thought enough of a hint to make the Germans believe the real attack was going to be on Sardinia.

The members of the Double Cross Committee were highly inventive in their choice of other documents to be planted on the body. Two 'used' West End theatre tickets for a few days before the intended launch of the body were in his pocket to show that he must have been travelling by air. A photograph of Martin's 'fiancée', actually that of a female MI5 clerk, was placed in his wallet. For several weeks, Cholmondley carried two love letters from the 'fiancée' around in his pocket to give them the proper crumpled look. There was even an irate letter from Martin's bank manager.

The body was floated ashore near the southern Spanish town of Huelva from a submarine. The Allies now had to find out if the Germans had swallowed the bait and the only sure way of knowing was from *Ultra*, and in particular from the *Abwehr* Enigma traffic between Madrid and Berlin. Following the death of Dilly Knox, his ISK section had been taken over by Peter Twinn with Mavis Lever still one of its key members. The *Abwehr* officers in Madrid were as anxious to find out Berlin's ruling on the documents as the codebreakers and the deception planners. 'We were asked to look out for German reactions and the delighted Double Cross Committee knew as soon as Berlin had decided, following a detailed investigation, that "no further doubts remain regarding the reliability of the captured documents",' Lever said.

Noel Currer-Briggs was still in Tunisia with 1 Special Intelligence Section, when the *Mincemeat* deception reached its denouement.

We were stationed at Bizerta on top of a hill just outside Tunis and I remember we were inspected one day by Alexander and Eisenhower. There we were working away at the German wireless traffic coming from the other side of the Mediterranean and we were saying: 'Oh yes. They've moved that division from Sicily to Sardinia and they've moved the other one to the Balkans' and these two generals were jumping up and down like a couple of schoolboys at a football match. We hadn't a clue why. We thought: 'Silly old buffers.' It wasn't until 1953 when Ewan Montagu's book *The Man Who Never Was* came out that we realised we were telling them that the Germans had swallowed the deception hook, line and sinker.

When Bletchley decyphered the *Abwehr* intercept confirming the results of the German investigation, which showed that the Germans were totally taken in by the deception, a message was sent to Churchill, then in the US for the Trident Conference with US President Franklin D. Roosevelt, saying simply: '*Mincemeat* swallowed whole.'

The ability the Allies now had, through *Ultra*, to tell whether or not the enemy had been fooled by deception operations was another crucial contribution made by the codebreakers to Allied intelligence operations, said Ralph Bennett.

> No other source could have proved the efficacy of the deception planners' rumour-mongering so conclusively, relieving the operational commanders' minds as they prepared an amphibious undertaking on an unprecedented scale. *Ultra* demonstrated *Mincemeat*'s success by showing, more clearly than any other source could have done, that German troops and aircraft movements over the following weeks conformed to the deception; this enabled planning for the assault to go ahead in an atmosphere of confidence.

Even two months later, when the invasion of Sicily had been launched, German intelligence continued to insist that the original plan had been to attack Sardinia and Greece and that it had only had been switched to Sicily at the last moment.

CHAPTER 10

THE BIRTH OF THE MODERN COMPUTER

The Allied landings first in Sicily in July 1943 and then in Italy itself in September, followed swiftly by the Italian surrender, provided *Ultra* with its first strategic test. Hitler's reaction was uncertain. Would he accept Rommel's advice and take the logical course and retreat to the Alps, saving men and material, or would he fight every inch of the way as proposed by the German commander in Italy, Field Marshal Albert Kesselring? Bletchley Park was able to follow Hitler's decision-making, as he initially agreed with Rommel and then accepted the argument of Kesselring that the Germans must make a stand on successive defence lines all the way up the peninsula. 'This was the strategic prize of the greatest moment,' said Ralph Bennett. 'It enabled the Allies to design the Italian campaign to draw maximum advantage from the willingness Hitler thus displayed to allow Italy to drain away his resources.'

The German ability during the Italian campaign to use long pre-established landline communications limited the ability of Hut 6 to produce useful material from the Enigma decrypts. The breaks into the *Red* continued but while other Enigma keys could be broken intermittently, sometimes in floods, it was more often in a trickle that could not be used to produce reporting of any great substance. One former Hut 6 codebreaker said:

> Brief spells of heavy traffic sometimes led to breaks which could not be followed up because the flow dried up as suddenly as it had begun. For the cryptographer this was dispiriting; for Hut 3 it meant that intelligence from Italian Army keys tended

to be fragmentary and mostly of low grade. The result was normally a grey picture of difficult breaking and low-grade intelligence, brightened occasionally by spectacular flashes of brilliant success and priceless information.

Fortunately, the Bletchley Park codebreakers now had another source of high-grade German intelligence that more than filled the gap in Italy, and ensured they not only knew what Hitler and his generals were thinking but also had a constant and comprehensive guide to all the German dispositions and intentions.

The Germans were using an encyphered radio teleprinter system for communications between Hitler and his senior commanders. The earliest indications of this encyphered radio teleprinter system came in the second half of 1940 when the Metropolitan Police unit at Denmark Hill under Harold Kenworthy picked up unidentified German non-Morse signals. No effort was put into intercepting these transmissions until mid-1941 when an RAF station at Capel-le-Ferne, near Folkestone, picked up similar signals. 'The transmissions were erratic,' said Kenworthy. 'But on one occasion, a secret teleprinter message in clear was intercepted reporting the removal of a Flak [*Fliegerabwehrkanone* – anti-aircraft gun] battery to the Eastern Front.' Denmark Hill was asked to take a closer look at the teleprinter signals with the assistance of the GPO intercept station at St Albans.

The first regular transmissions intercepted by the British were on an experimental *Wehrmacht* link between Vienna and Athens which used the Lorenz SZ40 cypher machine. The radio-teleprinter traffic had been mentioned in the Enigma traffic as *Sägefisch* (sawfish), probably because of the teeth on the SZ40's rotors, and as a result the Bletchley codebreakers gave the radio-teleprinter traffic the codename *Fish*, with the SZ40 traffic itself given the codename *Tunny*. Another teleprinter encyphering system, the Siemens and Halske T52 *Geheimschreiber*, was also detected in use by the Germans, mainly by the *Luftwaffe,* and was codenamed *Sturgeon,* but because of the lack of Army Enigma the codebreakers decided to concentrate on the *Tunny* material produced by the Lorenz machine.

This worked on a system invented in America in 1918 by Gilbert Vernam. Teleprinter transmissions are based on the international Baudot system, a binary code in which each letter is made up of a series of five elements, or 'bits'. Each of these 'bits' is either a 'mark' – the equivalent of the binary 1 and denoted by a cross – or a 'space' – the counterpart of the binary 0 and represented by a dot. Each 'bit' is transmitted as a separate negative or positive impulse.

'The letters were in the form of five elements, always preceded by a start signal and always followed by a stop signal,' said Ken Halton, one of the GPO teleprinter engineers who worked at Bletchley. 'So they were basically seven units in length, the middle five being the active code elements. The start signal and the stop signal were there to start and stop the machine at the receiving end.'

The Baudot Code as it is known was not secret, but Vernam's cypher system combined the five elements for one letter with those of another letter 'randomly' selected by a cypher machine to produce a third encyphered letter. Each of the five elements that made up the letter under the Baudot Code were added to each other on the basis that like and like, either two marks or two spaces, would produce a space, while like and unlike, i.e. a mark combined with a space, produced a mark. Once the cypher machine was introduced the new combination of marks and spaces constituted a third, encyphered letter. For example, if the letter A – which in the Baudot Code is represented by ××••• – is added to B – which is ×••×× – the result would be •×•×× or the letter G.

The beauty of this system lay in the decyphering process. Since, in binary mathematics, addition is the same as subtraction, an identically set cypher machine at the receiving end had only to add the same pattern of 'random' letters to the encyphered letters, or effectively re-encypher the message on the same setting, to come up with the original clear text. The Lorenz SZ40 took Vernam's idea one stage further, adding not one but two separate 'random' letters to the original letter in an attempt to make it even more difficult to decypher.

The Lorenz machine had twelve wheels, ten to encypher the message, paired in two separate rows of five, and two motor wheels. The movement of the wheels was very complex. Each of the encyphering wheels had a number of springed teeth equally spaced around its circumference which could be put into an active or inactive position to form either a mark or a space. The first wheels in each of the pairs, known as the 'chi' wheels, moved regularly one position with each letter. The 'chi' wheels were geared to move at different speeds and each had a different number of positions it could adopt. The second wheels, known as the 'psi' wheels, moved intermittently with their motion controlled by the remaining two wheels – the motor wheels. The five elements of the letter were passed through the first set of five wheels, each element through one wheel, and were either modified or left unaltered depending on the addition principle described above and whether or not the pin at that point was active or inactive. They were then passed through the second set of wheels where a similar process took place.

The intercepted teleprinter messages were sent to Bletchley Park where they were examined by John Tiltman and his research group. Tiltman himself did the initial work, quickly identifying the messages as being encyphered using the Vernam system and began to work on a method of unravelling the messages by hand. Tiltman realised that, because of the way that binary mathematics worked, if two messages were sent using the same setting, and they could be lined up so that the starting points matched, adding them together would eliminate the 'random' letters that the Lorenz machine had introduced. What would be left would be a combination of the letters in the two original messages, still in their original positions, as if their two binary values had been added together to form one.

A number of messages sent on the same setting, or as the codebreakers described it 'in depth', were recovered. But Tiltman was having difficulty separating the clear texts out. Then a lazy German operator came to his assistance. On 30 August 1941, the operator sent a message 3,976 characters long. When asked to repeat it, he sent it again with the exact same settings.

It should have produced exactly the same message which would have been no help to Tiltman at all. But although the codebreakers knew from the operator chat that the two messages were the same and they certainly began identically, within a few letters they had become different. The vital clue that allowed Tiltman to work out what had happened was the fact that this message had fewer characters. The operator had left something out of the original message.

Anxious to cut down the length of time the job would take, he had abbreviated a number of parts of the message, beginning with its introduction. He had cut the word *Spruchnummer*, message number, using the German abbreviation for number to make it *Spruchnr*. Tiltman now knew that if he lined the subsequent apparently different parts of the two messages up and added them together, it would strip off the keys, leaving him with two identical clear texts added together.

Because each character of the combined text represented only one letter, albeit it added to itself, the stripped text would have similar characteristics to the German language and could be recovered relatively easily by exploiting basic cryptanalytical tools such as letter frequency.

Sadly it was not quite as easy as that because the message had been abbreviated in a number of places. But Tiltman, who preferred to work alone, standing at a custom-built high desk, was a brilliant codebreaker. Gradually he worked his way through the message recovering the clear text up to the next abbreviation, working out what that was, realigning the two texts and reconstructing the next piece of plain language.

Eventually he managed to recover the complete text. This was in itself an amazing feat. But it was to be followed by one that was perhaps even more remarkable. Once Tiltman had completely decyphered the message all he had to do was add the clear text to the encyphered version to find the elements that had been added by the Lorenz machine. He gave these to the research section so they could try to reconstruct the machine that would have produced those 4,000 letters of key.

'They worked hard, guided by an ingenious theory, but to no avail,' recalled Bill Tutte, one of the other members of the research section. He later wondered if it was 'a gesture of despair' that led Captain Gerry Morgan, his immediate superior, to hand him the key strip and some other documents and say: 'See what you can do with this.' Tutte, a young Cambridge chemistry graduate who had subsequently become interested in mathematics, wrote out a stream of the first of the five individual 'bits' or 'impulses' that made up each of the encyphering characters, looking for some form of pattern. If only one wheel had been used then a repeating pattern would be found in which every repeat matched precisely with the pattern on the wheel. However if two wheels had been used the precise pattern repeated in each row produced by the first wheel would to some degree be altered by the effects of the second wheel in the pair. Tutte detected a pattern suggesting that one of the wheels might be able to produce twenty-three different positions, or possibly twenty-five. So he decided to test both out, multiplying the two together to form 575 and using that as a basis for his work. In doing so he realised that 574 was an even better fit.

> I wrote the first impulse on a period of 574 and marvelled at the many repetitions down the columns from row to row. But surely the Germans would not use a wheel of that length? Perhaps the true period was forty-one, this being a prime

factor of 574? So I wrote the first impulse a third time, now over a period of forty-one.

It clearly worked. One of the wheels on the machine did have forty-one positions. At this stage of the process, the rest of the section joined in the attack. It later transpired that Tutte's initial belief that one of the wheels had twenty-three positions was correct, but it was the last of the chi-wheels so it would have taken a lot longer for his attack to succeed, although it would have done so in the end. 'Then I suppose my success would have been attributed entirely to close logical reasoning,' Tutte later mused, suggesting that other members of the research section, frustrated in their own efforts, might not have been as generous in their praise as he deserved. 'As things were, I was supposed to have had a stroke of undeserved luck,' Tutte wrote. 'Think twice, O Gentle reader, before thou takest an unexpected and opportune short cut.'

Once Tutte began to make progress, other members of the research section joined in and they managed to work out its complete internal structure and how it operated right down to the intermittent movement of the second row of wheels.

Given that no one at Bletchley had any idea what a Lorenz machine looked like, Tutte had achieved a near miracle, but he remained unassuming and modest about his feat, recalled Shaun Wylie, who later moved from Hut 8 to work on *Tunny*. 'You could hardly get anything out of him,' Wylie said. 'I once wanted to hear from him the saga about how he'd done his astonishing bit of work and I think we got interrupted after about half an hour but I really hadn't got much out of him.'

But the importance of the breakthrough was not lost on those in charge. 'That the Research Section was in fact able to achieve this feat within a matter of a few months was one of the outstanding successes of the war,' said Nigel de Grey. With Tiltman and Tutte having shown that it was possible to break the *Tunny* traffic, it was decided to set up a section to exploit it, de

Grey added. 'The system was being fairly rapidly extended by the Germans over their high command networks and such messages as could be decyphered by "depth" reading left little doubt that their contents would have considerable intelligence value.'

The new section was run by Ralph Tester and therefore became known as 'the Testery'. Ralph Tester was a 39-year-old accountant who, having spent much of his working life in Germany, had an exceptionally deep knowledge both of the country itself and the language. He had been working with Tiltman on police cyphers having only recently transferred to Bletchley from the BBC Monitoring Service at Caversham, near Reading, which intercepted German public radio broadcasts. A small site at Knockholt, near Sevenoaks in Kent, which was owned by Section VIII, the radio section of MI6, was used to intercept the *Tunny* material.

The station, which was staffed mainly by ATS operators, came on line in mid-1942. The German transmissions were turned into a perforated teleprinter tape. The teleprinter tape could then be fed through a teleprinter to send it to the Testery but the tapes were themselves also sent to Bletchley by dispatch rider.

Everything was done twice to ensure there were no mistakes, Kenworthy recalled.

> An error in one character in several thousand was enough to cause trouble. A system was introduced to overcome this on the principle that two separate people would hardly be likely to make the same mistake. All tape was therefore measured by two girls before being read up.

The *Fish* link between Kesselring's headquarters and Berlin, codenamed *Bream* at Bletchley, was the first of many such links that now began to produce extremely high-grade intelligence on German dispositions and intentions, and because it was at such a high level this intelligence was not just limited to the specific area covered by that particular link.

As the Germans increased the number of links and the amount of *Tunny* traffic grew, new outstations would be opened at Forest Moor, near Harrogate; Wincombe, near Shaftesbury in Dorset; Kingask, near Cupar in Scotland; and Kedlestone Hall, near Derby. The codebreakers recruited to work in the Testery included Roy Jenkins, who subsequently became Chancellor of the Exchequer and, as Lord Jenkins of Hillhead, Chancellor of Oxford University; Peter Benenson, the founder of Amnesty International; and Donald Michie, a Classics scholar from Balliol College, Oxford, who subsequently became Professor of Machine Intelligence at Edinburgh University.

Peter Hilton, later a distinguished Professor of Mathematics at the State University of New York, but brought into Bletchley Park as a 21-year-old student, was one of those working in the Testery.

> I was recruited by a team looking for a mathematician with a knowledge of German. I wasn't a mathematician at the time. I was in my fourth year at Oxford. My knowledge of German was what I had taught myself in one year so I wasn't what they were looking for at all really. But I was the only person who turned up at the interview and they jumped at me and said: 'Yes, you must come.' I loved it. There is this enormous excitement in codebreaking that what appears to be utter gibberish really makes sense if only you have the key and I could do that sort of thing for thirty hours at a stretch and never feel tired.

Just as with the Enigma, German errors were helpful in breaking the system.

> Sometimes the German operator made the mistake of encyphering two successive messages using the same wheel setting. When he did this, we could combine the two encyphered texts and what we got was a combination of the two German messages. So you had one length of gibberish which was, in

a certain sense, the sum of two pieces of German text. So you were tearing this thing apart to make the two pieces of text. And it's absolutely a marvellous process because you would guess some word, I remember once I guessed the word '*Abwehr*'. So that means you have a space and then '*Abwehr*', eight symbols of one of the two messages.

By subtracting the Baudot elements for those letters from the characters in the combined text, Hilton would then be left with eight letters from the other message.

But the eight letters of the other message would have a space in the middle followed by '*Flug*'. So then you would guess, well that's going to be '*Flugzeug*' – aircraft. So you get '*zeug*' followed by a space and that gives you five more letters of the other message. So you keep extending and going backwards as well. You break in different places and try to join up but then you're not sure if top goes with top, or top goes with bottom.

Then of course when you've got two messages like that, as a codebreaker, you have to take the encyphered message and the original text and add them together to get the key and then you have the wheel patterns. But for me the real excitement was this business of getting these two texts out of one sequence of gibberish. It was marvellous. I never met anything that was quite as exciting, especially since you knew that these were vital messages.

Throughout 1942, the work on the *Tunny* material had to be done by hand and, although some useful material was gained on the German campaign against Russia and from the links between Italy and North Africa, many of the messages took several weeks to decypher.

Max Newman, one of the mathematicians working in the Testery, was a thin, bald academic from Manchester University, who like Tutte had worked in Tiltman's research section. He had been Turing's tutor at one stage. It was Newman's suggestion that machines might be able to prove mathematical statements that had led Turing to write his ground-breaking paper 'On Computable Numbers, with an Application to the *Entscheidungsproblem*', and Newman who had ensured that it was published.

Newman became convinced that, using similar principles to those advocated by Turing, it would be possible to build a machine that, once the patterns of the wheels had been worked out in the Testery, would find the settings of the first row of wheels, thereby making the codebreakers' task immeasurably easier.

'Newman judged that much of the purely non-linguistic work done in the Testery could and should be mechanised and that electronic machinery would be essential,' said Jack Good, who worked with Newman in what became known as the Newmanry. 'He convinced Commander Edward Travis, by then the head of BP, that work on such machinery should be begun, and so the Newmanry was born.'

Newman went to Wynn-Williams at the Telecommunications Research Establishment in Malvern and asked him to design the machine. It was known as *Robinson*, after Heath Robinson, the cartoonist designer of fantastic machines, and the first version was delivered to Bletchley Park in May 1943. It worked on the principle that although the encyphering letters were supposed to be random, they were not. No machine can generate a truly random sequence of letters. *Robinson* compared a piece of teleprinter tape carrying the encyphered text with a piece of tape on which the wheel patterns had been punched to look for statistical evidence that would indicate what the wheel-settings were.

But while *Robinson* could clearly do its job, there were problems, Travis told the weekly meeting of senior staff.

Although Mr Newman's new research machinery is still going through teething troubles, it is likely to prove better than anything they have yet produced in the USA. The only snag is that it needs a lot of personnel. It should be able to handle 28–30 *Tunny* messages a day which would be invaluable.

Robinson was designed to keep the two paper tapes in synchronisation at 1,000 characters a second but at that speed the sprocket wheels kept ripping the tapes. Turing, who, while working on the Bombe, had been impressed by the abilities of a bright young telephone engineer at Dollis Hill called Tommy Flowers, suggested to Newman that he might be just the man to get *Robinson* to work.

> I came into the project when the *Robinson* machine didn't work properly, because it was made almost entirely of telephone parts, telephone switching parts, which was my area. I was brought in to make it work, but I very soon came to the conclusion that it would never work. It was dependent on paper tape being driven at very high speed by means of spiked wheels and the paper wouldn't stand up to it.

Tester recalled long conversations with Flowers, Turing, Tutte and Newman over what should be done. Flowers, who had been developing telephone exchanges containing valves instead of the old fashioned relays used in *Robinson*, suggested that he could make an electronic machine built with valves that would do the same job much faster without the need for the synchronisation of the two tapes. The data on the wheel patterns would be generated electronically using ring circuits while the tape reading the cypher text would be read photo-electrically and could be run on smooth wheels rather than sprockets so it wouldn't rip.

The codebreakers asked Flowers how long it would take to produce the first machine. 'I said at least a year and they said that was terrible,' Flowers recalled. 'They thought in a year the war could be over and Hitler could have won it so they didn't take up my idea. They decided they would proceed hopefully with the *Robinson*.

> I was so convinced that *Robinson* would never work that we developed the new machine on our own at Dollis Hill. We made the first prototype in ten months, working day and night, six-and-a-half days a week, twelve hours a day sometimes. We started with the design of what was to be called *Colossus* in February 1943 and we had the first prototype machine working at Bletchley Park on 8 December.
>
> The purpose of the *Colossus* was to find out what the positions of the code wheels were at the beginning of the message and it did that by trying all the possible combinations and there were billions of them. It tried all the combinations, which processing at 5,000 characters a second could be done in about half an hour. So then having found the starting positions of the cypher wheels you could decode the message.

Flowers said the codebreakers were astounded at how reliable it was compared to *Robinson*.

> What they did with *Colossus*, the first day they got it, was to put a problem on it which they knew the answer to. It took about half an hour to do the run. They let it run for about four hours, repeating the processes every half hour, and to their amazement, it gave the same answer every time. They really were amazed. It was that reliable, extremely reliable.

Colossus was the world's first large-scale electronic digital computer and as such the forerunner of the computers most people use today. It was also the first to be programmable, albeit as a result of its specialised role, semi-programmable. Although it had a specialised function, it showed the theory could be turned into practice. The sequence of operations was determined mainly by the setting of external switches and plugboards, which were controlled by Wrens on the orders of the Newmanry codebreakers. Just like the *Robinson*, it was looking for sequences that were not random.

'The work on *Tunny* divided roughly between what you might call the machine work and the hand work,' said Peter Hilton.

> Machine work was of course putting messages on to *Colossus* which was a process whereby we would determine the starting positions of the first set of five wheels which were involved in making up the key. Then after that process had taken place, that is to say a process based on statistics, mathematics, the message shorn of part of its key, would come to the codebreakers in the Testery who would then have the job of using their knowledge of expected pieces of text in order to set the remaining wheels.

Each codebreaker was assisted by two Wrens who set the machine up. Jean Thompson was just nineteen when she was posted to Bletchley in 1944 to work on *Colossus*.

> Most of the time I was doing wheel setting, getting the starting positions of the wheels. There would be two Wrens on the machine and a duty officer, one of the cryptanalysts – the brains people, and the message came in on a teleprinted tape.
>
> If the pattern of the wheels was already known you put that up at the back of the machine on a pinboard. The pins were bronze, brass or copper with two feet and there were double holes the whole way down the board for cross or dot impulses to put up the wheel pattern. Then you put the tape on round the wheels with a join in it so it formed a complete circle. You put it behind the gate of the photo-electric cell which you shut on it and, according to the length of the tape, you used so many wheels and there was one moveable one so that could get it taut.

At the front there were switches and plugs. After you'd set the thing you could do a letter count with the switches. You would make the runs for the different wheels to get the scores out which would print out on the electro-matic typewriter. We were looking for a score above the random and one that was sufficiently good, you'd hope was the correct setting. When it got tricky, the duty officer would suggest different runs to do.

Another of the Wrens working in the Newmanry was Odette Murray.

I was offered the chance of joining what was known as *Pembroke V*, not knowing what it was all about. A group of us turned up at Bletchley Park where we were taught to be touch typists, still not knowing what it was all about, and eventually I got into the park itself in the Newmanry. I was head of a watch and I was given instructions by whoever was in charge at the time and, still not having the remotest idea what I was doing, I worked with a slide rule producing a lot of figures and gave the result to the next person who gave it to the next person and eventually it was run on a tape.

Shaun Wylie had just been transferred over from Hut 8 shortly after Odette Murray arrived at Bletchley. 'All the Wrens were swooning about Shaun Wylie,' she recalled.

They thought he was absolutely wonderful: 'Oh, Mr Wylie this, oh Mr Wylie that.' I didn't think much of him. I couldn't see what they saw in him. However, he thought something of me.
    He tried to explain to me exactly what my contribution had been in a successful thing. I just didn't understand. I'm not a mathematician, I'm not a linguist. I'm just somebody who's given instructions and does little funny calculations with a slide rule and bingo. A few days later a smiling Shaun comes in. I don't know what my contribution is but okay, satisfactory.

She was billeted in Woburn Abbey and on their days off Wylie
would cycle over there to visit her. 'Most of our courting was in
Woburn Park,' Odette recalled.

> The Abbey is a huge imposing building and the central part
> has a large podium on top of it, very high up, and I used to go
> casual climbing, leaping across two-foot, three-foot chasms so
> that I could sit on the top of this to watch Shaun on his bicycle
> coming up the drive. No way would I go up there now.

The atmosphere in the Newmanry was very happy, largely
because of Newman's influence. 'Max Newman was a marvellous fellow,' American codebreaker George Vergine recalled.

> I always sort of felt grateful to have known him really. We used
> to have tea-parties. These were just discussions on problems or
> developments, techniques, to a great extent mathematical. We
> used to meet in the small conference room. Somebody would
> write a topic up on the blackboard and all of the analysts, includ-
> ing Newman, would come with their tea in hand and chew it
> around and see whether or not it would be useful as far as crack-
> ing more communications. They were very productive and after
> it was over somebody would summarise it in the research log.

Once the encyphered messages had been stripped of the effect of
the first set of wheels, the part-decyphered message was passed
to the Testery where the cryptanalysts worked out the setting of
the second row of wheels. The work in the Testery was much
more like that in Huts 6 and 8 where the Enigma material was
decyphered. The human brain had to take over from the machine.
'We had to operate on a semi-intuitive basis and sometimes
your intuition worked and sometimes it didn't,' said Roy Jenkins.

> It was a curious life. It could be very wearing, particularly if
> it didn't succeed. You could spend nights in which you got

nowhere at all. You didn't get a single break, you just tried, played around through this bleak long night with total frustration and your brain was literally raw. I remember one night when I made thirteen breaks. But there were an awful lot of nights when I was lucky if I made one. So it was exhausting.

The codebreakers looked for differences between the Baudot elements for regular sequences of letters which occur commonly in German, or characters that denoted a common sequence of teleprinter instructions.

One of the methods used in the Testery to get into the *Tunny* transmissions originated from the tests conducted by the German operators before sending the message, Peter Hilton recalled.

We were fortunate that the Germans seemed to have been so convinced that we couldn't possibly be reading *Tunny* that they didn't take the precautions they should have done.

At the beginning of each message, the German operator would transmit by hand some little piece of text of his own in order that the other operator would be able to report: 'I am receiving you clearly.' He could then switch over from hand transmission to automatic and put through the tape of the real message. Some of the German operators began to reveal their own personalities by referring to their own conditions and circumstances.

I remember one message which the operator began: '*Mörderische Hitze*' – murderous heat. Well once I'd broken the first few letters to guess he was talking about *mörderische* and it was quite likely, because that's a sort of natural expression of an ordinary German when something is terribly bad. What could be bad? He was writing from southern Italy, so it was very likely it would not be the food. It was probably the heat.

So you got to know people. There was another one I remember from outside Leningrad who said: '*Ich bin so einsam*' – I'm so lonely. The next day came a message that said: '*Hier ist so traurig*'

– It's so sad here, and this fellow, I had the feeling that he didn't want to be there. He didn't want to be fighting the Russians. He didn't want to be besieging Leningrad, but he had to do it.

The officers drafting the messages made equally stupid mistakes, repeating predictable, and often completely useless, phrases, Hilton said.

I remember '*Nieder mit den Englander*', down with the English, as a phrase that certainly appeared very commonly in these messages and of course '*Heil Hitler*' was enormously valuable. You should never inculcate in your military the tendency to have exactly the same phrase opening every statement.

Once the settings of both rows of wheels had been worked out, the tape of the encyphered message was taken into the *Tunny* Room where there were a number of '*Tunny* machines' that had been built at Dollis Hill to replicate the action of the Lorenz cypher machine. The machine was set up in exactly the same way as the German cypher machine was set up and the clear language German came out.

Since they were Army messages, they were then passed to the Hut 3 intelligence reporters. The first really important reports to result from the decyphered *Tunny* messages covered the Eastern Front. They came between April and July 1943 when the complete German plans for the forthcoming Battle of Kursk were sent on the link between the headquarters of the German Army Group South and Berlin. A sanitised version, disguising the source, was passed to Moscow but this assistance was unnecessary. Stalin was already receiving full transcripts. Despite the strict security in force at Bletchley Park, a member of one of the watches in Hut 3 was a KGB spy.

John Cairncross, codenamed *Liszt* by the Russians because of his love of music, had already given Moscow Centre details of Bletchley Park's network of intercept sites while working in the section of the Treasury that dealt with the GPO in the months before the war. He had then become private secretary to Lord Hankey, the Minister without Portfolio, and passed the Russians details of the Anglo-American atomic weapons project, providing them with the information that formed the basis for their own atomic weapons programme.

But at the beginning of 1942, Cairncross was called up and was instructed to try to get himself into Bletchley Park, which the KGB codenamed *Kurort* (German for Spa). Moscow Centre was aware from one of its other agents that Colonel Frederick Nicholls, the head of MI8, was looking for new codebreakers and told Cairncross to seek him out. 'In the course of his professional duties, Liszt became acquainted with Nicholls and by rendering small services established friendly relations with him,' Cairncross's KGB handler told the Centre.

> During lunch at the Travellers Club, Liszt complained to Nicholls that he was about to be called up by the Army where he would be unable to use his knowledge of foreign languages. Nicholls started to persuade him to come to work in *Kurort*. After he received his call-up papers, Liszt told Nicholls about this, remained in his unit for one day and was then put at the disposal of the War Office which conditionally demobilised him and seconded him to *Kurort*.

Cairncross smuggled decrypts that were due to be destroyed out of Hut 3 in his trousers, transferring them to his bag at the railway station before going on to London to meet his KGB contact. The information that he handed the Russians is probably rightly credited with helping them to win the Battle of Kursk, the turning point on the Eastern Front. Despite the fact that a sanitised version of the *Tunny* messages was being passed to Moscow, Stalin was highly suspicious of any intelligence passed to him by the Allies, particularly if the source was unclear. But Cairncross was supplying the German language signals and it was coming via the KGB. 'The Russians were convinced,' Cairncross said, 'that in its German version the *Ultra* I supplied was genuine, giving the full details of German units and locations, thus enabling the Russians to pinpoint their targets and to take the enemy by surprise.'

It is impossible to tell how vital his contribution to the Battle of Kursk was. But the Russians' codes were being decyphered by the Germans and their brief liaison with Hitler had left them riddled with Nazi agents. His breaching of the *Ultra* secret risked informing the Germans that their most secret cypher systems had been broken.

The surrender of Italy saw all the linguists and codebreakers who were working on Italian codes and cyphers switched to Japanese systems and two separate Japanese courses were set up, one in Bedford by Tiltman and another by Josh Cooper's Air Intelligence Section which required linguists capable of listening to the clear speech passing between pilots and their ground controllers. Cooper's eccentric approach was reflected in the course he selected for his Japanese students. It was described by Tiltman, with some understatement, as 'a rather more tricky experiment' than the Bedford course.

What the Royal Air Force needed was interpreters who could read air-to-ground and air-to-air conversations. For this purpose my counterpart in the Air Section J. E. S. Cooper started an intensive 11-week course at which the students were bombarded incessantly with Japanese phonograph records, ringing the changes on a very limited vocabulary. The course was directed, not by a Japanese linguist, but by a phonetics expert. I remember taking a US Army Japanese interpreter, Colonel Svensson round the course. Stunned by the volume of sound in every room, Svensson mildly asked the Director whether all the students made the grade and the reply he received was: 'After the fifth week, they're either carried away screaming or they're Nipponified.'

The British codebreakers from the Far East Combined Bureau had moved from Singapore first to Colombo and then, in April 1942, to Kilindini, near Mombasa in Kenya, and in September 1943 back to Colombo. Although the Americans dominated the day-to-day breaking of Japanese codes and cyphers, it was the British who 'broke in' to most of them with John Tiltman leading the way. Having broken the main military encyphered code systems in 1938, he had followed that up with the main Imperial Japanese Fleet encyphered code, JN25, the Japanese Military Attaché code in mid-1942 and the Japanese Army Air Force General Purpose Code in early 1943. Other important Japanese codes were broken by British codebreakers in Kilindini and Delhi. Of the major Japanese codes and cyphers, the Americans 'broke into' only very few, but one of these was one of the most important, the *Purple* Japanese diplomatic machine cypher, and it was inevitably the Americans who made the most spectacular use of the Allied breaks into Japanese codes and cyphers, most emphatically before the Battle of Midway, in June 1942, when the US Navy codebreakers at Pearl Harbor decyphered the entire Japanese battle plan.

The number of Japanese sections increased dramatically in late 1943, with one long corridor in F Block known as the Burma Road because of the large number of Japanese sections all along it. Most of the sections dealing with Japanese Army material were a mixture of Intelligence Corps personnel, Foreign Office civilians and members of the Women's Auxiliary Territorial Service (ATS), many of whom did extremely repetitive work preparing messages for the codebreakers to tackle. Gladys Sweetland was sent to the mysterious 'Station X' as a young ATS corporal.

'I went for an interview at a place in Praed Street, in London,' she said.

We were there for several days being interviewed by lots of different people, most of them officers. Then finally we were told we were being transferred to Bletchley. It was really rather weird. I was taken into a hut and introduced to what I was supposed to do. Teleprinter sheets of coded messages were handed to me and I had to copy each message out in different coloured inks across one line on large sheets of graph paper, a bit tricky when some stretched across four different sheets. Each message was marked with a sign to indicate which colour ink I should use. I know it sounds ridiculous but we never asked what they did with the sheets of messages. It was all so secret. Even with the other girls in the ATS we only ever asked: 'Where do you work?' And they'd say: 'Oh, Hut 6' or 'Block F' or whatever. We never asked each other what we actually did.

We were given travel passes to come in by train during the day, which was similar to going to and from work in 'Civvy Street' and it was fairly easy. When we finished at midnight there was a bus which would take a whole load of us home, dropping everyone off at the various villages where they were billeted and it depended on how many of you there were, and what route the bus took, how long it took you to get home. The first woman I was billeted with was rather peculiar. She had two young children and wanted me to stay in and look after them all the time so she could go out. The second was much nicer. She was middle-aged. She had a son who was in the RAF and her attitude was that if she could treat people billeted with her kindly, then perhaps other people would treat her son the same way. She would insist on bringing me breakfast in bed after I had worked the late shift.

Bletchley Park was a wonderful location and sometimes we just sat in the grounds in fine weather for our break. There was a whole group of us who used to go around together to pubs and concerts. There was an assembly hall just outside and it was there I got my love for opera and ballet because I saw the D'Oyly Carte touring company and the Ballet Rambert. There were also discussion groups where people would play classical music records and then explain the merits of the various pieces. I shall never forget the comradeship and meeting all those different types of people who were there. I never thought, leaving school at fourteen and a half, that I would be able to have a proper conversation with a university professor.

The mix of people from so many different areas of British life is one of the recurring themes of the memories of those who worked at Bletchley Park. Jonathan Cohen, later Professor of Philosophy at Oxford, was rather shocked to discover that his girlfriend was from a very different social background to his own.

> There were very considerable class differences at Bletchley Park itself. I took up with a girl who I was quite surprised to find was a countess's daughter, because with my middle-class Jewish background that wasn't the kind of person you would normally mix with. But it was a place where all sorts met and there were dances and parties and we enjoyed ourselves to a certain extent. But there was always the background and the need to know criteria, that is to say you didn't ask questions about what other people were doing or working on. You never went beyond your own narrow field as it were.

Maurice Wiles was moved from the Japanese Military Attaché Section to the team decoding the Army Air material sometime in the first half of 1943.

> The main work was done by four of us. Alexis Vlasto, who was one of the few who had not come via the Bedford school, was in charge. He was a Japanese and Russian linguist. Very quiet, very relaxed with a nice ironic sense of humour. George Ashworth, later Registrar of Manchester University, was the quickest mind among us. He had a wonderful memory. He would say: 'Oh, I remember something similar to that four months ago.' The other was Mervyn Jones. He was rather

introverted with a lovely sense of humour, not particularly outgoing. I remember the day the war ended and there was nothing to do, he came in and pulled out an Aristophanes text and sat there chuckling away to himself. Then he put that away and pulled out a musical score.

There were also musical evenings organised by Alexis Vlasto who married Jill Medway, who was a very good musician. As a civilian, I belonged to the Home Guard, which was a bit like Dad's Army. We weren't very efficient. There was a good deal of competition between the two platoon commanders and we had night exercises. Max Aitken, the Scottish chess champion, was one of these people whose limbs are very uncoordinated. Marching alongside him was often very comical. There were a lot of very good chess players at BP. We used to have evenings when Hugh Alexander and Harry Golombek, both members of the British chess team, would take on twenty boards.

I found the codebreaking a stimulating mental activity. I think being a civilian it was very easy for me to have a very relaxed time with the senior hierarchy and the most junior person, although that was certainly true of many of those who were in the services as well. I felt it was a very relaxing way to work. There were certainly boring periods. It's a much longer-term thing than a crossword and it was vital in codebreaking to do the groundwork first, to read through the text first because that can be how you begin to spot the patterns.

The year 1943 was also notable for an invasion of more US liaison officers ahead of the invasion of Europe. Despite the initial agreement in 1941, there were continuing disputes between GC&CS and the US Army codebreakers over who should do what, and what each side should reveal to the other. There was a continuing distrust of the Americans at Bletchley, with a fear that they might too easily give the *Ultra* secret away. This was based on justified concerns. What leakages there were of signals intelligence had appeared in the US news media. There were immense problems on the Japanese side where the US frequently refused to assist and the British at one point threatened to break off relations entirely.

The Americans meanwhile were determined to set up an operation to break Enigma in America and did not want to be beholden to the British in any way. This was unrealistic. The British had by now made such advances that the Americans could not have possibly managed on their own. Telford Taylor, the head of the US Army liaison team, urged caution while at the same time being brutally candid about what the Americans wanted.

> What we really want at this time is to gain a foothold in 'Enigma' and develop technical competence, and gradually develop a supplementary operation so as to improve joint coverage. What we ultimately want is independence, but if we get a foothold and develop our technique, independence will come anyhow. As our position in Europe gets better established, we will be less dependent on the British for intercept assistance.

The British reluctance to allow the decrypts to cross the Atlantic for security reasons continued to mar the relationship. General George Strong, who as G-2 was the US Army officer in charge of signals intelligence, remained highly suspicious of British motives. 'The picture that emerges is of G-2 and the British authorities walking around and eyeing each other like two mongrels who have just met,' wrote Ted Hilles, one of the senior US Army officers at Bletchley Park. 'Presumably and quite naturally, the ministries in London were reluctant to risk source's neck sharing this precious information with an unproved and shadowy group in Washington.'

A US mission went to Britain in April 1943 and was involved in 'difficult and protracted negotiations' with Travis and Menzies. But in mid-May, the two sides signed a groundbreaking accord. The BRUSA agreement set out a division of responsibilities between Bletchley Park and Arlington Hall. The British would control the interception and decryption of German radio messages while the Americans concentrated on Japanese. US liaison officers would be based at Bletchley Park where they would have access to 'all decoded material' and the right to pass those they selected back to Washington or on to US commanders in the field.

'The proposal is now that the Americans, though not exploiting E [Enigma] in the USA, should have a party in this country working either here at BP or elsewhere,' Travis told the BP management committee. 'Moreover some American officers would be attached to Hut 3 and would report to the USA from there. In this way General Strong would make certain he was not cheated of information.'

But with concerns over American security a predominant factor in the negotiations, it was agreed that all this material should be passed 'through existing British channels'. Information that was to be sent to field commanders would be passed via the British Special Liaison Units, the agreement said.

> Where an American officer is commander-in-chief, an American officer, properly trained and indoctrinated at Bletchley Park, will be attached to the unit to advise and act as liaison officer to overcome difficulties that may arise in regard to differences in language. The preservation of secrecy is a matter of great concern to both countries and, if the highest degree of security is to be maintained, it is essential that the same methods should be pursued by both countries at every level and in every area concerned, since a leakage at one point would jeopardise intelligence from these sources not in one area only but in all theatres of war and for all services.

Telford Taylor was sent to Bletchley to head up the US Army intelligence team there. He persuaded Travis to send someone from Hut 3 over to America to pick out US intelligence officers who would fit into the hut's somewhat rarified atmosphere. The man selected for this task was Jim Rose, who was to remain close friends with Taylor for the rest of the latter's life.

'When Telford came over in 1943, he asked me to go out to Washington to interview candidates for Bletchley,' Rose said.

> Most of the officers who came to Bletchley I chose. There were some very bright people. One of them was Lewis Powell, who became a judge of the US Supreme Court. There was a man who became managing editor of the *Washington Post*, Alfred Friendly. There were quite a lot of lawyers and their reception in Hut 3 was extremely friendly and they all felt integrated.

While the Hut 3 reporters selected by Rose came, like Taylor, from the Special Branch, the US Army equivalent of the Intelligence Corps, the codebreakers came from the Signal Intelligence Service of the US Army Signal Corps and were under the command of Captain Bill Bundy, a law student from Harvard whose studies had been interrupted by the war.

> I went to Arlington Hall in the spring of '43. And I remember vividly, a group of us, a very small group, were convened in a room there and told: 'What you're going to hear today is something you will not discuss.' They went on with the briefing about what was then in that circle called Yellow, which was the whole Enigma-breaking operation. After considerable sparring back and forth an agreement had been reached between the American and the British governments that the Americans would keep the major role on Japanese material and the British would maintain the major role on German, but as a sort of codicil to that it was agreed that a small American contingent, thirty to fifty, should go to Bletchley Park to integrate right into the organisation there and I was picked to be the commanding officer of that outfit.

Amid conditions of great secrecy they were sent to England on board the SS *Aquitania*, Bundy recalled.

> I think we were twenty in our advance contingent and on the way over we had to bunk with other services. Our cover story was that we were pigeon experts in the Signal Corps. I don't think we used it very often, Lord knows it would have broken down very quickly, you didn't really have to explain what you were doing on a troopship, but that was the cover story we used.

Art Levenson, a young Jewish mathematician, was one of Bundy's advance party. 'We were a somewhat select group,' he said.

> But this was the first experiment in cooperating in the code-breaking business between any two countries in history and I don't know if you want to put your best foot forward, but you want to put one of your better feet forward. I don't think I'd ever met an Englishman in my life until that point. We went to Lichfield, which was the 'repo-depot', the reporting depot where everybody who was coming to the UK or the European theatre went to. Then we were in London for a few days, and then we were sent up to Bletchley. We were introduced to Brigadier Tiltman and they treated us like visiting generals.

But underlying the VIP treatment was a continuing mutual distrust. 'I remember with horror the American invasion when every section had an American,' said Jean Howard, who worked in Hut 3.

> We believed they had no sense of security and were terrified that material they took out of the Hut would go astray. We felt strongly that they would never have come into the war but for Pearl Harbor. They were different animals, and the English they spoke had different meanings. They were fat, we were

emaciated. They were smart (eleven different sorts of uniform), we were almost in rags. They were rich, we were poor. They brought in alcohol: 'Have a Rye sister.' 'We don't drink here.' We were overworked and exhausted, and having to teach people who barely knew where Europe was, was the last straw.

The mutual mistrust came to a head during celebrations to mark the 4 July, recalled Barbara Abernethy.

We were challenged by the Americans to a game of rounders. They nearly went home. Now in the United States, you don't need to get all the way home in one go to score. As long as you get all the way home eventually you score. Now our rules for rounders of course were very tough. You had to go all the way round in one go. It was a lovely day, we all played well, and at the end of the game we all sort of clapped each other on the back and the Americans said: 'Well, we're sorry we beat you' and the British captain said: 'I'm sorry, but we beat you.' The Americans were a little touchy. They were convinced that they'd won and it took a bit of explanation on somebody's part to soothe ruffled feathers. It all ended with drinks all round, actually we agreed we'd won by our rules and they'd won by their rules. So that was alright. But they never asked us to play again.

They might never play rounders again, but the Americans were placed in various parts of the Park and soon mixed in well. Both sides swiftly got over their prejudices. While the British had seen the Americans as brash and careless about security, the Americans had believed that the British would be too 'stiff-upper-lipped' to get on with. 'We thought they'd be aloof, hard to reach, buttoned up, as we say. That it would be very hard to get to know them and that they'd probably be rather cold,' Bundy recalled.

Well that broke down, I should say, in the first forty-eight hours and certainly the first time that you had a mug of beer with a Britisher. If we're talking original stereotypes, they didn't last.

One felt right away a concern on the British side whether Americans could keep their mouths shut and they dealt with this, I thought brilliantly, as they dealt with the whole security problem throughout. No stern lectures or anything of that sort, just quietly saying how important it was not to let a bit of this come out. So very quickly and in a very low key but totally persuasive way we were indoctrinated with the basic security principles that governed all the Enigma material and all the cypher and codebreaking materials at all grades, all levels throughout the war, it was just terribly well done.

Gradually as the two sides got to know each other, a level of mutual respect replaced the suspicion and relationships between the two sides became very much closer. 'We didn't have a separate American unit within the Enigma cypher breaking structure,' Bundy recalled. 'We were integrated on an individual basis in the various offices of Hut 6, or on the translation and exploitation side Hut 3, and it was, from the standpoint of personal relations, a terribly good relationship, taking people as they came, as they were, laughing about the national differences and customs, a very relaxed, very giving and taking relationship.'

Art Levenson recalled having a 'pretty heavy' social life at Bletchley Park.

We were a handful of Americans and we were, I guess, somewhat exotic. There were lots of Wrens around. They invited us to lots of parties and we had a great time. I made many friends that I still have. It was great fun, they were wonderful people, a great crowd. I had been full of stereotypes about the English. 'They're distant and have no sense of humour, they won't speak to you unless you're introduced' and all kinds of nonsense. But these were the most outgoing people, who invited us to their homes and fed us when it was quite a sacrifice, and with a delightful sense of humour. Maybe there were some English that fitted the stereotype but there were none at Bletchley, they were all a delight and just enough screwballs to be real fun.

One of the most striking thing about the Americans to the British, used to the weak wartime beer sold in the Bletchley Park beer hut or the local pubs, was their ability to drink spirits, and in particular whisky. 'It was astonishing,' said Christine Brooke-Rose, who was newly married to one of her fellow codebreakers.

> I don't know if it was just the war or me being terribly inno-cent. I remember my husband and I being invited to dinner to the local hotel in Leighton Buzzard where all the Americans were billeted, and after dinner, all the Americans, each one would order another whisky and another Drambuie and another round. It was absolutely amazing and we had to cycle back to the billet where we were living and I remember being really very zig-zaggy. It wasn't that they were alcoholics. It was just the war atmosphere. They did drink far more. That was part of the American culture.

As relationships became closer, there were inevitably romances between the Americans and some of the British women, a number of which would lead eventually to marriage. Telford Taylor, who was a married man, became involved in a torrid affair with the unhappily married Christine Brooke-Rose.

> It was just one of those things that happen. I was twenty-two and he was in his late thirties. He was very handsome, he looked like Gary Cooper, and he was a very interesting person. He was in charge of the American liaison section which was in one room just opposite where we were in Hut 3 so they would all come in for coffee and I knew them quite well. Telford had first arrived on his own and I was detailed to explain things

to him. It was quite an odd experience because he was much too high up to be interested in this kind of routine work. I don't know how these things happened. He was a very serious person. He had quite a good sense of humour. He was a nice man, a lawyer. He liked to tell me all about the American law system. But he was very musical.

When her husband was taken into hospital with pneumonia, they began an affair, sharing trysts in London away from the gossip of Bletchley Park. When her husband was released from hospital, Brooke-Rose told him of the affair.

He was very, very British and he and Telford talked together. Telford was terribly amused afterwards because he thought my husband was so British, shaking hands and saying that everything was alright which of course it wasn't because our marriage broke up. It just made him laugh because Americans don't face things the way gentlemen used to. It was so British.

With the tide finally turning in the Allies' favour, Christmas 1943 was a time of real celebration, particularly in Huts 4 and 8 which had come successfully through the *Shark* blackout. Phoebe Senyard recalled the occasion.

Mr Birch gave a wonderful luncheon party. We toasted the Naval Section and anything else that came into our heads. It was great fun and by the time we went into the room where the luncheon was served, we were prepared for almost anything but not for the wonderful sight which met our eyes. The tables were positively groaning with Christmas fare. They were arranged in a T-shape. The top of the T was loaded with turkey, geese, and chicken while the table down the centre at which we all sat was decorated with a game pie, and fruit salad, cheese and various other dishes. We set to and thoroughly enjoyed ourselves and I know that I was still beaming by the end of the day.

Pat Wright was working in Hut 8 and was not one of those invited to Birch's lunch. At the end of her shift she returned to her billet.

I remember it was the first house I had come across that had a toilet in the garden and I had spent five minutes of my first evening there with my toilet bag touring around looking for the bathroom. But Mrs Tomlin was very good to me. She had an engine driver husband and a fireman son and she never took the tablecloth off. She always had food on the table. She was a very capable woman with a range of language I had never encountered before. I had been brought up fairly strictly and she used words I hardly knew the meaning of. I was working Christmas day and so I finished work at four o'clock and went back to my billet. Christmas dinner was over by now but she said: 'Hello duck, saved you a bit of Christmas pudding. Here you are, this'll make your shit black.' I didn't know whether to laugh or what to do. So I said thank you very much and ate it.

CHAPTER 11

THE INVASION OF EUROPE

The intelligence collected by the British codebreakers ahead of D-Day and the invasion of Europe provided an extraordinarily comprehensive picture of the German defences and preparations. One of the most important pieces of intelligence came in late 1943 from the intercepted communications of Oshima Hiroshi, the Japanese ambassador in Berlin, who toured the German fortification along the French Coast, the so-called Atlantic Wall, that October, providing a detailed rundown of German forces in both France and Belgium. In a report decyphered and translated in Hut 7, Oshima listed the number of divisions with their locations and subordination. He reported the proposed reinforcements ahead of the expected invasion, which included three SS *Panzer* Divisions, provided the full strength of German forces in France, which was 1.4million, and critically noted that 'the Straits area', i.e. the narrowest point of the Channel along the Pas de Calais and towards the Belgian border, was 'given first place in German Army's fortification scheme and troops dispositions, Normandy and Brittany coming next in importance'. This told the Allies that the Germans remained susceptible to the suggestion, which was increasingly being planted in their minds through the deception operations of the Double Cross Committee, that the D-Day landings were to take place on the Pas de Calais. At around the same time, a report signed by Field-Marshal Gerd von Rundstedt, the German commander in chief in the West, and sent using the *Red* Enigma easily broken in Hut 6, warned,

'It is certain that the enemy is methodically and on the largest scale proceeding with his preparations to attack'.

The gaps in Oshima's report, and there had seemed at the time to be very few, were more than filled in by Colonel Ito Seiichi, the Japanese Military Attaché who had made his own tour of the entire German coastal defences sending a massive 32-part report back to Tokyo. It gave a comprehensive account of every building in the fortifications and every installation, detailing everything from the heaviest artillery battery to the smallest collection of flame-throwers.

The Japanese Military Attaché cypher had been broken by John Tiltman in 1942. Bill Sibley was one of the Japanese interpreters translating the Japanese Military Attaché's messages.

I was recruited from Balliol (I was a classicist, at the end of my first year) for the second Japanese language course at Bedford, which began, I think, in September 1942. We were summoned to a five-minute one-to-one interview with John Tiltman, having been pre-selected by the Master of Balliol A. D. Lindsay. I then went to Bletchley in the spring of 1943 and was set to work as a translator on the Japanese Military Attaché code until the end of the war, apart from a period of a few months when I was seconded to work on the Japanese Naval Attaché cypher. Our work began after the real cryptographers had done their work and identified where, in relation to the double substitution cypher keys, individual messages were located. The texts on which we worked were provided for us by 'key-breakers' who were not trained in the language, and whose task was to break the keys used in the messages relying on acquired familiarity with the frequencies of the bigrams in which the messages were composed before being encyphered. We lived an introverted existence, insulated from the real world. Our masters did occasionally send us words of encouragement, but I can't recall that at our level we were ever told of any examples of our work having produced any

positive results. Nobody knew what was going on in the rest
of the place. It was a funny life, very funny, particularly the
secrecy, and the oddity of some of the people. There was one
famous professor of English who used to read about three
detective novels a day. He used to walk around the grounds
reading them.

The codebreakers added to the significant intelligence they were
already providing to Allied commanders when they broke into
the *Fish* link between Berlin and von Rundstedt's headquarters
at St Germain, just outside Paris. The Germans had increased
the security of *Tunny*, introducing the SZ42, but the arrival of
Colossus in early 1944 led in March to the breaking at Bletchley
of the Paris–Berlin link, which they codenamed *Jellyfish*, decyphering all of von Rundstedt's high-grade communications
with Hitler.

The confirmation from the Japanese ambassador's report,
and other signals decyphered by Bletchley, that the Germans
believed the Allies would land on the Pas de Calais led the
Double Cross Committee to use the double agents to send false
intelligence to the Germans that would reinforce them in that
view, ensuring that large numbers of German forces were kept
there and cutting the numbers that would face the Allied troops
in Normandy.

The Double Cross deception, codenamed *Fortitude South*,
evolved rapidly during the early months of 1944, but the bare
bones of the plan remained the same. The Germans were to be
led to believe that the Normandy landings were a feint attack
aimed at drawing German forces away from the main thrust of
the Allied invasion, which would be against the Pas de Calais.
This would ensure that the bulk of the German forces would
be held back from the Normandy beaches, allowing the Allies
time to establish a strong foothold in northern France from
which they could break out towards Paris and then on to the
German border.

A completely mythical formation, the First United States Army Group (FUSAG), was supposedly commanded by Gen. George Patton, a hero of the invasion of Sicily and a man who the Germans would believe must be heavily involved in the invasion of Europe, as indeed he later would. FUSAG was supposedly grouped in East Anglia and south-eastern England and it was vital that the agents' reports were coordinated to show that this was the case, and to downplay the mass of troops waiting in the south and south-west to attack the German defences in Normandy.

The most spectacularly useful of the wireless agents deployed in the *Fortitude South* deception plan was the Spaniard Juan García Pujol, codename *Garbo*. He was an accomplished fraudster who originally offered his services to MI6 and was rejected as an obvious charlatan. Undaunted, he offered his services to the German *Abwehr* and agreed to go to England as a German spy. He then went not to London but to Lisbon where, armed with an out-of-date copy of *Jane's Fighting Ships* and a *Blue Guide to Great Britain*, he began feeding false intelligence to the Germans for cash. He was discovered by the British who, concerned that he might discredit their own operation, brought him to the UK and began running him back at the Germans under British control. *Garbo*'s network of agents, all of them completely fictitious, was so large and had become so vital to the overall deception picture that virtually everything had to be closely coordinated on a day-to-day basis. The most important of the other agents who, in the parlance of the Twenty Committee, 'came up for D-Day' was the triple agent *Brutus*. Roman Garby-Czerniawski, a Pole, had led the *Interallié* resistance network in France and, once it was uncovered, volunteered to work for the *Abwehr* in London in order to save the other members of his group from execution. On arrival in Britain he immediately told the authorities of his mission and was turned against the Germans. Two others should be mentioned as important to *Fortitude South*: the Yugoslav Dusko Popov, codenamed *Tricycle*, and *Treasure*, Natalie 'Lily' Sergueiv, a French citizen born in Russia whose family had fled in the wake of the Bolshevik revolution.

These four were the main agents used to build up *Fortitude South*, the false picture of the intended target of D-Day. *Tricycle* and *Brutus*, who was supposedly a member of a Polish unit attached to FUSAG, provided an order of battle for the fictitious formation so detailed that the Germans were not just supplied with details of individual units, strengths and locations, they were even given reproductions of the insignia painted on the side of the FUSAG vehicles.

Treasure's role was to report from the West Country that there were very few troops there, further pushing the Germans towards the view that the main thrust of the attack would be against the Pas de Calais. But she came close to blowing the whole plan. Sent to Lisbon to collect a radio set from the *Abwehr*, she told a former acquaintance she met in the street that she was now working for the British secret service. When she returned to London, she confessed to considering warning the *Abwehr* as retribution for the British refusal to allow her to bring her dog to the UK without going through quarantine. She was swiftly retired and replaced by an MI5 operator imitating her distinctive method of sending Morse and her loquacious messages. For several months after D-Day, the *Treasure* character was kept active for no other reason than that her messages were so long-winded that Bletchley Park was able to follow them through the *Abwehr* communications network and use them as cribs. Denys Page, who had taken over from Oliver Strachey as head of the ISOS section in early 1942, told Masterman that the cribs supplied by *Treasure* and *Brutus* had 'absolutely saved our bacon' after the Germans introduced more secure systems during 1944.

But by far the most important and complex role was played by *Garbo*. At one point, he had a network of twenty-seven supposed agents, some of whom still survived from his freelance period before the British recruited him. They included a Swiss businessman based in Bootle who had reported 'drunken orgies and slack morals in amusement centres' in Liverpool and an enthusiastic Venezuelan living in Glasgow who had noted the willingness of Clydeside dockers to 'do anything for a litre of wine'. The Swiss businessman died of cancer in the autumn of 1942. But his widow continued working for *Garbo*, becoming virtually his personal assistant. The Venezuelan also grew in stature becoming *Garbo's* official deputy and developing his own ring of agents in Scotland, one of whom was an ardent communist who actually believed he was working for the Soviet Union. The *Abwehr* codenamed this group of agents the Benedict Network. *Garbo's* mistress, a secretary working in the offices of the War Cabinet, provided useful opportunities for valuable pillow talk. She, like the wireless operator, believed that her lover was a Spanish Republican. *Garbo* had also successfully set up a large network of agents in Wales, mostly Welsh Nationalists but led by an ex-seaman, 'a thoroughly undesirable character' who was working for purely mercenary reasons. At this point, it is probably worth reminding the reader that none of these people actually existed.

Nevertheless, they all contributed to the German utter belief in *Garbo* as their most reliable source for intelligence on the Allied plans and set the scene for his key role in *Fortitude*. The German belief in the existence of FUSAG was steadily built up by a number of means apart from false reports from the double agents. Dummy invasion craft nicknamed 'Big Bobs' were left out in the open in east coast ports and mobile wireless vehicles travelled around south-east England broadcasting messages from a number of different locations to fool the German radio interception units.

So fantastic was *Garbo's* story that it would have been virtually impossible to imagine that the Germans would believe anything he said if it were not for the fact that, due to the breaking by Dilly Knox of the *Abwehr* Enigma, the British were able

to decypher the messages between the *Abwehr* headquarters and
Garbo's controller in Madrid. These showed that, as with the
Mincemeat deception, the Germans had swallowed it whole. This
was not just because *Garbo*'s story carefully fitted in with all the
other detail being sent by *Brutus*, *Tricycle*, *Treasure* and the other
double agents. It was also because it fitted in completely with
what the Germans were expecting, and that was known in detail
as a result of the intercepts of messages between von Rundstedt
and Hitler and between Oshima and his colleagues and their
government in Tokyo. All of these messages, decyphered at
Bletchley, were vital to the way in which the D-Day deception
was developed and carefully nurtured to ensure its success.

Throughout April and into May the intelligence from the
Japanese diplomats in Berlin and the *Jellyfish* link between von
Rundstedt and Berlin reaffirmed that the Germans believed the
main British attack would be on the Pas de Calais, although
there were also worrying occasional suggestions of an additional
attack on Normandy. Concerns over the German mentions of
Normandy led to a decision on 18 May to go all out on the
Fortitude South deception pointing to the main Allied landing
being on the Pas de Calais.

There were a series of assessments from von Rundstedt on the
Jellyfish link, broken with the aid of *Colossus*, which refined details
of the German defences and the strengths and capabilities of the
German forces. The *Jellyfish* link also included the complete order
of battle of the German armoured divisions drawn from the
detailed itinerary of a tour of inspection by the Inspector-General
of the German Armoured Forces General Heinz Guderian.

In early May, the Japanese naval attaché in Berlin made his
own tour of the German defences. Sent on the *Coral* cypher
machine – newly broken in a joint US/UK attack in which
Hugh Alexander had played a leading role – the naval attaché's
report was read at Bletchley. It was more authoritative than that
of Oshima, whose pro-German tendencies led him to accept
unquestioningly what he was told. Rommel, who had been

appointed to lead the main force resisting an invasion, intended 'to destroy the enemy near the coast, most of all on the beaches, without allowing them to penetrate any considerable distance inland,' the naval attaché said. 'As defence against airborne operations he plans to cut communications between seaborne and airborne troops and to destroy them individually.'

The number of staff at Bletchley Park had been dramatically increased in anticipation of the Allied invasion of Europe, reaching a total of 7,000 by June 1944. Morag Maclennan had by now been transferred out of the Bombe section into Hut 4, the Naval Section, where in the run-up to D-Day there was a minor security scare. 'The girl who was most closely concerned with the Normandy beach landings went up to the Admiralty and was fully briefed,' Maclennan said. '*Bigoted* was the name for anybody who was let into the great secret in the weeks leading up to D-Day. She was *bigoted* and immensely pleased with herself. We had this enormous map all the way down one wall of the coast of Holland right down to the south of France and she carefully underlined the beaches that they were going to land on. We were horrified at this and went along underlining every beach we could see from Holland down to France because the cleaners would come in and might notice.'

Tommy Flowers and his men at Dollis Hill were already working on an updated version of *Colossus*. 'The first processor contained 1,600 valves,' Flowers said. 'It worked, as designed, well enough, but we had not been able to make the processing fast enough, and with use we could see that it needed to be improved in several ways.' Flowers was told that if his new *Colossus* was not ready by the beginning of June, it would be no use at all, which he rightly assumed meant that D-Day was to be at the beginning of June.

> We worked flat out for four months and met the deadline, but only just. I was at Bletchley Park on that historic day and had been since the morning of the previous day, with a number of

other men, dealing with the last few difficulties that remained. In fact, the machine was fully ready for service for the first time during the small hours of the morning of 1 June.

The decyphering girls in the Big Room of Hut 8 went on night shift just before midnight on 4 June 1944, unaware that the Allied invasion was about to be launched, said Pat Wright.

They told us that D-Day was today and they wanted every possible message decoded as fast as possible. But then it was postponed because the weather was so bad and that meant we girls knew it was going to take place, so we had to stay there until D-Day. We slept where we could and worked when we could and of course then they set off on 6 June, and that was D-Day.

Although the heads of the main sections were all *bigoted* and most people at Bletchley Park knew that the invasion of Europe was imminent, even fairly senior staff were not told when it was to come. 'There was no point speculating when the balloon was going to go up,' said Bill Bundy.

So you didn't give day-to-day thought to it really and it just so happened that the evening of June 5 there was a long scheduled party. I'm sure there was a moment's thought given on high as to whether this ought to be kept and the instantaneous decision was that to cancel it would be far too much of a signal. So it went ahead and I remember we had a very pleasant group and drank martinis in which the role of vermouth was played by sherry and one had a really very nice time.

Anyway, at midnight those of us who were on the night shift reported to our sections to work, and there waiting in the outer room just outside the watch was the head of Hut 6, Stuart Milner-Barry. He had been at the party and he was just sort of standing there on one leg watching the whole proceeding and one said: 'Why is Stuart doing this at this hour?' So we went to work and suddenly about 3 o'clock there was a real rustle in the room that got the traffic first and it was patent that something was happening on a big scale. Very shortly the word spread that there had been German traffic in clear, saying that paratroopers were dropping all over the place and it happened to be nearer Calais than Normandy so I'm sure it was one of the deception operations. We later learned that they were not paratroopers, they were bunches of straw, something that would show up on the radar in the same way.

In the early hours of 6 June 1944, D-Day, *Garbo* made repeated attempts to warn his *Abwehr* controller that the Allied forces were on their way. This move was agreed by Allied commanders on the basis that it would be too late for the Germans to do anything about it but would ensure that they still believed in *Garbo* as their best-informed secret agent after the invasion had begun. As predicted it only served to increase their trust in him and paved the way for the next stage of the deception. Shortly after midnight on 9 June, as the Allied advance faltered and with the elite 1st SS *Panzer* division on its way from the Pas de Calais, together with another armoured division, to reinforce the German defences in Normandy, *Garbo* sent his most important message about the D-Day landings. Three of his agents were reporting troops massed across East Anglia and Kent and large numbers of troop and tank transporters waiting in the eastern ports.

After personal consultation on 8 June in London with my agents *Donny*, *Dick* and *Derrick*, whose reports I sent today, I am of the opinion, in view of the strong troop concentrations in south-east and east England, that these operations are a diversionary manoeuvre designed to draw off enemy reserves in order to make an attack at another place. In view of the continued air attacks on the concentration area mentioned, which is a strategically favourable position for this, it may very probably take place in the Pas de Calais area.

Garbo's warning went straight to Hitler who ordered the two divisions back to the Pas de Calais to defend against what he expected to be the main invasion thrust and awarded Pujol the Iron Cross. Had the two divisions continued to Normandy, the Allies might well have been thrown back into the sea. On 11 June, Bletchley Park decyphered a message from Berlin to *Garbo*'s controller in Madrid saying that *Garbo*'s reports 'have been confirmed almost without exception and are to be described as especially valuable. The main line of investigation in future is to be the enemy group of forces in south-eastern and eastern England.' Only the messages decyphered from the *Abwehr* Enigma could have provided Allied commanders with that sort of high-level reassurance that the deception was working.

The importance of the *Abwehr* Enigma and the *Jellyfish* link in confirming the D-Day deception cannot be overstated. One of Telford Taylor's Special Branch intelligence officers, Don Bussey, said:

> *Ultra* made a tremendous contribution to the success of the deception planning for the Normandy landing because we were able to follow through *Ultra* not only what the German forces were doing but also that *Fortitude* was working so well. The Germans still believed well into July that Patton had an Army in south-eastern England that was going to come across to Pas de Calais so they couldn't send reinforcements to Normandy. This is a very important aspect of how *Ultra* contributed to strategic consideration. That's big stuff and not to be minimised.

Brigadier Bill Williams, who was Montgomery's intelligence officer during the invasion of Europe, said that no army ever went to war better informed about the enemy.

> Intelligence officers at BP were briefed before D-Day and thereafter we made it our business in Normandy to send a daily ISUM [Intelligence Summary] from 21 Army Group

saying what we thought was happening in front of us and in general attempting in a friendly and unofficial fashion to keep the Park aware of what we were trying to do. The whole series of signals was conversational. One felt one was talking to friends and from that feeling of gratitude which we hoped was reflected in the casually worded terms sent to the Park emerged at least from the point of view of one consumer, a belief that because of them he was getting a better service. The people at the other end knew what he wanted and there seemed to be no hesitation in the answer. G (R), the staff branch responsible for deception and cover plans, was more dependent on *Ultra* than any of the rest of us. It was the only source revealing the enemy's reaction to a cover plan. Without *Ultra* we should never have known. In the case of *Fortitude South* (the Pas de Calais cover plan) it is arguable that without *Ultra* confirmation that it was selling, it might have been dropped.

Senior administrators at Bletchley Park were very well aware that some of the young men working there wondered whether they shouldn't be fighting alongside their friends and relatives, who were now thrust into the thick of battle. Eric Jones, the head of Hut 3, the military and air intelligence reporting section, told his staff that the work they were doing might not be so dangerous but it was just as important to the war effort. One recent report sent out by Hut 3 had shown that enemy dispositions in the Cotentin peninsula in Normandy had changed. US paratroopers from the 82nd Airborne had been due to drop in the area around La Haye du Puits on the west of the Cotentin peninsula, but a Bletchley decrypt showed in late May that several German divisions had moved into the area and that any landing there would have had disastrous consequences. The resultant change to 82nd Airborne's dropping zone had saved the lives of up to 15,000 men, Jones said.

At this moment, in far the biggest combined operation in

history, the first of the airborne troops are down. Sailors and airmen are facing frightful dangers to transport the first ground troops across the Channel and protect them on their way; more sailors and airmen are daring everything to blast holes in the German defences; and the ground troops themselves, in their thousands, will soon be literally throwing away their lives in the main assault by deliberately drawing enemy fire so that others may gain a foothold; and we are in complete, or almost complete, safety; some of us are even enjoying something akin to peacetime comfort. It's a thought we cannot avoid and it's a thought that inevitably aggravates an ever-present urge to be doing something more active; to be nearer the battle, sharing at least some of its discomforts and dangers. Such feelings cannot be obliterated, but they can be subjugated to a grim resolve to serve those men to the very utmost of our capacity. There is no back-stage organisation (and I think of Hut 3, Hut 6, Sixta and the *Fish* Party as an indissoluble whole) that has done more for past Allied operations and Allied plans for this assault; and none that can contribute more to the development of the invasion once the bloody battles for the beaches have been won.

Amid concern at the damage the U-Boats might inflict on the invasion forces, Frank Birch had arranged for a number of Royal Navy radio intercept positions to be set up in Bletchley Park. All signals indicating danger to the invasion force were dispatched from the Hut 4 'Z' Watch on what was known as a 'Rush' basis and the OIC was normally able to pass them on to the naval escorts within thirty minutes of the Germans sending them. Birch's initiative was the first and only time that any messages were actually intercepted at Bletchley Park.

'This step was taken with some hesitation in view of the risk associated in having GC&CS associated with masts and aerials,' said Harry Hinsley.

But it was fully justified by the exceptional speed with which the Naval Enigma was decrypted during the crucial days in which the assault forces were crossing the Channel and getting ashore. We were able to watch the expedition going across as well as getting the first German response. We quickly realised they weren't expecting invasion and as soon as the assault waves were ashore we started reading all the emergency messages from the German navy and sending them straight on to the invasion force leaders in their command ships off the beaches. Throughout the assault phase the average time-lag between the interception of the German signals and the delivery of the decrypts to the OIC was to be thirty minutes during those large parts of each day in which the Enigma keys were being decrypted currently.

Within forty-eight hours of the initial landings, the first of twenty-eight British and American Special Liaison Units set up to pass the *Ultra* intelligence on to the Allied commanders were reporting through their Special Communications Units that their positions were secure and they were ready to receive and pass on the reports from Bletchley.

'Shortly after the Normandy landings, I was assigned to the European theatre to be one of the field representatives handling the *Ultra* information with the US military command, both air force and Army,' said Don Bussey.

All US commands had these *Ultra* representatives who would ensure the security of this information and that it was handled in the proper way. I had a Special Communications Unit manned by British officers, both Army and RAF, that supported me, and they were the ones who would receive the messages over the air from Bletchley Park. It's very important to realise that day in, day out, the most important thing that *Ultra* had to tell us was the complete German order of battle. We would know their divisions by number. We would know where they were. We would know their subordinations by corps and army and by army group. We'd know the boundaries between division and between other units, and all this gave us the kind of information which is absolutely indispensable. I would process all this information and pass it on to the people at headquarters who were authorised to receive it.

The mobile Y Service units were already producing large amounts of information about the German reaction. In conjunction with Bletchley Park, they produced the position of one of the most important German headquarters, allowing the British to mount a series of air strikes that put paid to a counter-attack which would have driven a gap between the American and British armies.

'One of the very first things that was noticeable was that there was a radio station very busy indeed in Normandy, near the front,' said Ralph Bennett, one of the Hut 3 intelligence reporters.

Now Y service could locate this place exactly and could monitor the number of signals coming in and out; it was obviously a very important headquarters. But on 10 June, Enigma revealed that it was the headquarters of *Panzergruppe West*, the headquarters of all the tanks in the invasion area. Monty knocked it out for three weeks and lots of the senior staff officers were killed.

There were gaps in the information provided by *Ultra*. The codebreakers were unable to provide a precise location for 32nd *Panzer* Division, which was defending the vital British objective of Caen and held up Montgomery's advance for more than a month. They had also missed the presence of a German infantry division defending Omaha beach. But these were the only blank spaces in an otherwise complete and detailed picture of the German order of battle.

Although the *Red* Enigma remained a constant source of

intelligence until July 1944, when the Germans realised it was compromised, Army Enigma circuits began to be broken and as the Allied invasion wore on Army Enigma networks became more important than their *Luftwaffe* counterparts. There was a major potential problem when von Rundstedt's *Fish* link to Berlin became temporarily unreadable.

'Until D-Day, they changed the wheel patterns once a month,' said Art Levenson.

> So once you had them recovered, you were in. But after we invaded, they changed the patterns every day, so the job became much more difficult. We went to the boss Edward Travis and said: 'We need four more *Colossi* because they're changing the patterns too often.' He went to Churchill who said: 'Anything they want.' So we got the four new *Colossi* and they were absolutely necessary. We used them to recover the links, which we never would have done without them.

On 20 July, a group of senior Army officers, among them Colonel Claus von Stauffenberg, attempted to assassinate Hitler. Stauffenberg took a bomb, hidden in a briefcase, to a staff conference at the Rastenberg *Führer HQ* and placed it under the table. As soon as he heard the explosion and unaware that Hitler had escaped serious injury, he left for Berlin to tell the generals planning the military takeover that the *Führer* was dead.

Alex Dakin said one of his most vivid memories from Bletchley was being on duty in the Hut 4 'Z' Watch 'when not much was happening'. The messages coming into the Watch in the wire tray by which messages were passed from Hut 8 'were nothing exciting – but then in the next almost empty tray, one of the most exciting messages ever.'

The message read: *OKM AN ALLE EINSATZ WALKUERE NUR DURCH OFFIZIER ZU ENTZIFFERN OFFIZIER DORA DER FUEHRER ADOLF HITLER IST TOT DER NEUE FUEHRER IST FELDMARSCHALL VON WITZLEBEN…*

'Naval Headquarters to all. *Operation Valkyrie*. Officer only
to decypher. Officer setting Dora [D]. The *Führer* Adolf Hitler
is dead. The new *Führer* is Field Marshal von Witzleben.'

Sadly, Hitler wasn't dead. By 11 o'clock that night, the
attempted military coup was over and von Stauffenberg and a
number of other senior officers had been executed.

As the Allied forces poured into Normandy, they had been
held back by heavy German resistance, orchestrated by Field
Marshal Günther von Kluge. But at the beginning of August,
the American 12th Army Group under General Omar Bradley
swept south though Avranches turning west into Brittany and
eastwards behind the German tanks.

'I remember after the invasion there was a long period
of time when Montgomery's forces and the US forces under
General Bradley were being built up,' said Selmer Norland, one
of the Americans working in Hut 3.

> Units were being ferried across the Channel and, after they
> captured the initial bridgeheads, they were sort of pinned
> down for quite a long period of time while this build-up was
> taking place. And I remember a particular night when I was
> working on a message and some German unit reported that
> the American tank spearheads were in the outskirts of Rennes.
> I told the Army adviser who was on duty at the time and we
> dashed for a map to find out where Rennes was. We were
> astonished to find that it was almost all the way across the
> Brittany peninsula.

Convinced of his own infallibility as a military strategist, Hitler
now decided that von Kluge should force his way through to the
western Normandy coast at Avranches, cutting the American thrust
in half. 'We must strike like lightning,' he told his chiefs of staff.

> When we reach the sea the American spearheads will be cut
> off. We might even be able to cut off their entire beachhead.

We must not get bogged down in cutting off the Americans who have broken through. Their turn will come later. We must wheel north like lightning and turn the entire enemy front from the rear.

There was certainly an element of reason in the idea but with more than a million Allied troops now firmly established in Normandy, von Kluge had little hope of carrying it out and, far worse, with Montgomery's 21st Army Group pressing down on him from the north and the Americans sweeping westwards along his southern flank, he risked becoming trapped in an Allied pincer movement.

The Allies, fully informed by Bletchley Park of the German plans, ensured the initiative failed. As von Kluge's counterattack faltered with its only route of retreat through a small gap south of the town of Falaise, Hitler insisted that it should be carried through to the bitter end. 'On its success depends the fate of the Battle of France,' Hitler said in a message sent in the early hours of 10 August and decyphered in Hut 6 almost immediately. 'Objective of the attack, the sea at Avranches, to which a bold and unhesitating thrust through is to be made.'

John Prestwich was on duty in Hut 3 when Hitler's orders came through the hatch from Hut 6.

I remember it. My goodness I remember it. I remember we queried it at the time. We said: 'It cannot be true.' It seemed to us inconceivable. But what made sense was that the Americans had broken out of their base in the Cotentin peninsula and the Germans had made what was a perfectly sensible limited spoiling attack on the American lines of communication. Then there came through this detailed order that four or five German armoured divisions were to go hell for leather for Avranches and this opened up the whole possibility of wiping out the cream of the German armed forces. All you had to do was to close the Falaise Gap and there was this great pocket. But it was an order from Hitler. The German generals might have thought it was lunatic, and Rommel clearly did on at least one occasion, but they obeyed on the spot because they were under oath.

Within a few days, it was clear that von Kluge had no hope of carrying out Hitler's orders and, fearing that at any moment the Allies would surround his forces, he ordered the withdrawal. Susan Wenham was one of the codebreakers on duty in Hut 6 on duty on 16 August when von Kluge's orders came through.

> It was the most exciting night I had. The Germans were making plans to make their last terrific push to try to get out of the pincer they were in. I was on the night shift and the day shift had had an enormous message. They came in sections; they weren't allowed to do them more than a certain length. It was a ten-part message and only six of the parts of the message, the *Teile*, came through. They had managed to break those during the day and the message was to say how the Germans were planning to get out of this impasse. Then during the night, a very obvious re-encodement of this came in, all ten of the parts, and we could see by looking at it that it was a word-for-word re-encodement, which was absolutely not allowed. So we let Hut 3 know and we got all the Bombes cleared. We worked like mad on this thing during the night and by morning it was all put through and finished. So that was a very exciting night.

Allied timidity allowed 300,000 German soldiers to escape from the Falaise Pocket, but a further 250,000 were either killed or captured. With the Germans now in full retreat, the Allies poured out of Normandy towards the the Belgian and German borders. Paris was liberated on 25 August as Montgomery's 21st Army Group raced towards Belgium, heading for the Ruhr and, with the newspaper headlines trumpeting 'Berlin by Christmas', an unwarranted level of over-confidence set in.

The intelligence supplied by Bletchley Park had proved invaluable to the Allied generals, giving them a comprehensive picture of their opponents' positions and plans. But now the picture coming out of Hut 3 seemed to contradict that suggested by the speed of the breakout from Normandy and the race across northern France.

Montgomery's reputation had been built on the back of the codebreakers' advance knowledge of Rommel's plans in North Africa. But he ignored their reports that Hitler had ordered his troops to maintain control of the Scheldt estuary. This typically arrogant decision to disregard the *Ultra* intelligence was to lead to a major defeat for the British on the banks of the Rhine. Anxious to beat the Americans to Berlin, Montgomery pushed on into Holland to mount *Operation Market Garden*, a three-stage airborne offensive with landings at Eindhoven, Nijmegen and Arnhem, the infamous bridge too far.

'Elements retreating from the pocket in August and September filled the air with reports of their movements and strength,' said Ralph Bennett.

> Among much else these showed that II SS *Panzer* Corps was to refit in the general area of Arnhem where Montgomery was planning to make a bridgehead across the lower Rhine. So firmly entrenched however was the conviction that German resistance was nearing its end that this knowledge was not enough to cast doubt on the wisdom of launching *Operation Market Garden*.

Although the American airborne troops dropped onto Eindhoven and Nijmegen secured their positions and managed to link up with the main advance, the British 1st Airborne Division which was to seize a bridgehead across the Rhine at Arnhem was not so fortunate. It succeeded in capturing the only surviving bridge across the Rhine and held it for several days, expecting reinforcements to arrive at any minute. But surrounded by vastly superior forces from two SS *Panzer* divisions, the British paratroopers were eventually forced to withdraw. Only 2,200 of the 10,000-strong division managed to get out.

'It should have been no surprise that 9 and 10 SS *Panzer* Divisions were encountered somewhere between Eindhoven and Arnhem,' said Bennett.

> *Ultra* had placed them in this general area with certainty over ten days before *Market Garden*, although it had not located them precisely. The *Ultra* evidence was amply strong enough to shake the confidence of men with minds as open as they had been on D-Day, but the high command had lately become so over-confident that it was allowing itself to spend more time in disputes over future strategy than in studying the ground immediately under its own feet.

Yet even the mistake over Arnhem failed to dissuade the Allied generals from their over-optimistic belief that the Germans were finished and that there was little they could do to slow the advance on Berlin. They continued to ignore the evidence of the *Ultra* decrypts which now pointed to a major counter-attack being prepared in the Ardennes.

Jim Rose, one of the Hut 3 air advisers, and Alan Pryce-Jones, one of the military advisers, flew to SHAEF headquarters in Paris in November and briefed General Kenneth Strong, Eisenhower's intelligence officer, on the *Ultra* decrypts.

> Strong had a very weak chin. He said: 'This is the way we read it. Right across the front from the North Sea really to Switzerland the Germans are losing a division a day and this can't be maintained. They're bound to crack.' Alan Pryce-Jones was just a major. He had his own form of battledress, he wore suede shoes. He just sort of sat on the corner of the desk and he said to Strong: 'My dear sir, if you believe that you'll believe anything.' Three weeks later was the Ardennes offensive.

The warning signs that the Germans were planning a major counter-attack were not as obvious from *Ultra* as they had been at times during the war. Nevertheless, there was no failure of intelligence collection, simply a lack of long-term analysis of German intentions born out of the belief that the war was virtually over, said Ralph Bennett.

> The high-ups on our side became convinced that the Germans were weakened by their failures and they couldn't do anymore. By that time we'd got too damn cocky. I still don't understand and I don't think I shall understand, how it was that sign after sign that they were planning something was ignored. Who knows what it was, we never did know until it happened. They [the Germans] never told us. They were getting very security conscious by then. Time after time, we simply neglected to add two and two together and say well it might make a total of four rather than seventeen and a quarter.

The clearest evidence from the codebreakers came in decrypts of the messages from the Japanese diplomatic representatives in Berlin to their bosses in Tokyo which spoke of 'the coming offensive'. But there was plenty more besides, said Bennett.

> The evidence about what turned out to be the Battle of the Bulge began in September 1944 and went on until 16 December when the attack happened. If anybody had ever thought of putting all the bits of information together they would surely have come to the conclusion that there was going to be an attack.
>
> We had continual signals recording that the rest of the *Panzer* divisions were moving across from the Rhineland into Belgium and no one was saying: 'Why are they doing all this? That's very funny: it happens to be just the area where Ike and Bradley have put our defences at their thinnest.' Because the Ardennes is very difficult countryside, Bradley had weakened

that front, put the least trained divisions there because it was most unlikely they'd be involved in urgent operations. Damn it, Rommel and 7th *Panzer* Division had gone through there in 1940. Easily the most striking evidence was that the Germans had just brought in the ME262s, the first jet aircraft, and these ME262s, the latest, fastest kind of aircraft were making almost daily aerial reconnaissance of the same area, the area in front of the Ardennes, over and over again every day. No one seems to have thought: 'This is rather a rum thing.' So consequently we were deceived into thinking there was nothing going to happen, and when I say we, I don't mean Hut 3, I mean the British. It never occurred to us to think that something might happen down there.

Hitler intended a massive armoured attack to rip through the Allied forces, splitting them in two before recapturing Antwerp and cutting off their lines of supply. It was a massive gamble. Hitler's attempted reprise of his earlier *Blitzkrieg* assault was checked by the Americans, first at St Vith, and then, fatally for the Germans, by the US 101st Airborne Division at the Battle of Bastogne. His refusal to shift the weight of the attack to that part of 'the Bulge' in the German lines that was making most forward progress prevented his tanks from overrunning the Allied fuel depots to replenish their supplies and within four weeks the counter-attack had run out of steam.

The Battle of the Bulge was a massive defeat for the Germans, who lost 120,000 men, killed, wounded or captured, compared to a little over half that figure for the Americans. But it had held up the Allied advance by around six weeks. 'Hut 3 was asked to do a post-mortem,' said Jim Rose. 'It was done by Peter Calvocoressi and F. L. Lucas. It was an extremely good report and showed the failure of intelligence at SHAEF and at the Air Ministry.'

The Germans had dropped the complications to the Lorenz machine by October 1944, easing the problems faced in the

Newmanry and Testery, and in January 1945, as the Allies advanced towards the Rhine, a new intercept station for *Fish* was set up at Genval, near Brussels. Kenworthy recalled:

> This was the only station connected with Knockholt which received any damage from enemy action. A V1 dropped very close to the building rendering it unserviceable. Very little damage was done to the gear and it was then installed in the wireless transmitter vans. The Brussels station moved up later in the year with the 21st Army Group advance.

Colossus was constantly updated as new variants were introduced and by the end of the war, there were around ten *Colossi* actually operational, said Donald Michie, another member of the Newmanry.

> Each one was like a very big wardrobe in size and the place looked almost like an aircraft hangar. At the end, it was looking like a scene that you didn't see again until about 1960 with huge main-frames all over the place, the whole thing going flat out around the clock, twenty-four hours a day, 365 days round the year, a total staff of 300 Wrens, maybe fifty on duty on any particular shift, and a duty officer taking decisions. Very often when things got really hot, in the sense of being on to something which had been resisting, you would work on. So that there would be people who were officially on shift and people who weren't but just couldn't tear themselves away and would catch another transport out of the place and flop in their digs for a few hours and then come back again. They were very exciting times.

By now Bletchley Park had little effect on the Allied advance across Germany although its intelligence on the V-weapon launch sites at Peenemünde and the ISOS traffic carrying the reports of the Double Cross agents was invaluable in *Operation*

Crossbow, the effort to counter the last-ditch German bombard-ment of London.

The double agents were repeatedly being asked for infor-mation on where the missiles were falling. The mean point of impact of the V-weapons was in south-east London, four miles short of their target. But by carefully manipulating the times and locations of the blasts reported back by the double agents in conjunction with the times of the launches reported by an RAF Y station sent to the continent to monitor them, the Double Cross Committee persuaded the Germans that they were overshooting and the range of the V-weapons was shortened, moving the danger still further out of London.

As the threat from the Germans receded, increasing numbers of people were moved on to Japanese codes and cyphers and new recruits arrived, many of them Wrens like Rosemary Calder, who was put to work in the Japanese Navy traffic analysis section which was run by the Cambridge historian Sir John Plumb.

'I was interviewed by Jack Plumb who told me, "We analyse traffic",' said Calder.

I had no idea what this meant. I had this picture in my mind of people sat on camp stools by the side of the road count-ing lorries and gun carriages. I spent most of my time at BP, attached to the room of which Angus Wilson the famous novel-ist was head. We considered ourselves to be a small exclusive group who were all given scope for initiative and intelligence despite the bulk of the work (as I recall) being of a repetitive clerical nature. Any of us could do any of the jobs in the office. It was a very democratic place. Wrens mixed up with civilians. We might as well as not been in uniform. We were having a marvellous time. It was like being back at college. Angus was a great darling who spoilt us all and we spoilt him in return. He called us all Ducky and he had this special friend called Bentley Bridgewater who took over the traffic analysis section from Jack Plumb and later went on to become Secretary of the British Museum. Angus was known to be very brilliant but crazy. He had at least one nervous breakdown before I got there and was still going to Oxford to see a psychiatrist, writing all his dreams down. But he was very good-natured most of the time and if he started getting agitated, we would just give him a copy of *Vogue* or *Tatler* and he could go off and sit down by the lake flicking through it and come back as happy as a sandboy.

Anne Petrides, another of the young Wrens in Hut 7, worked on an index of merchant shipping movements.

I joined Naval Section at BP the day after my eighteenth birthday 'celebrated' at the WRNS training centre at Mill Hill on 31 May 1944 and was flung into the work of cataloguing ships, entering brief notes on their cards about the decoded signals as they came to us from the translations. Most of their warships had been sunk by then and we were dealing with *Maru* – merchant ships. The naval officers in my office included Gorley Putt and 'Shrimp' Hordern, brother of Michael Hordern, the actor. As a very young girl, I was petrified to be left all alone at lunchtime, in four interconnecting rooms – and in fact justifiably so, as a senior officer from the Admiralty phoned and said 'Can we go over...' followed by a burble of words. He came back in clear language and was outraged to find that not only had no one seen fit to tell me which button to press for the scrambler but that no 'duty officer' was present. A regular visitor from 'down the passage', usually on quieter night watches was Angus Wilson, the novelist. His first book of stories was said to have originated in a series of sessions he had with a psychiatrist. I believe the men cracked more easily under the strain whereas girls found it easier to have a crying breakdown. We Wrens were extremely spoilt in our accommodation, nothing but the best country houses in the area, including Woburn Abbey, while the

ATS lived in barracks at the back of the Park. I started out at Wavendon House. Then I lived at Stockgrove Park. It had been rather knocked about by the 51st Highland Division which had been there before us. I remember dances attended by locally billeted GIs and drinking draught cider, very heady.

Olive Humble, one of the Temporary Women Assistants drafted in to work on Japanese cyphers, was put into another sub-section of Hut 7. She had been called up in early 1943 for the WRNS but there were no places and she found herself sent off instead to the Foreign Office as a civil servant.

So in February 1943 I arrived at BP and was escorted to the Billeting Office by an armed soldier, to my great consternation. I had never left home before, having worked in an insurance office in the City when I left school. I was suitably impressed with my new surroundings, until I saw the Mansion, which no one can say is beautiful to the eye. I was parcelled off to a Commander Thatcher, a fierce naval man who put the fear of God into me. He informed me that I was in the Japanese Naval Section, which confused me even further, that from then on I would not be allowed to leave the Park other than through death or disablement, that if I said one word of what I or anyone else was doing, even to my nearest and dearest, I would get thirty years without the option. He stood over me while I digested the Official Secrets Act, and dutifully signed it.

My billet was in Bedford – the lady of the house was not a willing billetor, and for the few months I was there she made my life miserable, I was turned out in the evenings as I was in the way, and so roamed round Bedford which was manned by the American Army Air Force. I was petrified. Later I made a friend in another part of my Section and we joined forces and went to another billet again in Bedford, to a Mr & Mrs Buick, who had two children. They were completely and absolutely magnificent, never probed, always there for us.

Olive was put to work on the JN40 Merchant Shipping Code which had been broken by British codebreakers working at Kilindini in Kenya.

One half was manned by a host of civilian women, who seemed to be dealing with coloured flimsy sheets of paper. I never did know what they did. The other half of the room was manned by the Navy, and there we went. I was put on to three shifts immediately, the civvies were always on days, and I found myself sitting at a table with six to eight Wrens. In the centre of the room was the boss Major W. E. Martin, he was older than us of course, and looked after his youngsters like a benevolent father. At the other end were three or four Navy boys. All were young and bright, and I was quite happy, as I had really wanted to join the Wrens. We put the five-figure blocks, typed on flimsy paper, into clear English letters from pads, and constructed clear messages, such as: 'Otaru Maru leaving Manila at 0200 hrs for Singapore arrives such and such.' These messages were then passed to Major Martin, who I suppose with hindsight passed them on. We didn't know what was happening in any other part of the section, the need to know syndrome was very much to the fore.

The social life at BP was for me rather mixed, as being on shift work did curtail it to a certain extent. When I did get enough time off, in between shifts, I would remain in Bedford, sometimes with a Wren, whose name I have forgotten but who introduced me to Mozart. She would drag me into her favourite music shop, and we would land in the booths and listen to records, my recollection of hearing *Eine Kleine Nachtmusik* for the first time is still very vivid. I met some odd characters there. One was a very brainy lad, who could only work well while under the influence of whisky, so the caring FO provided him with a bottle a day or equivalent, until he broke and was taken away. I remember passing him in the corridors, always dressed in a pin-stripe suit, papers under his arm, muttering to himself, and a strong smell of malt wafting by with him. Another bright specimen divested himself of all his clothing and galloped round the lake with the Army in hot pursuit, cheered on by we spectators on the banks, and the Wrens rowing lustily on the lake.

CHAPTER 12

AN EXTRAORDINARY GROUP OF PEOPLE

As the Allies advanced across western Europe towards Berlin, and German commanders and radio operators came under increasing pressure, the Army Enigma keys finally began to be broken on a more regular basis and, by March 1945, Hut 6 was breaking more Army Enigma than *Luftwaffe* Enigma for the first time in the war. The effect of the battle on Army units forced them to use communications to a far greater extent and limited the number of Enigma keys they could use, leading to productive breaks into *Bantam*, the key used by the German Commander-in-Chief in the West; *Duck*, the German 7th Army's key; and *Puffin*, the main key in use between Berlin and German forces in Italy, which also produced important intelligence on German intentions on the western front. Inevitably, as units came under pressure in battle there were a lot more plain language communications that helped to provide cribs.

Despite new German security measures, improved *Colossus* computers ensured continued coverage of the *Jellyfish* encyphered teleprinter link between the western front and Berlin and the *Bream* link between Italy and Berlin, which was also producing high-grade intelligence on German intentions in the West. Although individual U-Boats began using unique keys, Hut 8 continued to break the main *Shark* and *Dolphin* keys and as a result increasing numbers of U-Boats were sunk, leading to their withdrawal from the English Channel. Increased captures of cypher material and the sheer pressure of battle ensured that the improved German security measures failed to prevent Bletchley from producing vital intelligence to the very last.

'The new German security measures of all kinds might, properly handled, have virtually stopped the flow of operational intelligence from Hut 6 to Hut 3,' said J. M. 'Max' Aitken, the official historian of Hut 6.

Very largely through German mistakes, this result was never achieved. This is not to say that our success was unaffected but on the whole the luck of Hut 6 held good and to the end we decoded currently most of the vital operational traffic. On the Army side, in particular, 1944 witnessed an immense advance. Though we should not forget the valuable intelligence provided by the African Army keys in 1942–43, still Hut 3 had never previously seen Army traffic of such high quality as on the best keys of 1944 – the *Bantams*, *Ducks* and *Puffins*. The importance of Army keys relative to Air constantly increased and towards the end when the Air difficulties were most acute the Army decodes sometimes surpassed the Air in number as well as quality. This was of course a reversal of the situation that prevailed for most of the war, but the Army experts who had in general the hardest cryptographic tasks cannot be grudged this final hour of triumph. In 1944–45, first Italy, then the West, finally even the East was held in fee and, on the Army as on the Air, the cryptographic encirclement of Germany was complete.

Asa Briggs, later the distinguished official historian of the BBC but then just another of the students pulled in from Sidney Sussex, Cambridge, to work in Hut 6, was on duty in the early hours of 7 May 1944, his twenty-fourth birthday, when one of the most important messages of the war was received. There was no need to decypher it, it was in plain text.

I was working in the Watch on Monday 7 May, my birthday, when I received and passed on to Hut 3 a message in clear from Grand Admiral Dönitz, Commander-in-Chief of the German

Navy and Hitler's successor, saying that Germany had surrendered unconditionally. This was one of many messages in clear received in Hut Six during the last days of the war. I felt that I was participating in history as I received it and passed it on with a mingled sense of excitement and relief.

Stuart Milner-Barry, the head of Hut 6, recalled that the content of the message

was known all over the Hut on the night shift. It is worth recording, I think, that my appeal to all rooms that it should not be passed on to the day shift was honoured in full, and that the first news they had was in the public announcement, after lunch, on the German wireless. That seems to me of its kind to be one of the most remarkable episodes in our history.

The need for utter secrecy had not disappeared with the fall of Germany. With the war against Japan still continuing and a new Cold War with Russia already anticipated, Travis hammered that message home in a 'special order' to the staff congratulating them on their work against Germany.

On this historic occasion I want to express my personal thanks to all of you for your loyal cooperation in our common effort to defeat the enemy. The general standards of keenness, discipline, personal behaviour and security have been admirable and have combined to produce a direct and substantial contribution towards winning the war. But our work is by no means ended yet. Three main problems face us now: to finish off the Japanese war; to ease the transition from war to peace conditions as much as possible for everyone; to ensure that nothing we do now shall hinder the efforts of our successors. I cannot stress too strongly the necessity for the maintenance of security. While we were fighting Germany it was vital that the enemy should never know of our activities here. We and our American allies are still at war with Japan, and we are faced with great responsibilities arising out of the preliminaries to peace in Europe. At some future time, we may be called upon again to use the same methods. It is therefore as vital as ever not to relax from the high standard of security that we have hitherto maintained. The temptation now to 'own up' to our friends and families as to what our work has been is a very real and natural one. It must be resisted absolutely.

Seven weeks later, on 28 June, the head of the armed forces Field Marshal Sir Alan Brooke visited Bletchley Park to thank the codebreakers for their work. He was accompanied by the First Sea Lord, Admiral of the Fleet Sir Andrew Cunningham, the victor at Matapan. Malcolm Kennedy recorded the event in his diary.

A great day at Bletchley Park, the Combined Chiefs of Staff paying a visit to express their thanks and appreciation of our work. [Air Chief Marshal Sir Arthur] Tedder, unfortunately, was prevented at the last moment from coming, but Sir Alan Brooke and Admiral Cunningham both came, and Brooke made a speech on behalf of all three. It is pleasant to have one's work recognised in this way by the powers-that-be; and some of the examples he quoted to show how valuable our work had been were of great historical interest although, unfortunately, they are not of a kind that can ever be made public.

The war against Japan continued with Japanese codes and cyphers broken by British codebreakers at Bletchley, in Delhi and in Colombo, until the dropping of the atomic bombs on Hiroshima and Nagasaki in August 1945. Even before the news that an atomic bomb had been dropped on Hiroshima was officially announced, the Japanese messages arriving in Hut 7 at Bletchley Park provided a frightening vision of what had happened. 'I was on a day watch by myself and all this stuff came in and it was total gibberish,' said Rosemary Calder. 'I didn't know the bomb had been dropped but you could tell from the disruption of all the messages that something terrible had happened. You could just feel the people standing there screaming their heads off.'

Later messages were more specific. An Army-Air message sent to the chief of staff of the General Army Air Command in Tokyo and decyphered at Bletchley Park gave one of the first descriptions of the now familiar mushroom cloud associated with the atomic bomb. 'There was a blinding flash and a violent blast – over the city centre, the flash and burst were almost simultaneous but in the vicinity of the airfield the blast came two or three seconds later – and a mass of white smoke billowing up into the air.'

Messages decyphered previously by British and US code-breakers had shown that the Japanese would have surrendered before the bombs were dropped if the Allies had been prepared to assure them that the Emperor could remain on the throne. Given that they received this assurance in the subsequent peace deal, it is impossible to comprehend why the horrors of Hiroshima and Nagasaki were inflicted on the Japanese.

❧

Churchill called the codebreakers 'the geese that laid the golden eggs and never cackled' and it was not until the mid-1970s that the lifetime ban on them disclosing that they worked there was lifted. Olive Humble was on leave from the Hut 7 Naval Section when Japan surrendered in August 1945.

> I came back to Bletchley Park two days later to find all the civilians had shipped out. I was sent to the fearsome Commander Thatcher, who lectured me again about keeping my mouth shut for all time, had to re-sign the Official Secrets Act, and

was threatened with the thirty years and or firing squad if I went off the straight and narrow.

But like many of the people who worked at Bletchley Park, Humble had spent the war in what was seen as a 'cushy billet' unable to tell even her parents what she was doing.

> One thing I regret deeply. I was an only child, on my first day home my father at dinner said: 'What do you do at the Foreign Office?' I replied: 'I cannot tell you sorry, please don't ask me again' – and he didn't, nor did my mother at any time. She died in the early 1960s and he in 1976, before I realised the silence had been lifted.

The contribution made by the codebreakers to the allied victory is truly incalculable. Bletchley Park did not win the war. No single organisation could make that claim. Certainly not of a war that was fought all too often by soldiers killing and dying by the bullet or bayonet. But Bletchley Park's contribution to the allied victory was enormous. While intelligence was passed intermittently to British officers during the German invasions of Norway and France, and might have helped in small ways, it made no real contribution in either of those campaigns. It was not until late 1940 and the *Blitz* that Bletchley made its first substantial contribution to the British war effort. The breaking by Hut 6 of the *Brown* Enigma cypher allowed Bletchley to predict the targets and routes of the *Luftwaffe* bombers, which ensured that RAF fighter aircraft could ambush them on their way to their targets and that the authorities on the ground could anticipate and prepare for the raids, limiting the numbers of deaths and amount of damage so far as was possible.

The Royal Navy victory over the Italian fleet at Matapan in March 1941 was just one of a number of individual incidents where Bletchley played a direct result in the allied victory. While the extensive knowledge of German intentions in the Balkans that derived from the *Ultra* intelligence produced by Bletchley did not prevent the German occupation of Greece in mid-1941, it did allow an orderly British withdrawal. Intelligence from Bletchley on German and resistance operations in the Balkans also played a key role in persuading Churchill to back the Yugoslav Partisan leader Tito rather than the Royalist resistance leader Draža Mihailović.

The second half of 1941 saw Hut 8 make the breakthrough on the *Dolphin* Enigma key used by the U-Boats attacking the trans-Atlantic convoys, allowing the Admiralty's Operational Intelligence Centre to re-route the convoys around the U-Boat Wolf Packs. Despite the ten-month 'blackout' after the German navy introduced the four-wheel *Shark* Enigma system, the contribution the codebreakers made here was immense. The Battle of the Atlantic is a good example of how Bletchley did not win the war on its own, but it did at numerous points during the war make the difference between success and failure. The U-Boat problems did not stem simply from the fact that the Admiralty knew their locations and intentions. New Allied direction-finding and radar systems became more efficient at tracking them and the US very long-range Liberator aircraft, flown by the RAF in the eastern Atlantic and the Canadians and Americans in the west, ensured that there was no point on the convoy routes where the U-Boats were themselves safe from attack. Nevertheless, as is shown by the horrific losses of merchant shipping when first *Dolphin* and then *Shark* were not broken, compared to the much reduced losses once they were being read, *Ultra* played a critical role in ensuring that Britain continued to receive the vital supplies across the Atlantic.

It was in North Africa where Bletchley Park came into its own, assisted by its outpost in Cairo, the Combined Bureau Middle East. The Enigma decrypts provided vital intelligence in August 1942 ahead of the Battle of Alam Halfa and, from then on, a constant stream of intelligence on Rommel's vulnerabilities and intentions. British military commanders had until that point seen far less intelligence of value from Bletchley than their naval and RAF equivalents. Now they, and the codebreakers themselves, had tangible evidence of the value it could give in a long-running military campaign. This ensured confidence that the codebreakers could play a critical role in winning the land battle that was to come in the invasion of Europe. It also provided, or should have provided, a number of lessons to commanders not just in how to use *Ultra* but also in its limitations.

The *Mincemeat* operation ahead of the Allied invasion of Italy in July 1943 gave an early taste of the usefulness of *Ultra* in the running and creation of deception operations. The campaign in Italy itself, with the Germans able to use well-established landline communications, provided far less scope for Hut 6 to become heavily involved. But the advent of the *Fish* teleprinter links and particularly the *Bream* link between Kesselring's headquarters and Berlin provided a large amount of intelligence, not all of it limited to operations in Italy.

During the invasion of Europe, Bletchley's involvement was absolutely vital across the board. The codebreakers' ability to read the Japanese diplomatic and naval and military attaché cyphers and the *Jellyfish* encyphered teleprinter link from Paris to Berlin provided the vast bulk of the intelligence on the German defences and allowed Allied planners to ensure that the invasion plans had the greatest chance of success. The breaking of the high-level *Abwehr* Enigma messages which confirmed that the Germans believed the Double Cross Committee's deception plan was absolutely critical to the success of the D-Day invasion and also assisted in *Operation Crossbow*, deflecting the V-weapons attacks on London.

Brigadier Bill Williams, Montgomery's top intelligence adviser, credited *Ultra* with providing military commanders with the intelligence that would ensure the victory over the Germans.

Few armies ever went to battle better informed of their enemy. It is recognised by those who ostensibly provided the information that they were but useful hyphens between the real producers at Bletchley Park and the real consumer, the soldier in the field whose life was made that much easier by the product.

At the end of the war in Europe, the Allied commander General Dwight D. Eisenhower wrote to Stewart Menzies, the head of MI6, asking him to pass on his 'heartfelt admiration and sincere thanks' to everyone at Bletchley Park 'for the magnificent services which have been rendered to the Allied cause'. Eisenhower said he was only too aware of the enormous amount of work and effort involved in producing the *Ultra* intelligence and the setbacks and difficulties the codebreakers had faced down and overcome.

> The intelligence which has emanated from you before and during the campaign has been of priceless value to me. It has simplified my task as a commander enormously. It has saved thousands of British and American lives and, in no small way, contributed to the speed with which the enemy was routed and eventually forced to surrender.

The achievements of the British codebreakers against Japanese codes and cyphers have been persistently underplayed. For many years, largely the result of a more lax US approach to releasing historical information, there was a general belief that the Americans broke the Japanese codes and cyphers. In fact we now know that, as with the Enigma and *Fish* cyphers, the British skill at making the initial breaks into the cyphers was mirrored in the Japanese systems. The Japanese introduced a whole stream of new codes and cyphers in advance of the war. John Tiltman had broken the new Japanese Army super-encyphered codes in 1938 and when the new Japanese Navy General Operational Code was introduced in June 1939, it was broken by Tiltman at Bletchley using material sent back by the British

Far East Combined Bureau in Singapore. This was the most important Japanese naval code of the war. Like the Japanese Army codes, it was 'super-encyphered' by adding streams of figures to the five-figure code groups.

British codebreakers based in Bletchley, Colombo, Delhi and for a while Kilindini in Kenya made the initial breaks into many of the main Japanese codes and cyphers. But while the British were the 'break-in' experts, getting into the codes and cyphers at the outset, the US had a far greater interest in keeping on top of Japanese codes and cyphers, as well as the ability to throw endless amounts of analytical machinery and manpower into the effort. This ensured that the Americans led the way in keeping on top of the Japanese codes and cyphers and therefore produced the great codebreaking coups of the Pacific War like the breaking of the Japanese orders for the Battle of Midway in June 1942, which was critical in the US victory, and the shooting down of the Japanese naval chief Admiral Isoruku Yamamoto in April 1943.

Quite aside from the codebreaking triumphs, there is the simple fact that Bletchley Park was the birthplace of the modern computer. The creation of *Colossus* was a tremendous achievement and if that was all that had happened at Bletchley Park it would still now be hailed as a demonstration of British brilliance. It is not for nothing that George Steiner, the philosopher and writer, has described Bletchley Park as 'the single greatest achievement of Britain during 1939-45, perhaps during the [20th] century as a whole.'

❧

So who were the very best of the codebreakers who worked at Bletchley Park? There were in fact so many great men and women working at Bletchley during the Second World War that it is invidious to make such a judgement, but even among the great names four figures do stand out above all the others. These were the truly great codebreakers.

Dilly Knox was a one of the leading experts in breaking hand codes and cyphers on the staff of the First World War codebreaking institution 'Room 40' and has never been given the proper credit for his role in 'breaking in' to the Zimmermann Telegram. After the First World War, he not only broke the cyphers used by Moscow to talk to its agents around the world, he also decyphered the *Mimiambi* of the Greek poet and playwright Herodas in his spare time. For most of the 1930s, Knox was probably the only person in British intelligence who believed the German Enigma cyphers could be broken. He broke into the less complex Enigma cypher machines used by Spanish Republican forces and their Italian allies during the Spanish Civil War and it was his ability and understanding of the machine that ensured that the Polish codebreakers felt able to share their own remarkable achievement against the pre-war *Wehrmacht* Enigma with the British.

Few people in the pre-war GC&CS shared Knox's confidence that Enigma could be broken. Indeed, Denniston and Admiral Sinclair both believed it an unlikely feat. Without Knox it is likely that the vital wartime breaks into Enigma would have taken far longer to achieve. The breaking of the *Abwehr* Enigma, a feat deemed too costly in terms of time and manpower by Hut 6 and so abandoned by them, was a fitting climax to Knox's career, and sixteen months after his untimely death in February 1943 would be a major factor in the success of D-Day. It is even possible that Knox's work extended still further. In the months before his death, he was working at home on what are believed to have been Soviet high-grade cyphers, so he may even have had an influence on the codebreaking feats of the early Cold War.

The second name in this small group of the very best of the Bletchley codebreakers is John Tiltman, whose experience dated back almost as far as Knox's – in Tiltman's case to shortly before the creation of GC&CS in 1919. His ability to break anything from the Double Playfair type systems used by the German police troops carrying out the killings in Eastern Europe to the high-grade machine cypher produced by the Lorenz SZ40 encyphered teleprinter system would set him apart even if he had never broken anything else. Tiltman's hand is everywhere in the history of Bletchley Park, the first man on either side of the Atlantic to break JN25, the Japanese Navy's main code system throughout the war, as well as several other main Japanese systems, including the Japanese Military Attaché's cypher which was to be so productive on the German defences against D-Day. Tiltman was used against any code or cypher that no one else at Bletchley Park could break. His leading role in British codebreaking continued into the Cold War. Although we do not yet know what his full impact was, we know it must have been substantial because he continued to work for Bletchley Park's Cold War successor GCHQ for a decade beyond the normal civil service retirement age of sixty and even then, at the age of seventy, was recruited by GCHQ's US counterpart, the National Security Agency, to work for them as a trouble-shooter, yet again dealing with codes and cyphers that no one else could break. He died in Hawaii in 1982.

Many of the bright young mathematicians who joined GC&CS shortly before the war or once it had started were to distinguish themselves but none more so than Alan Turing. The inevitable interest in Turing as a result of his pioneering role in computing, which had an immeasurable impact on the world today from the small hand-held computers now seen every-where to the internet, has tended to obscure and distort his role at Bletchley. Turing's ideas on computing machines were undoubtedly highly influential on Max Newman, his former tutor, who initiated the use of computers to help break the *Fish* encyphered teleprinter systems. Turing was also involved in the discussions surrounding Newman's proposals. But contrary to popular belief he was not involved in the Newmanry and the construction of the *Colossus* computer at all.

Like Knox, with whom he collaborated very closely in the initial attempts to break Enigma, Turing was a firm believer that it could and would be broken. He took on the far more difficult Naval Enigma system, with its various complex security measures, when no one else dared try, justifying this ambitious move 'because it would be so interesting to break it'. Hugh Alexander lauded Turing's leading role in breaking the U-Boat cyphers, a feat that kept the supply convoys going and ensured British survival in the darkest days of 1940 and 1941 when the UK stood virtually alone against the Nazi threat.

'There should be no question in anyone's mind that Turing's work was the biggest factor in Hut 8's success,' Alexander said.

> In the early days he was the only cryptographer who thought the problem worth tackling and not only was he primarily responsible for the main theoretical work within the Hut but he also shared with Welchman and Keen the chief credit for the invention of the Bombe. It is always difficult to say that anyone is absolutely indispensable but if anyone was indispensable to Hut 8 it was Turing. The pioneer work always tends to be forgotten when experience and routine later make everything seem easy and many of us in Hut 8 felt that the magnitude of Turing's contribution was never fully realised by the outside world.

Turing's 1952 trial on charges of homosexuality, which ended his continued post-war links to GCHQ as a consultant, and his subsequent suicide in 1954 are now well-known. It was a truly tragic and bitter end to a life which produced so much and could have produced much more, giving added meaning to Alexander's final comments.

The last of the four leading codebreakers to be singled out here is Hugh Alexander himself. Like Tiltman he continued to work for GCHQ as a codebreaker through the Cold War. At Bletchley, Alexander worked initially in Hut 6, then as Turing's deputy and successor as head of Hut 8, before moving on to cover other problems as they emerged. When the Americans ran into problems trying to break the Japanese naval attaché machine cypher *Coral* in the summer of 1943, Hut 8 joined the attack employing procedures used against the *Shark* Enigma. Led by Alexander, the British codebreakers began to make headway in September 1943 and, in February 1944, he flew to Washington to lead the final break in time for a major Japanese report on the German defences in Normandy to be deciphered ahead of D-Day. At the end of the war, Alexander initially went back to his previous work as Director of Research for the John Lewis Partnership but in mid-1946 decided to join GCHQ, becoming head of the codebreaking division in 1949 and refusing further promotion so as to remain at the coalface. Like Tiltman he was persuaded to stay beyond the standard civil service retirement date, retiring two years after his sixtieth birthday in 1971, and like Tiltman he was then approached by NSA to join them, an offer he declined. He died in Cheltenham in February 1974. Noel Gayler, the then Director of NSA, said Alexander had made a 'monumental' contribution to joint Anglo-American codebreaking operations and to 'the special relationship' between Britain and the United States. That 'special relationship' was in fact founded on the wartime cooperation between Bletchley Park and its US counterparts and the continued and extensive exchange of intelligence between Britain and the United States remains by far the most tangible evidence of its continued existence.

A list of codebreakers, intelligence officers and administrators who made substantial contributions to the work at Bletchley Park would be bound to omit others who also deserved recognition. Welchman's invention of the diagonal board for the Bombe, for example, was absolutely vital, Tutte's unpicking of the *Tunny* secrets astonishingly brilliant, but to continue the list would risk missing the point.

The History of Hut 6, one of the internal GCHQ histories of the work at Bletchley that were written after the war, begins appropriately with the so-called 'Dodo Bird Verdict' from *Alice's*

Adventures in Wonderland, a quote that would no doubt have delighted the devoted Carrollian Dilly Knox: 'Everybody has won and all must have prizes.' This is perhaps particularly true of Bletchley Park where the work of the brilliant few was only possible because of the hard, often mind-numbing labour of very many others whose names were always less likely to go down in history. More than 10,000 people were working for GC&CS at the highest point in the war, at the beginning of 1945. This included the 2,000 Wrens and mechanics working on the Bombes at the out-stations at Adstock and Gayhurst Manor, in Buckinghamshire, and Stanmore and Eastcote in Middlesex, but not the thousands of intercept operators based at ninety locations in the UK and others around the world. Every one of these people played their part.

Counter-factual history is a very risky undertaking but few could argue that the work at Bletchley did not help to ensure the war ended quicker than it would otherwise have done, saving countless lives on both sides of the conflict. Harry Hinsley, who went on to write the official history of British intelligence in the Second World War, argued that the intelligence produced at Bletchley Park cut at least two years, if not three, off the length of the war. 'The U-Boats would not have done us in, but they would have got us into serious shortages and put another year on the war,' Hinsley said. '*Operation Overlord* would certainly not have been launched in June 1944 without *Ultra.* Or at least, if it had been launched, it would probably not have been successful.' It was still possible that the Russians might have gone on to capture Berlin in 1945 or that Britain might have been so badly hit by Hitler's V-weapons that the Allies might have responded by using the atomic bomb, he said. 'But my own belief is that the war, instead of finishing in 1945, would have ended in 1948 had GC&CS not been able to read the Enigma cyphers and produce the *Ultra* intelligence.'

George Steiner's judgement on the work of Bletchley Park reflects that achievement but it cannot just be pinned to the organisation itself. The success of Bletchley Park was the result of a lot of hard work by all of the people who worked there or at the many GC&CS outstations or intercept sites around the world. The recruitment difficulties which provoked the letter to Churchill written by Welchman, Turing, Alexander and Milner-Barry meant that there was no room for passengers at Bletchley Park.

In his history of the work on German Naval Enigma, Alexander said:

> The graphs and figures in the appendices give a statistical estimate of our work; it is harder to give a real impression of what we felt about it. Even the people who had the dullest and hardest work (and a great deal of the routine work was very dull and still more of it extremely exhausting) felt that it was worthwhile to an extent that few jobs in peace-time can be and they did not spare themselves in any way – through staff shortage they frequently had far more to cope with than they should ever have been asked to do; they always got it done somehow and I am sure that a number of the breakdowns in health that occurred were caused chiefly by overwork. As for these of us who did the skilled technical work, I think we all felt that it was impossible that we should ever again have a job which would give us in the same way a sense of the greatest importance and urgency combined with the fascination of a highly ingenious and complicated game – we all thought ourselves extremely fortunate to have had the chance to do it.

Although Alexander was talking specifically about Hut 8, it was the same across 'the Park'. The opinion of an American who worked at Bletchley might be seen as providing as close as we can come to a genuinely unbiased inside view of this truly great British institution.

Bill Bundy, who was in his mid-twenties when he led the US codebreakers working in Hut 6, went on to be a key foreign affairs adviser for both the Kennedy and Johnson administrations, ending his government service as Assistant Secretary of State. Bundy said he never worked with 'a group of people that was more thoroughly dedicated and with a range of skills, insight and imagination' than those he worked with at Bletchley.

> It was a terrific human experience and I've never matched it since. I had other jobs with superb people, important and worthwhile pursuits but certainly for me personally this was the high point. This was a totally dedicated group working together in absolutely remarkable teamwork. Their whole structure was one where you might readily find a major working under a lieutenant or under a civilian, somewhat younger. Whoever was in charge was the person who had been judged to be more effective at doing it. It was an extraordinary group, and that was true right across the board in BP, whatever system of selection they used, and I've heard lots of narratives and lots of colourful stories about it, the result was an extraordinary group of people in an extraordinary organisation.

ENDNOTES

Pages 1–2 Bletchley beginnings: The National Archives, Public Record Office (hereafter TNA PRO) HD 3/15. Mystery of its future use: *Bletchley District Gazette*, 28 May 1938.

Pages 2–3 Bletchley purchase: interview with former MI6 officer who managed the service's archives, 17 October 1995. The official MI6 history cites evidence in the Land Registry files that 'strongly suggests' Sinclair was reimbursed, but these documents, the details of which were already known, do not in fact strongly suggest anything. They show that Sinclair left the Park to his sister Evelyn who signed it over to MI6. If he had been reimbursed it would be unlikely that he would have left it to his sister; he could have signed it over to MI6 himself. It may have been of course that she was reimbursed after her brother's death but there is certainly no evidence of this. The only money exchanged when she signed the Park over was a 10-shilling legal fee. The Sinclair family wealth was such at the time that Evelyn did not need the money and having spent the last years of his life with her brother she would certainly have known what he wanted done with the Park before he left it to her. Without any further evidence, and there is none in the MI6 archives, it is unlikely that the truth will ever be known. The words of the MI6 archivist, reflecting the absence of any evidence of repayment in the MI6 archives, are the closest we can come to an answer: 'We know he paid for it, we're not even sure if he was ever repaid. He died soon afterwards, so he probably wasn't.'

Page 3 Evelyn Sinclair worked at GC&CS: TNA PRO HW 14/147, Temporary Staff, 5 March 1941, p.5.

Page 3 Move of various sections to Bletchley: TNA PRO HW 62/21, Move of Service Sections to War Station, 15 August 1939, dated 2 August 1939.

Page 4 Walsingham: TNA PRO HD 3/15.

Page 4 Secret Man and Secret Decyphering Branch: TNA PRO HD 3/14; HD 3/15; HD 3/16; HD 3/17; HD 3/22; HD 3/35.

Pages 4–5 Gill and Christmas message: TNA PRO WO 32/10776, History of Military Intelligence Directorate 1920–21.

Pages 5–6 Members of Room 40: TNA PRO HW 3/182, Records of W. F. Clarke of Room 40 and Head of Naval Section, Government Code and Cypher School.

Page 6 Zimmermann telegram: TNA PRO HW 3/177, Nigel de Grey account of decyphering of the Zimmermann telegram, January 1917.

Page 6 Denniston on rivalry: A. G. Denniston, 'The Government Code and Cypher School Between the Wars', *Intelligence and National Security*, vol. 1 (January 1986), pp.58–9.

Page 7 Post-war amalgamation: TNA PRO HW 3/33, Record of Conference held at the Admiralty on 5 August 1919 on amalgamation of MI1b and NID25; HW 3/33, Nigel de Grey, Notes on Formation and Evolution of GC&CS, p.1.

Page 7 Public and private roles: Denniston, 'The Government Code and Cypher School Between the Wars', pp.58–9.

Page 7 Curzon on need for secrecy: Keith Jeffery (ed.), 'The Government Code and Cypher School: A Memorandum by Lord Curzon', *Intelligence and National Security*, Vol. 1, No. 3 (October 1986).

Page 7 Supply of material: J. Johnson, *The Evolution of British Sigint 1653–1939*, HMSO, Cheltenham, 1997, pp.45,50.

Pages 7–8 Sinclair takeover and lack of funds: TNA PRO HW 3/182, Records of W. F. Clarke of Room 40 and Head of Naval Section, Government Code and Cypher School.

Pages 8–9 Cooper recruitment: TNA PRO HW 3/83, J. E. S. Cooper, Personal Notes on GC&CS 1925–39, p.1.

Pages 9–10 'Devotee of his art': TNA PRO HW 3/12, translation of German newspaper article by former Russian codebreaker.

Page 10 Role in capture of the Magdeburg codebook: Christopher Andrew, *Secret Service, The Making of the British Intelligence Community*, Sceptre, London, 1992, pp.143, 376.

Page 10 Details of Fetterlein's flight from Russia: P. William Filby, 'Bletchley

Park and Berkeley Street', *Intelligence and National Security* 3(2) (1988), p.272.

Page 10 Fetterlein's wartime work: TNA PRO HW 3/35, Work Done by Staff of ID25 During the War, Summary, 15/5/1919.

Page 10 Fetterlein's working practice: Filby, 'Bletchley Park and Berkeley Street'.

Pages 10–11 Cooper recollections of Fetterlein: TNA PRO HW 3/83, Cooper, Personal Notes on GC&CS 1925–39, paras 2–3.

Page 12 Cooper on lack of training. TNA PRO HW 3/83, Cooper, Personal Notes on GC&CS 1925–39, para 6.

Pages 12–13 Intercept sites: Johnson, *The Evolution of British Sigint*, pp.50–53; TNA PRO HW 3/81, H. C. Kenworthy, A Brief History of Events Relating to the Growth of the Wire Service; HW 3/33, de Grey, Notes on Formation and Evolution of GC&CS, pp.1–2; C. L. Sinclair-Williams, H. C. Kenworthy (unpublished paper kindly provided by Mrs Hazel Sinclair-Williams).

Page 13 Cooper on lack of work on German cyphers: TNA PRO HW 3/83, Cooper, Personal Notes on GC&CS 1925–39, paras 25–6.

Page 14 Germans begin using machine cyphers: Denniston, 'The Government Code and Cypher School Between the Wars', p.54.

Page 14 Foss asked to test Enigma machine for British use: TNA PRO HW 25/10, H. R. Foss, Reminiscences on the Enigma, p.2.

Pages 14–16 Working of Enigma and results of Foss test: ibid; Johnson, *The Evolution of British Sigint*, p.55.

Page 16 Wehrmacht starts using Enigma: TNA PRO HW 25/10, de Grey, Enigma History, p.2.

Page 16 Knox success against Italian machine: ibid; TNA PRO HW 25/10, Cooper handwritten memo on de Grey's Enigma History.

Page 16 Knox knowledge of Stecker-board: Robin Denniston, *Thirty Secret Years: A. G. Denniston's Work in Signals Intelligence 1914–44*, Polperro Heritage Press, Clifton-upon-Terne, Worcestershire, 2007, p.107; TNA PRO 62/21, Tiltman memo dated 9 September 1938.

Page 17 Move to Bletchley Park for 'rehearsal': TNA PRO HW 43/1, F. L. Birch, History of Sigint, p.49.

Page 17 Atmosphere at GC&CS: TNA PRO HW 3/83, Cooper, Reminiscences on GC&CS at Bletchley Park, para 5.

Pages 17–18 Barbara Abernethy recruitment: interview with Barbara Eachus, 23 March 1998.

Page 18 Timings of rehearsal: TNA PRO HW 43/1, Birch, History of Sigint, p.49.

Pages 18–19 Clarke memories: TNA PRO HW 3/16, W. F. Clarke, History of GCCS and its Naval Section, 1919–45, BP Reminiscences, pp.49–51.

Page 18 Cooper memories: TNA PRO HW 3/83, Cooper, Air Section GC&CS and the Approach to War 1935–39, pp.12–13.

Page 19 Meeting with Bertrand: TNA PRO HW 25/12, AGD to the Director, 2 November 1938.

Page 20 Hans Thilo Schmidt: Mavis Batey, *Dilly: The Man Who Broke Enigmas*, Dialogue, London, 2009, p.64.

Pages 20–21 Denniston on main reason for liaison with French: TNA PRO HW 25/12, AGD to the Director, 2 November 1938.

Page 21 Cooper memories: ibid; TNA PRO HW 3/83, Cooper, Air Section GC&CS and the Approach to War 1935–39, pp.16–17.

Pages 21–2 January 1939 meeting in Paris: TNA PRO HW 25/10, H. R. Foss, Reminiscences on the Enigma, p.3.

Pages 22–3 Turing and Twinn recruitment: interviews with Twinn, April 1998.

Pages 23–4 Dilly eccentricities: Batey, Dilly. Vincent memories: Corpus Christi Archives, Cambridge, Professor E. R. P. Vincent, Unpublished Memoirs, p.107.

Page 24 Peter Twinn: interviews with Twinn, April 1998; F. H. Hinsley & A. Stripp, *Codebreakers: The Inside Story of Bletchley Park*, Oxford University Press, Oxford, 1993, pp.125–7.

Pages 25–6 Polish work on Enigma: Ralph Erskine & Michael Smith (eds), *The Bletchley Park Codebreakers*, Biteback, London, 2011, p.42; Batey, *Dilly*, pp.74–9.

Pages 25–6 Mayer quoted in J. Stengers, 'Enigma, the French, the Poles and the British', in C. M. Andrew & D. N. Dilks (eds), *The Missing Dimension: Governments and Intelligence Communities in the Twentieth Century*, Macmillan, London, 1984, pp.130–32.

Page 26 Knox reaction: TNA PRO HW 25/12, A. G. Denniston, How News was brought from Warsaw at the end of July 1939.

Page 26 Twinn on QWERTZU: Michael Smith, *Station X, Decoding Nazi*

Secrets, TV Books, New York, 1999, pp.30–31; Hinsley & Stripp, *Codebreakers*, p.127.

Page 26 Delivery of Enigma machine to Menzies: Gustave Bertrand, *ENIGMA ou La Plus Grande Enigmé de la Guerre 1939–45*, Plon, Paris, 1973, p.60.

Pages 27–8 Recruitment of staff: TNA PRO HW 62/21, Denniston to Howard Smith, 25 November 1938; Undated memo on 'Available Emergency Staff'; TNA PRO HW 3/83, Cooper, Air Section GC&CS and the Approach to War 1935–39, pp.17–18.

Pages 29–30 Wilkinson recruitment: Hinsley & Stripp, *Codebreakers*, p.61.

Page 31 Vincent recruitment: Andrew, *Secret Service*, p.452.

Pages 31–2 Diana Russell Clarke: interview with Diana Barraclough, May 1998.

Page 31 Orders for move to Bletchley: TNA PRO HW 62/21, Move of Service Sections to War Station 15 August 1939, dated 2 August 1939.

Pages 31–3 De Grey memories: TNA PRO HW 3/95, History of Air Sigint, Chapter II, Sitz and Blitz: 1939–1940, pp.76–7.

Pages 33–4 Lack of German coverage: TNA PRO HW 43/1, Birch, History of Sigint, pp.68–69.

Pages 34–5 Green memories: TNA PRO HW 3/146, Edward Green, Memories of Naval Section.

Page 35 Cooper on secrecy and staff put up in hotels: TNA PRO HW 3/83, Cooper, Air Section GC&CS and the Approach to War 1935–39, p.22.

Page 35 Diana Russell Clarke: interview with Diana Barraclough, May 1998.

Pages 35–6 Senyard memories: TNA PRO HW 3/135, The History of Miss Senyard's Party, German Naval Section BP 1939, p.3.

Page 36 Rounders and attitude of academics: Smith, *Station X*, pp.35–6.

Page 37 Abernethy: interview with Barbara Eachus, May 1998.

Page 37 Dryden: Hinsley & Stripp, *Codebreakers*, p.195

Page 37 Cooper on start of war: TNA PRO HW 3/83, Cooper, Air Section GC&CS and the Approach to War 1935–39, p.22.

Page 38 Denniston on overcrowding at Bletchley: TNA PRO HW 14/1, Denniston to Menzies, 12 September 1939.

Page 39 Construction of the huts: TNA PRO HW 3/95, de Grey, History of Air Sigint, pp.77,91; HW 14/1, Denniston to Sinclair, 16 September 1939; Denniston, 29 September 1939.

Page 39 Abernethy memories: interview with Barbara Eachus, May 1998.

Pages 39–40 Senyard memories: TNA PRO HW 3/135, The History of Miss Senyard's Party, p.33.

Page 41 Attempts to get Polish codebreakers to Britain: TNA PRO HW 14/3, Denniston to Menzies, 9 January 1940; Menzies to Rivet, 10 January 1940; Menzies to Denniston, 25 January 1940.

Page 41 Poles' treatment in Bucharest: Stephen Budiansky, *Battle of Wits*, Viking, New York, 2000, p.121.

Page 41 Dryden memories: Hinsley & Stripp, *Codebreakers*, p.198.

Pages 41–2 Turing: TNA PRO HW 25/3, A. M. Turing, Mathematical theory of ENIGMA Machine, p.136.

Pages 42–3 Cillies: TNA PRO HW 43/70, History of Hut 6, pp.53–4; interviews with Susan Wenham and Mavis Batey, May 1998.

Page 43 Knox resignation threat: TNA PRO HW 14/3, Knox to Denniston, 7 January 1940.

Page 43 Turing visit to France: TNA PRO HW 43/70, History of Hut 6, pp.53–5; HW 3/95, de Grey, History of Air Sigint, p.90

Page 44 Creation of Hut 6: TNA PRO HW 3/95, de Grey, History of Air Sigint, p.91.

Pages 45–6 Need to find a way of reporting and protecting Enigma decrypts: TNA PRO HW 3/95, de Grey, History of Air Sigint, p.97.

Page 46 GCHQ covername: TNA PRO HW 14/3, CSS Memo dated 21 February 1940.

Page 46 Barred Zones: TNA PRO HW 3/95, de Grey, History of Air Sigint, p.99.

Page 46 Lyddekker memories: Smith, *Station X*, p.53.

Page 47 Cooper on German ladies: TNA PRO HW 3/83, Cooper, Air Section GC&CS and the Approach to War 1935–39, p.29.

Pages 47–8 Davies memories: Smith, Station X, pp.53–4 and Gwen Watkins, Cracking the Luftwaffe Codes: *The Secrets of Bletchley Park*, Greenhill Books, London, 2006, p.54.

Page 48 Wenham: interview with Susan Wenham, May 1998.

Page 49 Information on 'Y stations': TNA PRO HW 3/92, History of UK Military Sigint; TNA PRO HW 3/83, Cooper, Air Section GC&CS and the Approach to War 1935–39, p.28.

Pages 49–50 Joan Nicholls: Smith, *Station X*, pp.37–8.

Page 50 For detailed papers on DF, RFP and TINA see TNA PRO HW 18/89; HW 14/12, Saunders to Travis, Possibilities of RFP, 28 February 1941.

Pages 50–51 Joan Nicholls: Smith, *Station X*, pp.37–8, 112–4.

Page 52 Cooper on Blandy refusal: TNA PRO HW 3/83, Cooper, Air Section GC&CS and the Approach to War 1935–39, p.27.

Page 52 Cheadle agrees to put 20 sets on Enigma: TNA PRO HW 14/4, Interception of Enigma Traffic, 20 March 1940.

Page 52 Bletchley Park Control: Erskine & Smith (eds), *Bletchley Park Codebreakers*, pp.73–74.

Pages 52–3 Joan Nicholls: Smith, *Station X*, p.49.

Page 53 Blisters: Hinsley & Stripp, *Codebreakers*, p.91; Erskine & Smith (eds), *Bletchley Park Codebreakers*, p.69.

Page 55 Twinn on codebreaking: interview with Peter Twinn, May 1998.

Pages 55–6 Lever on codebreaking: interview with Mavis Batey, May 1998.

Page 56 Twinn on codebreaking: interview with Peter Twinn, May 1998.

Page 56 Russell Clarke on machine room: interview with Diana Barraclough, May 1998.

Page 57 Hut 3 reporting: TNA PRO HW 3/95, de Grey, History of Air Sigint, p.30.

Page 58 Number of officers in the know: TNA PRO HW 14/4, CX/FJ signal to Head of GC&CS dated 8 April 1940.

Page 58 Hut 3 reporting to MI6 Sections II and IV: TNA PRO HW 14/4, Minute Sheet on CX/FJ Information, dated 14 April 1940.

Page 58 Hut 3 beginning only 'small beer': TNA PRO HW 3/119, F. L. Lucas, History of Hut 3.

Page 59 Lucas quotes: TNA PRO HW 3/119, Lucas, History of Hut 3, pp.27–8.

Page 60 De Grey on invasion of Denmark and Norway and effect on Bletchley: TNA PRO HW 3/95, de Grey, History of Air Sigint, pp.102–104.

Page 61 Hut 3 shifts double in size: TNA PRO HW 3/119, Lucas, History of Hut 3, p.28.

Pages 61–2 Jones on Gilbert Frankau: R. V. Jones, *Most Secret War: British Scientific Intelligence 1939–45*, Hamish Hamilton, London, 1978, p.79.

Pages 62–3 Hut 3 early days: TNA PRO HW 3/119, Lucas, History of Hut 3, pp.24–5.

Page 64 Use of MI6 secure link to send Enigma decrypts to Norway: Michael Smith, *Foley: The Spy Who Saved 10,000 Jews*, Politicos, London, 2004, pp.161–9; TNA PRO WO 106/1904, 'Sickle' Force: General Paget's report on operations; WO 106/1912, Scandinavia Operations; general; HW 5/1, Operations mainly in Norway and Northern Europe.

Pages 64–5 Battle of France and changes to indicating system: TNA PRO HW 3/95, de Grey, History of Air Sigint, p.105; HW 43/70, History of Hut 6, p.4.

Pages 65–7 Herivel: interview with John Herivel, May 1998.

Pages 67–8 Milner-Barry: TNA PRO HW 43/70, History of Hut 6, pp.3–5.

Page 68 Calvocoressi: Smith, *Station X*, p.63.

Page 69 Birch on value of intelligence and use of Ultra, plus MI6 link to GHQ France: TNA PRO HW 43/1, Birch, History of Sigint, pp.113–5; HW 3/119, Lucas, History of Hut 3, p.221; HW 3/95, de Grey, History of Air Sigint, p.108.

Pages 70–71 Information on SCUs and SLUSs: TNA PRO HW 43/1, Birch, History of Sigint, p.118; Hinsley & Stripp, *Codebreakers*, p.23; Geoffrey Pidgeon, *The Secret Wireless War*, USPO, London, 2003, passim; Frederick Winterbotham, *The Ultra Secret*, Weidenfeld and Nicolson, London, 1974.

Page 71 Increase in size and attachment of MI6 officers: TNA PRO HW 14/14, Hut 3, 4 April 1941.

Pages 71–2 Ralph Bennett comments: Smith, *Station X*, p.58.

Pages 72–3 Process in Hut 3 and Lucas on Sorter's role: TNA PRO HW 3/119, Lucas, History of Hut 3, p.32.

Page 73 Millward: Hinsley & Stripp, *Codebreakers*, pp.20–23.

Page 74 Jim Rose comments: interview with Jim Rose, May 1998.

Page 74 De Grey section, initially known as 'Distribution and Research': TNA PRO HW 14/10, de Grey, Report on Work of Hut 3a, 8 January 1941; HW 43/1, Birch, History of Sigint, p.198.

Page 75 Senyard on French officers: TNA PRO HW 3/135, History of Miss Senyard's Party, p.21.

Page 75 Lever: interview with Mavis Batey, May 1998.

Page 75 French re-location: Budiansky, *Battle of Wits*, p.146; Smith, *Station X*, p.65.

Pages 75–6 Bombes: TNA PRO HW 3/164, Squadron-Leader Jones' Section; Gordon Welchman, *The Hut Six Story* (revised ed.), M. & M. Baldwin, Cleobury Mortimer, 1997; Smith, *Station X*, pp.72–3.

Pages 76–7 De Grey on Sea Lion: TNA PRO HW 3/95, de Grey, History of Air Sigint, pp.129–30.

Page 77 Kennedy: *The Diaries of Captain Malcolm Duncan Kennedy, 1917–1946*, Kennedy Collection, Sheffield University Library, entry for 15 May 1940.

Pages 77–8 Twinn on Turing: interview with Peter Twinn, May 1998.

Page 78 Ann Harding on Turing and Twinn: Imperial War Museum interview with Ann Harding, ref 05/67/1.

Page 78 Currer-Briggs: interview with Noel Currer-Briggs, May 1998.

Pages 78–9 Senyard on threat of invasion: TNA PRO HW 3/135, History of Miss Senyard's Party, pp.20–21.

Pages 79–80 Column BQ emergency mobile unit: TNA PRO HW 14/10, Head of GC&CS [Denniston] to The Director [Menzies] 8 January 1941; HW 14/12, Denniston, BQ Party, 22 February 1941; Smith, Station X, p.71.

Pages 80–81 Bonsall quotes: A. W. Bonsall, *An Uphill Struggle: The Provision of Tactical Sigint Support to the Allied Air Forces in Europe in WWII*, Bletchley Park Trust, Bletchley, 2011 (the author is grateful to Bill Bonsall for making the text of this invaluable paper available ahead of publication).

Page 81 Bonsall recruitment: email from Bill Bonsall, 20 September 2010.

Page 82 Cooper creates Computor Clerks: TNA PRO HW 3/83, Cooper, Air Section GC&CS and the Approach to War 1935–39, p.29; HW 14/11, Cooper to Boyle, 25 January 1941, Folio 8a.

Page 82 Bonsall quotes: Bonsall, An Uphill Struggle.

Pages 82–3 Home Defence Units: TNA PRO HW 3/119, Lucas, History of Hut 3, pp.124–6.

Page 83 Birch on Air Section: TNA PRO HW 43/1, Birch, History of Sigint, p.169.

Pages 83–4 Lavell comments: interview with Ann Cunningham, May 1998.

Page 84 Jones on Cooper: Jones, *Most Secret War*, pp.61–2.

Page 85 Davies on Cooper: Smith, *Station X*, p.69

Pages 85–6 Milner-Barry and breaking of the Brown: TNA PRO HW 43/70, History of Hut 6, pp.5,75,199.

Pages 86–7 Jones on implications of the breaking of the Brown Enigma: Jones, *Most Secret War*, pp.85–95, 135–9.

Pages 87–8 Intelligence on Coventry raid: F. H. Hinsley et al., *British Intelligence in the Second World War*, Vol. 1, HMSO, London, 1979, pp.528–48.

Page 88 'Vital intelligence' and concerns over security of Enigma: TNA PRO HW 14/10, Saunders to Vivian, Security of Source CX/JQ, 20 January 1941.

Page 88 Memories of Keith Batey kindly supplied by Mavis Batey. His memory matches that of R. V. Jones as stated in Jones, *Most Secret War*, p.149.

Pages 88–9 Kennedy on bombing of Bletchley Park: *Kennedy Diaries*, 21 November 1940.

Page 89 Air Section intelligence reports allowed (from June 1942): Bonsall, *An Uphill Struggle*; John Stubbington, *Kept in the Dark*, Pen & Sword, Barnsley, 2010, pp.41–2, 179.

Page 90 Alexander and Birch on Naval Enigma difficulties TNA PRO HW 25/1, C. H. O'D. Alexander, Cryptographic History of Work on the German Naval Enigma, pp.19–20; HW 43/1, Birch, History of Sigint, p.93.

Pages 90–91 Alexander on Turing: TNA PRO HW 25/1, Alexander, Cryptographic History of Work on the German Naval Enigma, p.20.

Page 91 Hinsley recruitment: Hinsley & Stripp, *Codebreakers*, p.77; email to author from Bill Bonsall.

Pages 91–2 Senyard: TNA PRO HW 3/135, The History of Miss Senyard's Party, pp.10–11.

Page 92 Hinsley on links to OIC: Hinsley & Stripp, *Codebreakers*, pp.77–8.

Pages 93–4 Hinsley on Glorious: Hinsley, *British Intelligence*, Vol. 1, pp.141–3; Smith, Station X, pp.78–9; Hinsley & Stripp, *Codebreakers*, p.78.

Page 94 Morgan: TNA PRO ADM 223/297.

Page 94 Birch: TNA PRO HW 43/1, Birch, History of Sigint, p.164.

Page 95 Green: TNA PRO HW 3/146, E. Green, Genesis, p.4.

Page 95 Birch on types of Naval Enigma: TNA PRO HW 43/1, Birch, History of Sigint, p.93.

Page 96 Senyard: TNA PRO HW 3/135, The History of Miss Senyard's Party, p.19.

Pages 96–7 German patrol boat looted: TNA PRO HW 43/1, Birch, History of Sigint, p.93; HW 25/1, Alexander, Cryptographic History of Work on the German Naval Enigma, pp.24–25.

Page 97 Wolf Packs: I. C. B. Dear and M. R. D. Foot (eds), *The Oxford Companion to the Second World War*, OUP, Oxford, 1995, pp.62–9.

Page 98 Clarke on recruitment into Hut 8: Hinsley & Stripp, *Codebreakers*, pp.113–4.

143 Pages 98–9 Noskwith on Kendrick: Erskine & Smith (eds), *Bletchley Park Codebreakers*, p.194.

Page 100 Birch on Turing and Twinn: TNA PRO HW 25/2, A. P. Mahon, History of Hut 8, p.23.

Page 100 Knox on Turing: TNA PRO HW 14/1, ADK to Denniston (undated), Folio 16.

Pages 100–101 Twinn on Turing: interview with Peter Twinn, May 1998, and Smith, *Station X*, pp.83–4.

Pages 101–103 Details of Ruthless: TNA PRO ADM 223/464, Operation Ruthless; HW 25/2, Mahon, History of Hut 8, p.25; Hugh Sebag-Montefiore, *Enigma: The Battle for the Code*, Phoenix, London, 2002, pp.113–5.

Page 101 Birch 'fair does': TNA PRO HW 25/2, Mahon, History of Hut 8, p.29.

Page 103 Effect of Lofoten pinch: Erskine & Smith (eds), *Bletchley Park Codebreakers*, p.169.

Page 104 Tandy: Smith, *Station X*, p.87.

Page 105 Noskwith on 'gardening': Erskine & Smith (eds), *Bletchley Park Codebreakers*, pp.190–91; Smith, Station X, p.87.

Page 105 24-hour working and Scarborough teleprinting to Hut 8: TNA PRO HW 25/2, Mahon, History of Hut 8, p.27.

Pages 105–106 Successes in June to September: TNA PRO HW 25/1, Alexander, Cryptographic History of Work on the German Naval Enigma, p.30; Erskine & Smith (eds), *Bletchley Park Codebreakers*, pp.169–70.

Page 106 Yoxall break into Offizier: TNA PRO HW 25/1, Alexander, Cryptographic History of Work on the German Naval Enigma, p.33.

Pages 106–107 Time taken for Bombes to find wheel orders: ibid, p.12.

Page 107 Noskwith on Banburismus: interview with Rolf Noskwith, May 1998.

Page 107 Mahon on Banburismus: TNA PRO HW 25/2, Mahon, History of Hut 8, pp.16–18.

Pages 108–109 Twinn on Banburismus process: interview with Peter Twinn, May 1998.

Pages 109–110 Halcrow: interview with Marjorie Halcrow, June 1998.

Page 110 Welchman on Freeborn: Welchman, *Hut Six Story*, pp.181–2.

Page 111 U-Boat sinking of allied shipping: Hinsley, *British Intelligence*, Vol. 1, p.169.

Pages 112–113 Maclennan: Smith, *Station X*, pp.91–3.

Page 113 Numbers of Wrens working on Bombes and where: TNA PRO HW 3/164, History of Sqn-Ldr Jones' section, the Bombe Hut, 1940–45.

Page 114 Quirk: interview with Barbara Quirk, May 1998.

Page 114 Joan Baily: Smith, *Station X*, pp.93–4.

Page 115 German preparations for occupation of the Balkans: Hinsley, British Intelligence, Vol. 1, pp.353–73. Tiltman and Rocket: Hinsley & Stripp, *Codebreakers*, p.116.

Page 115 Tiltman: Ralph Erskine & Peter Freeman, 'Brigadier John Tiltman: One of Britain's Finest Cryptologists', *Cryptologia* 27, 2003.

Pages 115–6 P. W. Filby, 'Floradora and a Unique Break into One-Time Pad Cyphers', *Intelligence and National Security*, Vol. 10, No. 3 (Autumn 1995).

Pages 116–7 Milner-Barry and Welchman and expansion of Hut 6 operations: TNA PRO HW 43/1, Birch, History of Sigint, p.206; HW 43/70, History of Hut 6, p.6.

Page 117 Light Blue broken: TNA PRO HW 43/70, *History of Hut 6*, p.4; F. H. Hinsley et al., *British Intelligence in the Second World War*, Vol. 2, HMSO, London, 1981, p.660.

Page 117 Italian codes and cyphers: Hinsley, *British Intelligence*, Vol. 1, pp.198–205.

Pages 117–21 Matapan: interview with Mavis Batey, May 1998; Batey, *Dilly*, pp.114–28; Dear & Foot (eds), *Oxford Companion*, pp.190–91.

Pages 122–3 Crete: TNA PRO HW 3/174, The Use of 'U' in the Mediterranean and North West African Theatres of War, pp.3–4; HW 43/1, Birch, History of Sigint, p.215; Ralph Bennett, Ultra and Mediterranean Strategy 1941–1945, Hamish Hamilton, London, 1989, pp.51–62.

Page 123 Herivel on Crete: interview with John Herivel, May 1998.

Pages 123–5 Bismarck: Hinsley & Stripp, *Codebreakers*, pp.53–5, 103; Hinsley, *British Intelligence*, Vol. 1, pp.342–5.

Page 125 Kennedy on Bismarck: *Kennedy Diaries*, 27 May 1941.

Pages 125–6 Krakow assembly: TNA PRO HW 1/3, Large troop movement April 3: Romania to Krakow; Hinsley, *British Intelligence*, Vol. 1, pp.451, 460, 465.

Page 126 Hut 3 report: Smith, *Station X*, p.99.

Page 126 Distressing decrypts; Hinsley, *British Intelligence*, Vol. 2, pp.669–73.

Page 126 Move to Chicksands from Chatham: TNA PRO HW 43/1, Birch, History of Sigint, p.192.

Page 127 Messages broken by Tiltman and then in Hut 5: TNA PRO HW 3/82, Notes on Military Section – German Police Section; HW 14/4, Denniston to Menzies, 29 April 1940.

Page 127 Message on 1,153 Jewish plunderers: TNA PRO HW 16/45, selected reports illustrating GP (German Police) war crimes in Russia and the Ukraine, 18 July 1941.

Page 127 3,274 Partisans: TNA PRO HW 16/45, 4 August 1941, item 9.

Page 127 More than 30,000: TNA PRO HW 16/45, 7 August 1941, item 24.

Page 127 Bletchley Park analyst: TNA PRO HW 16/6, bound volume of BP GP periodic summaries, p.4.

Page 128 Winston Churchill, BBC broadcast, 24 August 1941.

Pages 129–30 Germans kill 367 Jews: TNA PRO HW 1/30, Police Regiment South Shot 367 Jews, 28 August 1941.

Page 130 Germans kill 603 Jews: TNA PRO HW 1/35, Partisans and Jews shot, 30 August 1941.

Page 130 Germans kill 1,342 Jews: TNA PRO HW 16/45, 25 August 1941.

Page 131 Cypher changing twice a day: TNA PRO HW 3/155, History of the GC&CS German Police Section 1939–45.

Page 131 1,246 Jews killed: TNA PRO HW 1/40, Report for Himmler that Soviets are retreating, 1 September 1941.

Page 131 Killings for 30 August to 11 September: TNA PRO HW 16/45, 30 August 1941, 31 August 1941, 2 September 1941, 6 September 1941; HW 1/51, item 6.

Page 132 Gathering of evidence: Michael Smith, 'Bletchley Park and the Holocaust', *Intelligence and National Security*, Vol. 19, No. 2 (Summer 2004), pp.271–2.

Pages 132–5 Cunningham: interviews with Charles Cunningham, May 1998.

Page 135 Looting of Winter Palace: Smith, *Station X*, p.104.

Page 136 Welchman on Churchill visit: Welchman, *Hut Six Story*, p.128.

Page 137 Herivel: interview with John Herivel, May 1998.

Page 137 Churchill on 'no stone unturned': Brian Oakley, *The Bletchley Park War Diaries*, Bletchley Park Trust, 2011, p.67.

Page 137 Kennedy: *Kennedy Diaries*, 6 September 1941.

Page 138 Lavell: interview with Ann Cunningham, May 1998.

Pages 138–9 Codebreakers' letter and Churchill 'Action This Day' minute: TNA PRO HW 1/155.

Page 139 Milner-Barry: TNA PRO HW 43/70, History of Hut 6, p.7.

Page 140 Rebuilding programme: TNA PRO HW 14/21-24 passim.

Page 140 Tiltman sets up intelligence school: TNA PRO HW 43/1, Birch, History of Sigint, p.168.

Pages 140–42 *Daily Telegraph* crossword puzzle: correspondence with the late Stanley Sedgewick.

Pages 142–3 Y stations: TNA PRO HW 3/92, History of UK Military Sigint, pp.197–8, 204–207; HW 43/1, Birch, History of Sigint, p.192.

Page 143 Joan Nicholls: Smith, *Station X*, pp.112–3.

Page 143 Lever: interview with Mavis Batey, May 1998.

Pages 143–4 Abernethy: interview with Barbara Eachus, May 1998.

Page 144 Maclennan and Lydekker: Smith, *Station X*, p.115.

Pages 144–5 Lavell: interview with Ann Cunningham, May 1998.

Page 145 Prestwich: interview with John Prestwich, May 1998.

Pages 145–6 Milner-Barry on discipline: TNA PRO HW 43/70, History of Hut 6, p.24.

Page 146 Lavell on tolerance: interview with Ann Cunningham, May 1998.

Pages 147–52 Co-operation with Americans: see TNA PRO HW 14/45 (This file contains a copy of the undertaking signed by Currier not to reveal to anyone other than Safford what he had received from the British and an exchange of messages about the initial difficulty the Americans had understanding the British paper model of Enigma due to a missing document which was later found to have been mislaid in Washington); HW 4/25; ADM 223/297; ADM 199/1477; Prescott Currier, 'My Purple Trip to England in 1941', *Cryptologia*, Vol. 20, No. 3, 1996; Prescott Currier, NSA Oral History OH-38-80, November 1980; various conversations with Barbara Eachus (née Abernethy); Ralph Erskine, 'Churchill and the Start of the Ultra-Magic Deals,' *International Journal of Intelligence and Counterintelligence*, Vol. 10, 1997; Ralph Erskine, 'The Holden Agreement on Naval Sigint: The First BRUSA?', *Intelligence and National Security*, Vol. 14, No. 2 (Summer 1999). Safford: Laurance F. Safford, 'A Brief History of Communications Intelligence in the United States', March 1952 (obtained from the Federation of American Scientists website <http://www.fas.org/irp/nsa/safford.pdf>, 11 June 2011).

Pages 152–3 Eachus: Smith, *Station X*, pp.169, 179.

Pages 153–4 Double Cross System: Erskine & Smith (eds), *Bletchley Park Codebreakers*, pp.255–6.

Page 154 Details of code sent to GC&CS: TNA PRO KV 2/453, Robertson to Vivian, 19 September 1939. Alert operator and GC&CS scepticism: John Curry, *The Security Service 1908–45: The Official History*, PRO, London, 1999, pp.206–207.

Pages 154–5 Broken by Gill and Trevor-Roper and creation of GC&CS Abwehr section: ibid, pp.178–179, 206–207; TNA PRO ADM 223/793, 'ISOS', 25 September 1945.

Page 155 Operations of XX Committee: Erskine & Smith (eds), *Bletchley Park Codebreakers*, pp.255–7.

Pages 156–7 Knox working on Abwehr Enigma: Erskine & Smith (eds), *Bletchley Park Codebreakers*, pp.270–81.

Pages 157–8 Knox on need to have access to Abwehr material: TNA PRO HW 25/12, Knox to Denniston, undated but beginning: 'As I think you are aware…'

Page 159 Knox 'a small grouse': TNA PRO HW 14/23, Knox to Denniston, 10 November 1941.

Pages 159–60 Denniston Rolls-Royce response: TNA PRO HW 14/22, Denniston to Knox, 11 November 1941, folio 105.

Page 160 Denniston on breaking of Abwehr Enigma: TNA PRO 14/24, Folio 53, Denniston to Menzies, 10 December 1941.

Page 160 Lever solution of GGG: Batey, *Dilly*, p.145.

Page 161 Robertson on messages: Michael Howard, *British Intelligence in the Second World War*, Vol. 5, HMSO, London, 1990, pp.20–21.

Page 161 Keynes quote: Batey, *Dilly*, p.166.

Pages 162–3 Denniston on Strachey: TNA PRO HW 14/3, Denniston to Travis, 16 November 1940.

Page 163 Foss setting up Japanese section and remit: TNA PRO HW 43/1, Birch, History of Sigint, p.408–9, 445–6.

Pages 163–4 Browning on Foss: Elizabeth Hawken, *Recollections of Bletchley Park*, the unpublished memoirs of Elizabeth Hawken (née Browning), kindly provided to the author by her daughter Miss S. C. J. Hawken.

Page 164 Senyard: TNA PRO HW 3/135, The History of Miss Senyard's Party, p.33.

Pages 164–7 Revues: various conversations with Barbara Eachus (née Abernethy); interview with Pamela Rose (née Gibson); interview with Christine Brooke-Rose, May 1998; correspondence with the late Stanley Sedgewick; Smith, *Station X*, p.118.

Page 168 Lavell: interview with Ann Cunningham, May 1998.

Page 168 Diana Russell Clarke: interview with Diana Barraclough, May 1998.

Pages 168–9 Rows in Hut 3 and reorganisation: TNA PRO HW 3/119, Lucas, History of Hut 3, p.34; HW 43/1, Birch, History of Sigint, pp.436–442. Denniston 'very bitter': Robin Denniston, *Thirty Secret Years*, p.122.

Pages 170–71 Bennett and Rose on Denniston and Hut 3: Smith, *Station X*, p.123.

Pages 171–2 Dönitz on U-Boat cyphers: Patrick Beesly, *Very Special Intelligence*, Sphere, London, 1978, p.219.

Page 172 U-570 and British solving wiring of new wheel: Erskine &Smith (eds), *Bletchley Park Codebreakers*, p.171; David Kahn, *Seizing the Enigma*, Arrow, London, 1996, p.214.

Page 173 Mahon: TNA PRO HW 25/2, Mahon, History of Hut 8, pp.55, 62.

Page 173 Change to Shark: TNA PRO HW 25/1, Alexander, Cryptographic History of Work on the German Naval Enigma, pp.36–7.

Page 174 Wylie dismay: Smith, *Station X*, p.144.

Page 174 OIC Tracking Room: TNA PRO ADM 223/92, OIC Report No. 86, 9 February 1942.

Page 174 Noskwith: interview with Rolf Noskwith, May 1998.

Page 175 BP researches being too academic: Smith, *Station X*, p.146.

Page 176 Sailors abandoned: Budiansky, *Battle of Wits*, p.280.

Pages 176–7 Noskwith on guilt: Erskine & Smith (eds), *Bletchley Park Codebreakers*, p.189.

Pages 177–8 Drumbeat and US failure to institute convoys: Dear & Foot (eds), *Oxford Companion*, p.66.

Page 178 Hinsley on doubly fortunate: Hinsley, *British Intelligence* (Abridged), HMSO, London, 1993, p.158.

Page 179 U-Boat successes: Hinsley, *British Intelligence*, Vol. 2, p.679.

Page 179 Herivel: interview with John Herivel, May 1998.

Page 180 U-559: Smith, *Station X*, p.149.

Page 181 Noskwith: interview with Rolf Noskwith, May 1998.

Pages 180–181 Wylie on Shark break: Smith, *Station X*, pp.149–50.

Page 182 Beesly: Beesly, *Very Special Intelligence*, p.207.

Pages 182–4 Pat Wright: interview with Pat Bing, June 1998.

Page 184 Sarah Norton on Shark Blackout: interview with Sarah Baring, May 1998.

Page 184 Move to new blocks: Hinsley & Stripp, *Codebreakers*, p.309.

Page 185 Sarah Norton on Wrens: interview with Sarah Baring, May 1998.

Page 185 US Bombes and Holden Agreement: Erskine & Smith (eds), *Bletchley Park Codebreakers*, pp.179–80.

Pages 185–6 Eachus on working in Hut 8: Smith, *Station X*, p.169.

Page 186 Americans take over Shark: TNA PRO HW 25/2, Mahon, History of Hut 8, p.91.

Pages 186–7 US Navy Bombes used to run menus for Hut 6: TNA PRO HW 25/1, Alexander, Cryptographic History of Work on the German Naval Enigma, p.63.

Page 187 Birch: TNA PRO HW 43/1, Birch, History of Sigint, p.273–4.

Pages 187–8 Beesly: Beesly, *Very Special Intelligence*.

Page 188 Hinsley on U-Boat Commanders fears: Hinsley, *British Intelligence* (Abridged), pp.316–7.

Page 189 Number of people at Bletchley: TNA PRO HW 14/9, GC&CS Personnel, 2 December 1940; *Kennedy Diaries*, 14 December 1942.

Page 189 Women's Committee: TNA PRO HW 14/139.

Page 190 BP argues that Ultra will play large part in North Africa: TNA PRO HW 14/13, JQ Information in Middle East, 1 March 1941.

Page 191 Creation of CBME: TNA PRO HW 14/3, Memo to DDMI(O), 14 January 1940; HW 14/9, Denniston to Jacob, Ref 2949, 4 December 1940, and Winterbotham memo, 31 December 1940.

Page 191 Italian Air Force message: Hinsley, *British Intelligence*, Vol. 1, p.387.

Page 192 Dryden: Hinsley & Stripp, *Codebreakers*, pp.202–203.

Page 192 Rommel halted at Tobruk after Paulus talks: Bennett, Ultra Mediterranean, p.41.

Page 193 Limits of Ultra on Rommel advance: ibid, p.42.

Pages 193–4 SCU/SLUs: TNA PRO HW 3/119, History of Hut 3, p.250.

Page 194 Ultra regulations: Smith, *Station X*, pp.105–106.

Pages 194–5 Hut 4 C38m break: Hinsley & Stripp, *Codebreakers*, p.33.

Page 195 Tracking convoys: TNA PRO HW 3/119, History of Hut 3.

Pages 195–6 Importance of secondary source: TNA PRO HW 3/174, 'The Use of "U" in the Mediterranean and Northwest African Theatres of War', pp.2–3.

Page 196 Rose: interview with Jim Rose, May 1998.

Pages 196–7 Breaks into German Army keys: Hinsley, *British Intelligence*, Vol. 2, pp.295,310.

Page 198 Bill Williams: TNA PRO WO 208/3575, Brig. E. T. Williams, The Use of Ultra.

Page 198 Bennett on misunderstood message: Bennett, *Ultra Mediterranean*, pp.106–108.

Page 198 Churchill on Tobruk defeat: Sir Winston Churchill, *Memoirs of the Second World War*, Houghton Mifflin, New York, 1959.

Pages 198–200 Creation of traffic analysis units: TNA PRO HW 3/92, History of UK Military Sigint, pp.6–12, 92; James Thirsk, *Bletchley Park: An Inmate's Story*, Galago, Bromley, 2008.

Page 200 Luftwaffe callsign book captured: TNA PRO HW 3/92, History of UK Military Sigint, p.11.

Pages 200–201 Robinson and Faraday Davies: Smith, *Station X*, pp.126–7.

Page 201 Improvement in breaking of Afrika Korps Enigma: Hinsley, *British Intelligence*, Vol. 2, pp.374–6.

Pages 201–202 Wenham: interview with Susan Wenham, May 1998.

Page 202 Milner-Barry: TNA PRO HW 43/70, History of Hut 6, p.8.

Pages 202–203 Scorpion broken and reported in Cairo: Hinsley & Stripp, *Codebreakers*, p.37.

Page 204 Bennett on 'Monty': interview with Ralph Bennett, May 1998.

Page 204 Rommel messages: Bennett, *Ultra Mediterranean*, pp.147–8.

Page 205 Williams: TNA PRO WO 208/3575, Williams, The Use of Ultra.

Page 205 Bennett: interview with Ralph Bennett, May 1998.

Page 206 Rommel–Hitler exchange: Bennett, *Ultra Mediterranean,* pp.165–6.

Page 206 Rommel says fuel situation 'catastrophic': Hinsley, *British Intelligence*, Vol. 2, pp.454–5.

Page 206 Bennett: Hinsley & Stripp, *Codebreakers*, p.37.

Page 207 Thomas: ibid, p.48.

Page 207 Churchill messages: Hinsley, *British Intelligence*, Vol. 2, p.456.

Pages 207–208 Bennett: interview with Ralph Bennett, May 1998.

Page 209 Bletchley support for Torch: TNA PRO HW 14/56, Sigint Support for Torch in Mediterranean.

Pages 208–209 Currer-Briggs: Hinsley & Stripp, *Codebreakers*, p.225.

Page 209 Kasserine failure of Ultra: Bennett, Ultra Mediterranean, pp.203–207.

Pages 209–210 Currer-Briggs: Hinsley & Stripp, *Codebreakers*, p.225.

Page 210 Thomas on saving rations for PoWs: Hinsley & Stripp, *Codebreakers*, p.48.

Pages 210–211 Rose: interview with Jim Rose, May 1998.

Pages 211–2 Lucas on change of Army attitude towards Ultra: TNA PRO HW 3/119, History of Hut 3, pp.65–9.

Page 212 Bennett on new professionalism at BP: Hinsley & Stripp, *Codebreakers*, p.37.

Pages 212–3 Keefe: correspondence with Bernard Keefe, August 1998.

Pages 213–6 Details of Mincemeat: TNA PRO PRO ADM 223/794, 'Operation Mincemeat'; Erskine & Smith (eds), *Bletchley Park Codebreakers*, pp.262–4; Mavis Batey, *From Bletchley With Love*, Bletchley Park Trust, 2008. Bennett on Ultra effect: interview with Ralph Bennett, May 1998; Bennett, *Ultra Mediterranean*, p.223; interview with Noel Currer-Briggs, May 1998.

Page 218 Bennett on Hitler draining away resources: interview with Ralph Bennett, May 1998.

Pages 218–9 Intelligence in Italy from Enigma limited: TNA PRO HW 43/70, History of Hut 6, p.226; F. H. Hinsley et al., *British Intelligence in the Second World War*, Vol. 3, Pt 1, HMSO, London, 1984, p.75.

Pages 218–22 Original discovery of the encyphered teleprinter system: TNA PRO HW 3/163, H. C. Kenworthy, History of interception of German teleprinter communications; Hinsley, *British Intelligence*, Vol. 3, Pt 1, p.477; Smith, Station X, pp.184–5.

Pages 222–3 Tutte on how he broke Tunny: B. Jack Copeland (ed.), *Colossus: The Secrets of Bletchley Park's Codebreaking Computers*, OUP, Oxford, 2006, pp.356–7. (The author is grateful to Frank Carter for his advice on the breaking of Tunny.)

Page 223 The breaking of Tunny: Erskine & Smith (eds), *Bletchley Park Codebreakers*, pp.314–5; Hinsley & Stripp, *Codebreakers*, p.161; Hinsley, *British Intelligence*, Vol. 3, Pt 1, pp.477–82.

Page 223 Wylie on Tutte reticence: Smith, *Station X*, p.187.

Page 224 Knockholt and Kenworthy: TNA PRO HW 3/163, Kenworthy, History of interception of German teleprinter communications.

Pages 225–6 Hilton: Smith, *Station X*, pp.189–90.

Pages 225–6 Newman and Turing: Copeland (ed.), *Colossus*, p.178.

Page 227 Good: Hinsley & Stripp, *Codebreakers*, p.162.

Pages 227–8 Travis and Newman on Robinson: TNA PRO HW 14/66, EWT appoints Newman to coordinate centralised research on special machinery for breaking cyphers, 1 February 1943; HW 14/70, Newman to EWT on recent machine developments, 12 March 1943; HW 14/79, Newman to Travis on problems with new processing equipment being installed by GPO engineers.

Pages 229–30 Flowers: Copeland (ed.), *Colossus*, pp.78–80.

Page 230 Hilton: Smith, *Station X*, pp.189–90.

Pages 230–31 Thompson: Smith, *Station X*, p.195.

Pages 231–2 Murray: interview with Odette Wylie, May 1998.

Page 232 Vergine: Smith, *Station X*, p.197.

Pages 232–3 Jenkins: ibid, p.198.

Pages 233–4 Hilton: ibid, pp.199–200.

Pages 234–6 Cairncross: John Cairncross, *The Enigma Spy*, Century, London, 1997; Nigel West and Oleg Tsarev, *The Crown Jewels*, HarperCollins, London, 1998, pp.216–9.

Page 236 Tiltman on Cooper Japanese course: US National Archives NARA RG457 OD4632, John H. Tiltman, Some Reminiscences.

Page 237 Breaking of Japanese codes: Michael Smith, *The Emperor's Codes: Bletchley Park's Role in Breaking Japan's Secret Ciphers*, Dialogue, London, 2010, passim.

Pages 237–9 Sweetland: interview with Gladys Sweetland, February 2000.

Page 239 Cohen on friendship across classes: interview with Jonathan Cohen, December 1999.

Pages 239–40 Wiles: interviews and correspondence with Maurice Wiles.

Pages 240–41 Tensions over Japanese material and threat to break off relations: Smith, *Emperor's Codes*, p.154.

Page 241 Telford Taylor on cooperation: Erskine & Smith (eds), *Bletchley Park Codebreakers*, p.213.

Page 242 Travis on US change of mind: TNA PRO HW 14/72, Minutes of Joint Management Committee.

Page 243 Rose: interview with Jim Rose, May 1998.

Pages 243–5 Bundy, Levenson and Howard: Smith, *Station X*, pp.172–174.

Page 245 Rounders match: interview with Barbara Eachus, May 1998.

Pages 245–7 Bundy and Levenson on stereotypes: Smith, *Station X*, pp.177–8.

Pages 247–8 Brooke-Rose affair with Taylor: interview with Christine Brooke-Rose, May 1998.

Pages 248–9 Senyard on Christmas 1943: TNA PRO HW 3/135, History of Miss Senyard's Party, pp.48–9.

Page 249 Pat Wright: interview with Pat Bing, May 1998.

Pages 250–51 Detail of Oshima tour of defences and Rundstedt appreciation: F. H. Hinsley et al., *British Intelligence in the Second World War*, Vol. 3, Pt 2, HMSO, London, 1988, pp.32–4.

Page 251 Seiichi report: Hinsley, *British Intelligence* (Abridged), pp.436–7.

Pages 251–2 Bill Sibley on Japanese Military Attaché: interviews with Bill Sibley, July 1999 and January 2000.

Page 252 Breaking Jellyfish from March 1944: Hinsley, *British Intelligence*, Vol. 3, Pt 2, p.779.

Pages 252–3 The evolution of Fortitude South: Roger Hesketh, *Fortitude: The D-Day Deception Campaign*, St Ermin's Press, London, 1999, pp.25–7.

Pages 253–4 Main Fortitude South agents: Hesketh, *Fortitude*, pp.46–56.

Page 254 Treasure nearly gives game away: TNA PRO KV 2/464, Summary of Treasure Case.

Page 254 Treasure saves Bletchley's bacon: TNA PRO KV 2/464, Page to Masterman, 29 November 1944.

Pages 254–5 Garbo network: Howard, *British Intelligence*, Vol. 5, pp.231–3.

Page 255 Radio deception operations: TNA PRO WO 208/5050, Notes on Army Wireless Deception for Operation Overlord.

Page 256 Jellyfish link: Hinsley, *British Intelligence*, Vol. 3, Pt 2, p.779.

Pages 256–7 Alexander and Coral: Erskine & Smith (eds), *Bletchley Park Codebreakers*, pp.124–125.

Page 257 Maclennan: Smith, *Station X*, p.205.

Pages 257–8 Flowers on D-Day deadline: Copeland (ed.), *Colossus*, p.80.

Page 258 Pat Wright: interview with Pat Bing, May 1998.

Pages 258–9 Bill Bundy on D-Day: Smith, *Station X*, pp.206–207.

Pages 259–60 Garbo messages on D-Day and Hitler: Howard, *British Intelligence*, Vol. 5, pp.188–9.

Page 260 Bussey on importance of Ultra to Fortitude: Smith, *Station X*, p.208.

Pages 260–61 Williams on Ultra contribution: TNA PRO WO 208/3575, Williams, The Use of Ultra.

Pages 261–2 Jones: TNA PRO HW 3/125, Eric Jones, Memo to All Hut 3 Personnel, 6 June 1944.

Pages 262–3 Birch intercept decision and Hinsley: Hinsley, *British Intelligence*, Vol. 3, Pt 1, pp.129, 784.

Pages 263–4 Bussey and Bennett: Smith, *Station X*, pp.209–10.

Pages 264–5 Germans realise Red is compromised: TNA PRO HW 14/108, Milner-Barry, Compromise of Red, 9 July 1944.

Page 265 Fish changing daily and new Colossi: Erskine & Smith (eds), *Bletchley Park Codebreakers*, p.303; Smith, *Station X*, p.211.

Pages 265–6 Dakin on Stauffenberg plot: Hinsley & Stripp, *Codebreakers*, p.56.

Page 266 Norland: Smith, *Station X*, pp.212–3.

Pages 267–8 Prestwich: interview with John Prestwich, May 1998.

Page 268 Wenham: interview with Susan Wenham, May 1998.

Pages 269–70 Bennett on Market Garden: Ralph Bennett, *Ultra in the West*, Hutchinson, London, 1979, p.148.

Page 270 Rose on Ardennes: interview with Jim Rose, May 1998.

Pages 271–2 Bennett on Ardennes: Smith, *Station X*, p.217.

Page 273 Damage to Fish intercept site at Genval: TNA PRO HW 3/163, Kenworthy, History of interception of German teleprinter communications.

Page 273 Donald Michie: Smith, *Station X*, pp.218–9.

Pages 273–4 Double Cross on V-weapons (Operation Crossbow): Smith, *Foley*, p.229.

Pages 274–5 Calder: conversations and correspondence with Rosemary Merry, July 1999 and January 2000.

Pages 275–6 Petrides: letter from Anne Petrides dated 20 November 1999.

Pages 276–8 Humble: letter from Olive Humble dated 11 July 1999.

Page 279 Bletchley contribution during advance into Germany: TNA PRO HW 43/70, History of Hut 6, p.120; Hinsley, *British Intelligence*, Vol. 3, Pt 2, pp.845–54; Oakley, War Diaries, pp.162–71.

Page 280 Aitken quote: TNA PRO HW 43/70, History of Hut 6, p.120.

Pages 280–81 Briggs: Asa Briggs, *Secret Days: Codebreaking in Bletchley Park*, Frontline, Barnsley, 2011, p.124.

Page 281 Stuart Milner-Barry: TNA PRO HW 43/70, History of Hut 6, p.21.

Pages 281–2 Travis special order dated 8 May 1945: TNA PRO HW 14/140.

Page 282 Kennedy: *Kennedy Diaries*, 28 June 1945.

Page 283 Calder: conversations and correspondence with Rosemary Merry, July 1999 and February 2000.

Page 283 Army-Air message detailing effects of bomb and lack of need for bomb: Smith, *Emperor's Codes*, p.274.

Pages 283–4 Humble: letter from Olive Humble dated 11 July 1999.

Page 285 For an examination of the decrypts of the Yugoslav resistance see Erskine & Smith, *Bletchley Park Codebreakers*, pp.217–39.

Pages 286–7 Bill Williams: TNA PRO WO 208/3575, Williams, The Use of Ultra.

Page 287 Eisenhower message: TNA PRO HW 14/140, Eisenhower to Menzies, 12 July 1945.

Pages 287–8 For a detailed description of the respective US and UK successes against Japanese codes and cyphers see Smith, *Emperor's Codes*.

Page 289 Anyone wanting to learn more about Knox should read Mavis Batey's wonderfully affectionate biography *Dilly: The Man Who Broke Enigmas*, published in paperback by Dialogue.

Pages 289–90 Tiltman: Erskine & Freeman, 'Brigadier John Tiltman: One of Britain's Finest Cryptologists'.

Page 291 Alexander on Turing: TNA PRO HW 25/1, Alexander, Cryptographic History of Work on the German Naval Enigma, pp.42–3.

Pages 291–2 Information on Hugh Alexander: Harry Golombek, 'Alexander, (Conel) Hugh O'Donel (1909–1974)', rev. Ralph Erskine, *Oxford Dictionary of National Biography*, Oxford University Press, 2004; online edn, May 2008 <http://www.oxforddnb.com/view/article/30756>, accessed 23 June 2011.

Page 293 More than 10,000 at Bletchley: TNA PRO HW 14/154, Personnel at BP, 14 January 1945. Intercept sites: HW 14/114, Y Stations at 19 October 1944.

Page 293 Hinsley: Smith, *Station X*, p.232.

Page 294 Alexander on Bletchley work: TNA PRO HW 25/1, Alexander, Cryptographic History of Work on the German Naval Enigma, p.85.

Page 295 Bill Bundy: Smith, *Station X*, pp.177,228–9.

INDEX